IMAGES
of America

TAZEWELL

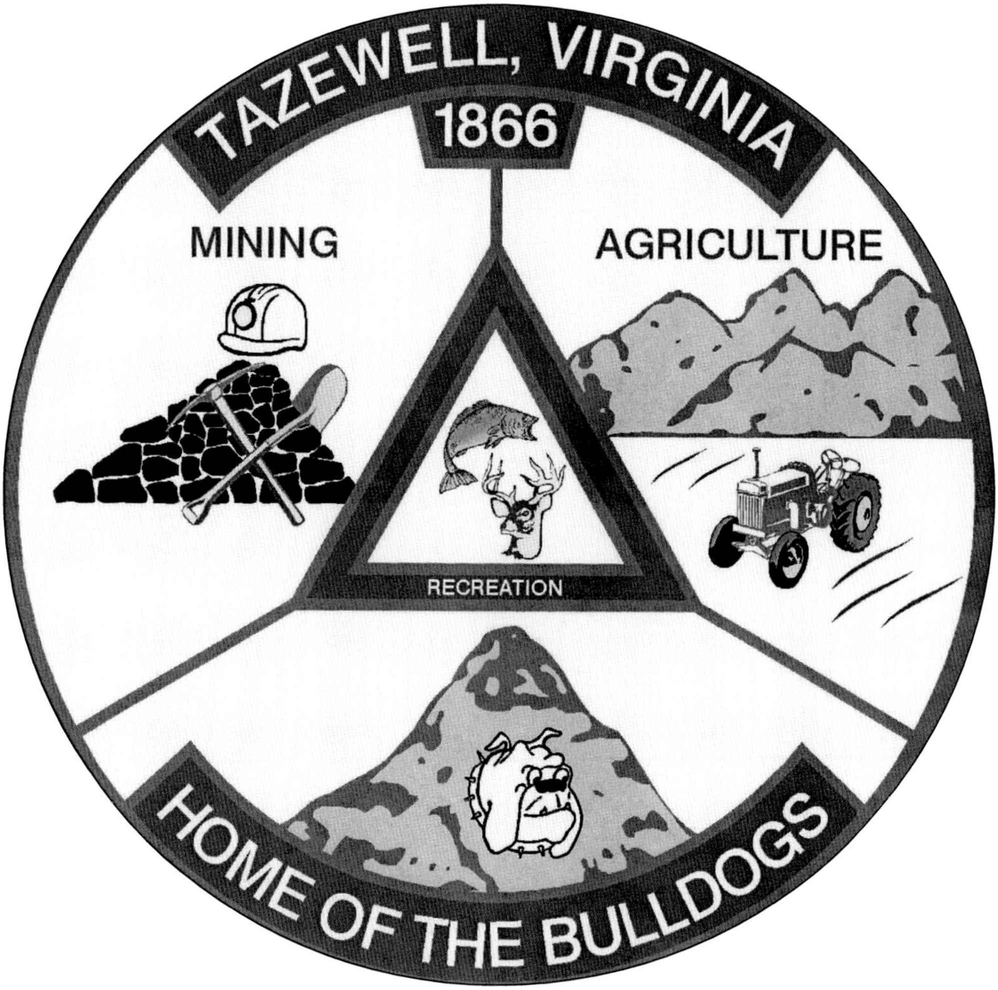

The Tazewell town seal was chosen following a competition open to the public in 1982. The seal features the major economic activities of the area: coal mining, agriculture, and recreational opportunities. At the base of the seal is the "Peak," which towers above the town of Tazewell, and the Bulldog, the mascot of Tazewell High School, the first high school in Tazewell County. The date shown is 1866, the year that Jeffersonville, later Tazewell, secured its charter. The seal was created by Billy Stanton when he was a student at Tazewell High School in the 1980s. (Courtesy of Town of Tazewell.)

ON THE COVER: The Tazewell depot and the Tazewell streetcar were important to the business community in many ways. One was providing transportation for the "drummers" (traveling salesmen) who made frequent trips to the merchants of Jeffersonville and Kelly and later to the newly named towns of Tazewell and North Tazewell. They usually stayed at the Central Hotel on Main Street or at the Clinchview Hotel close to the depot. When the first passenger train came into the North Tazewell Depot in 1887, the engineer was a jovial Irishman named Jim Carey. A large crowed gathered at the depot to welcome the "iron horse." As the train approached, the whistle was tied down to make a spectacular loud entrance. The steam chests were wide open. As the steam cleared away and the whistle was silenced, Carey shouted, "look out, I'm going to turn around." He caused a panic in the depot and a near stampede as people ran for safety. (Courtesy of Norfolk and Western Historical Photograph Collection at Virginia Tech.)

IMAGES
of America

TAZEWELL

Louise B. Leslie and
Dr. Terry W. Mullins

ARCADIA
PUBLISHING

ISBN 978-0-7385-4386-4

Published by Arcadia Publishing
Charleston, South Carolina

Printed in the United States of America

Library of Congress Catalog Card Number: 2006934167

For all general information contact Arcadia Publishing at:
Telephone 843-853-2070
Fax 843-853-0044
E-mail sales@arcadiapublishing.com
For customer service and orders:
Toll-Free 1-888-313-2665

Visit us on the Internet at www.arcadiapublishing.com

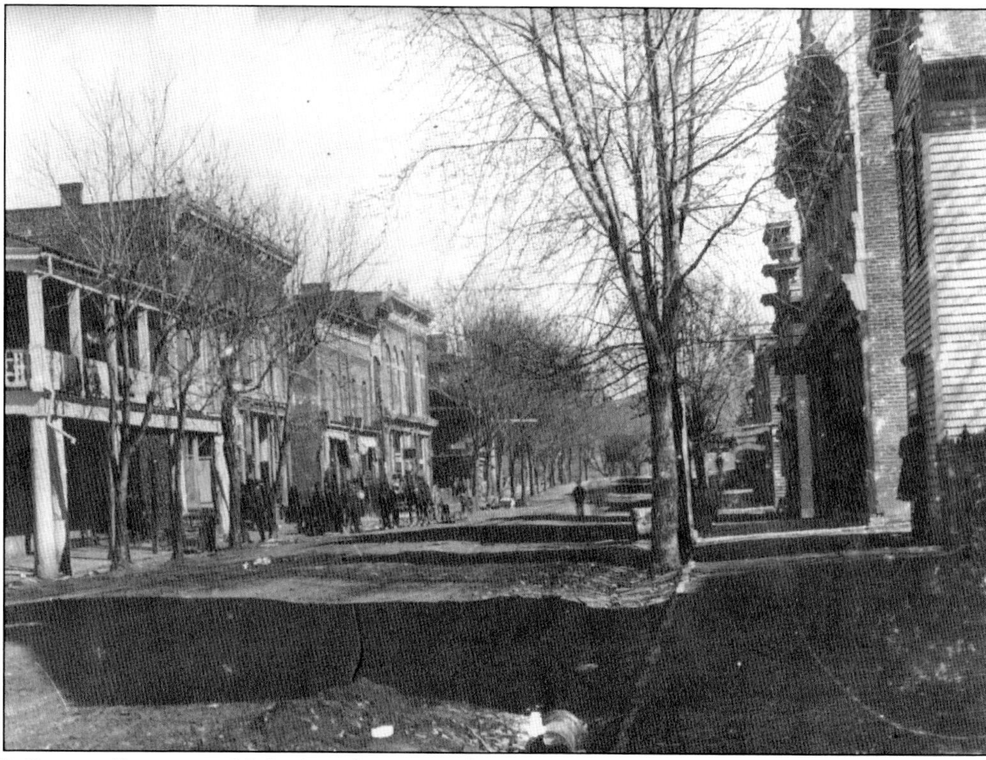

Jeffersonville was established as the Tazewell County seat in 1801. Tazewell's historic district today includes most of that original town of Jeffersonville, which was first incorporated in 1822. The town received charters again in 1840, 1850, and 1866. The name Jeffersonville was officially changed to Tazewell in 1892. By the early 1900s, Tazewell was a thriving town with a growing population that seemed to understand the coming development in the nearby coalfields, which had a great impact on the area. The trees that lined Main Street were later removed to make room for the days of the automobile. (Courtesy of Cindy Lowe.)

Contents

ACKNOWLEDGMENTS

Without the help and interest of our good friends throughout Tazewell County, *Tazewell* would not have been possible. We deeply appreciate everyone who helped by donating pictures, furnishing information, and encouraging us to complete the project. It is by no means a complete history of Tazewell, but we hope the pictures and text will give readers a feeling for our hometown as the community enters its third century of existence.

Special thanks go to the Tazewell County Historical Society, Cindy Lowe, Sandy Peery, the Tazewell County Public Library, Virginia Tech Archives, Jack Repass, Joe Evans, Emmy Dennison, Edythe Mullins, Nancy Peery Olson, Nancy Ward, Jesse Peery, Ella Greear, Mac Buchanan, Ross Gillespie, Elsie Jackson, Ralph Mullins, Rae Farley, Mary Barrett, June Friedl, G. Michael Alford, David Morrison, Tazewell County Farm Bureau office staff, Bob and Lori Moss, Shirley Mullins, Larry Hypes, Douglas Fleet, Mary June Wall, Marianna Rowlett Harris, Peyton L. Rowlett Jr., Bryan Warden, Louise McKinney, Faye Viney, Carolyn Harrold, Martha Ward Massie, Mary Bowen Peery Colley, Betty Leece Gillespie, Eric Robinson, Rick Farris, the *Clinch Valley News* files, the *Peak* Tazewell High School yearbook, Angie Patrick and the Tazewell Elementary Library, Keith Hovis, Barbara Gillespie, Regina Coleman, and the Tazewell High School Library.

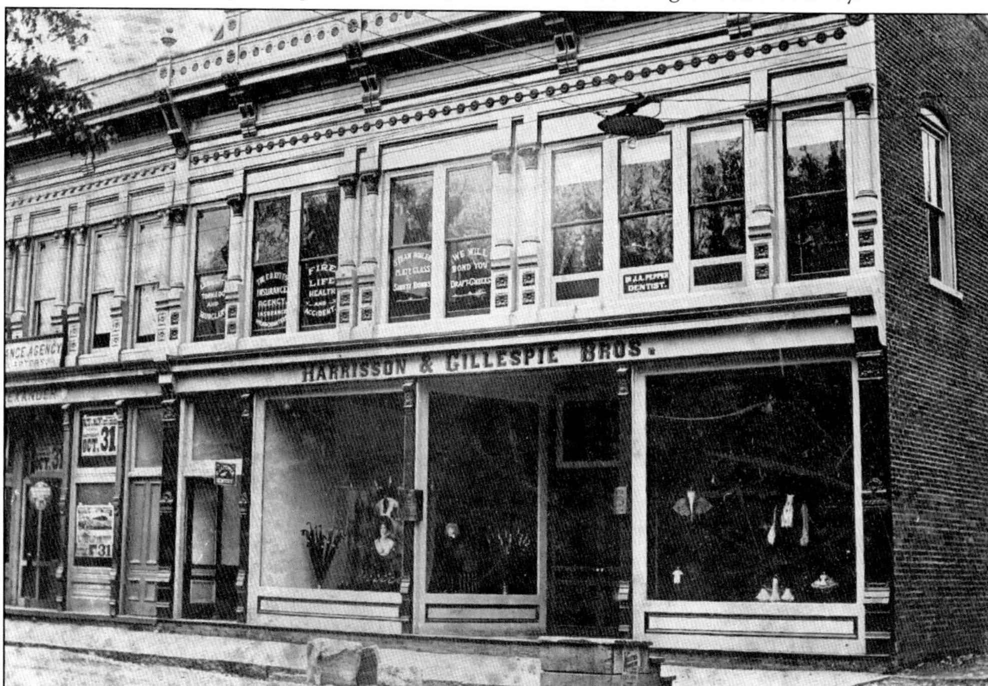

Main Street Tazewell has been designated a historic district by the Department of Historic Resources of Virginia. The historic district includes several older private residences on or near Main Street. Harrison and Gillespie Brothers was a well-known clothing store in early Tazewell. The business began in the 1890s and continued into the 1900s under the name of the Big Store or Jeff Ward's Store. Main Street was a busy place in 1900. Occupants of the second floor included the E. D. Kitts Insurance Company and Dr. J. A. Pepper, dentist. The stile in front of the store was used for the convenience of passengers in horse-drawn vehicles, those riding horses, or those arriving by streetcar. The building still stands on Main Street and is now occupied by county offices. (Courtesy of Martha Ward Massie.)

INTRODUCTION

Exploration of the area known today as Tazewell is traced to the first groups of hunters and explorers charting Southwestern Virginia from the eastern part of the state in the early 1700s. In fact, before any actual settlement, many trappers and hunters camped on the Clinch River. Indian traders were familiar with Tazewell's topography and had even given the river its first name, the Pellissippi. Such adventurers cannot, however, in any sense be claimed as actual settlers. It was, nevertheless, in 1769 that a small group of settlers including Thomas Witten, his son-in-law John Greenup, and other family members established the first permanent settlement by white pioneers at the Crab Orchard Tract on the Clinch River at Pisgah. This was the same site that had been a permanent settlement for the Woodland Indians as early as 200 years before. The population of this mountain and valley community grew slowly but steadily during the 18th century. As a result, a new county was proposed in the heart of the southern Appalachians to be created from portions of Russell and Wythe Counties. That new county, Tazewell, was created by the Virginia General Assembly on December 20, 1799.

The town of Tazewell is a picturesque community that was established to serve as the county seat for Tazewell County the following year. One of the oldest communities in Southwestern Virginia, Tazewell was first named Jeffersonville in honor of Thomas Jefferson, who received every local vote cast when he was elected president in 1800—the same year the town was established. Jeffersonville secured its first charter as an incorporated municipality in 1866, just after the Civil War. Tazewell and its neighboring town, North Tazewell, merged in 1963. The first recorded mayor of Tazewell was A. G. May in 1874. The first mayor of North Tazewell was William L. Britts in 1894. James W. Harman Jr. served as the first mayor of the merged municipality beginning in 1963.

During the first two centuries of the history of the town of Tazewell the population increased, transportation improved, streets were paved, sewers and electricity were added, and more houses and businesses were built. New communities grew up in and around the town. One of the first additions was the Tazewell Improvement Company's street of "new" residences, today known as Tazewell Avenue. Kelly grew up on the Clinch and, with the advent of the railroad and the train station, became North Tazewell and the commercial center of the Tazewell area. New Town and Riverjack were later additions to the North Tazewell community. Meanwhile, to the east of town, the Burkes Garden Siding addition grew up along the Clinch at the point where the railroad came closest to the farm-rich valley of Burkes Garden. This section would become a commercial center in its own right in late-20th-century Tazewell and gain the new name—the Four Way section.

Today the town of Tazewell is home to more than 4,000 residents. Tazewell is also the governmental seat to a county of more than 40,000 people. Located at the headwaters of the Clinch River, the springs of Tazewell eventually become part of the Tennessee, Ohio, and finally the Mississippi Rivers. Tazewell today is an energetic and vibrant community, proud of its heritage and excited about its future. The community is rich in a history that is matched only by its natural beauty. The hills of Tazewell with their myriad of seasonal colors and the beauty of the Clinch River Valley make Tazewell a truly beautiful place to live or visit. Welcome to this glimpse into the history and legacy of the people who call Tazewell and the mountains of Southwestern Virginia their home.

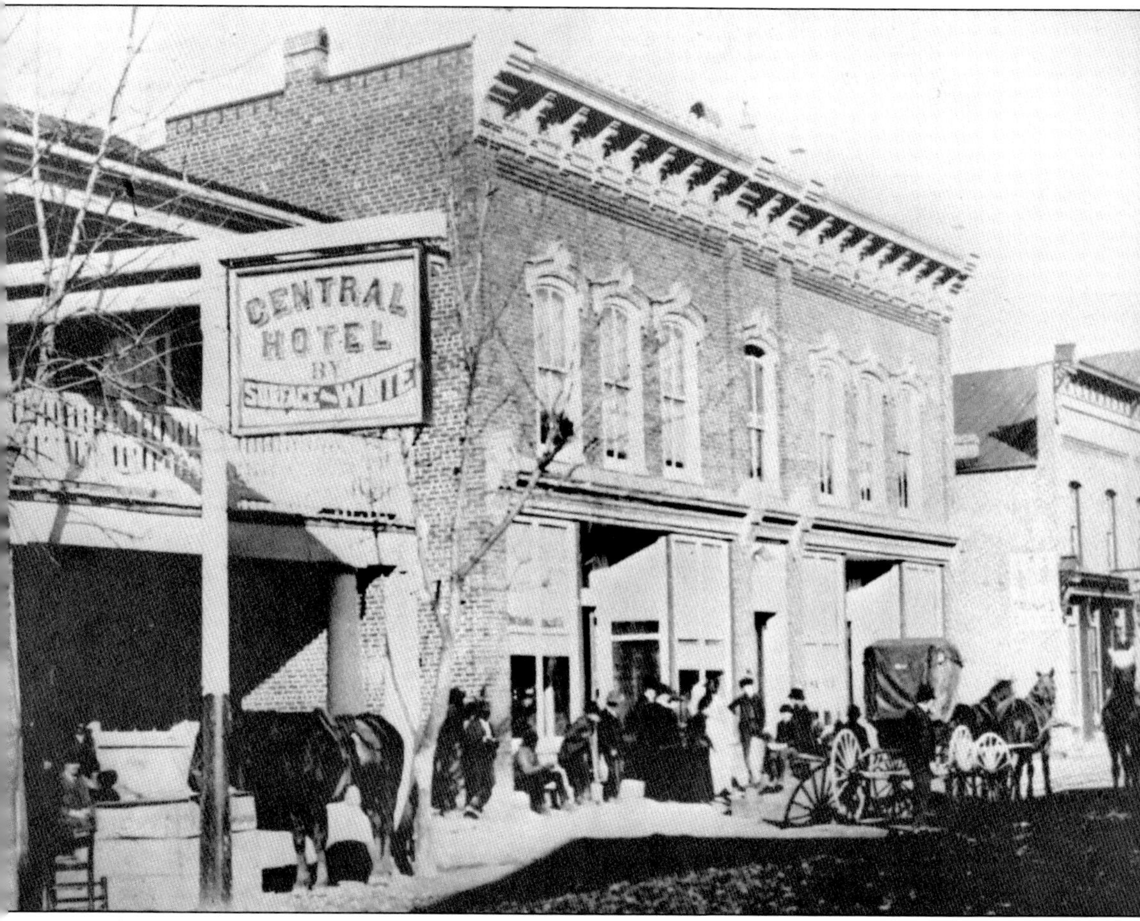

The Central Hotel was a busy place in the early days of Jeffersonville. It was owned by George Riley Surface and W. B. F. White and run by Surface. The hotel stood at the former site of the Western Auto on Main Street. The establishment burned in 1903. (Courtesy of Cindy Lowe.)

One

Old Towne Jeffersonville

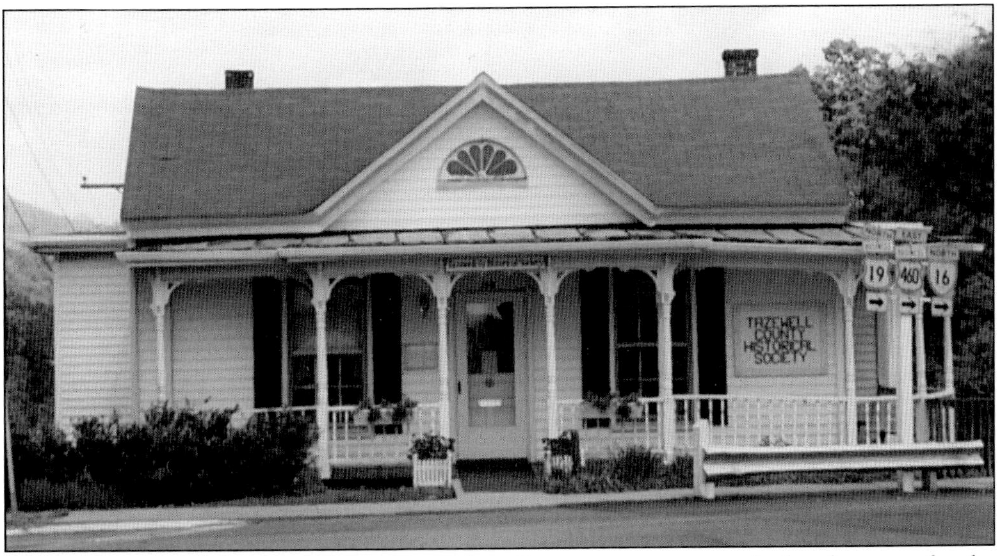

The C. W. Greever house, at the head of Main Street, now serves as the headquarters for the Tazewell County Historical Society. It was built about 1876 and is one of the town's oldest houses. Dr. Greever and his family lived here for their lifetimes, and his medical practice offices were in the small adjoining building. The Tazewell County Historical Society was organized in 1987. The society's purpose is "to keep history alive, bring together people who are interested in local history, accumulate and make available material about the area, collect and index historical materials, promote tourism, develop a speakers' bureau, and encourage genealogical research." (Courtesy of Mullins files.)

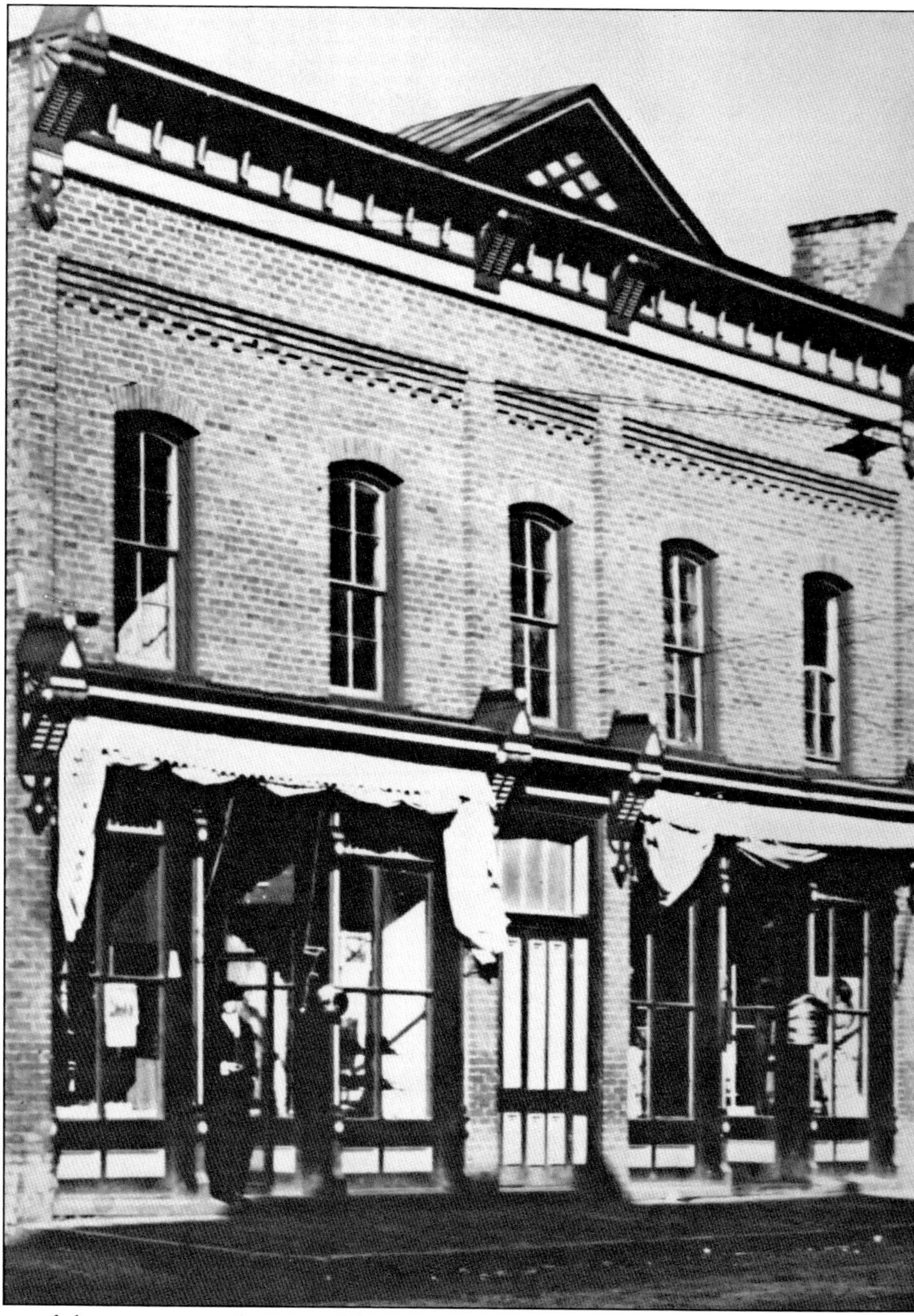

Many of the ornate storefronts on Main Street today date back to the first buildings of old Jeffersonville. The vernacular style predominates with many cast-iron storefronts. These iron artifacts are given credit for the development of commercial business centers throughout America during the latter years of the 1800s and the early years of the 20th century. The iron was cast in molds, so elaborate, ornate designs with repeating patterns were possible. Unlike stone or wood, which needed repainting often, one coat of paint on a cast-iron storefront would last and look new for years. Tazewell's ornate facades add a unique mixture of the old and new. (Courtesy of Cindy Lowe.)

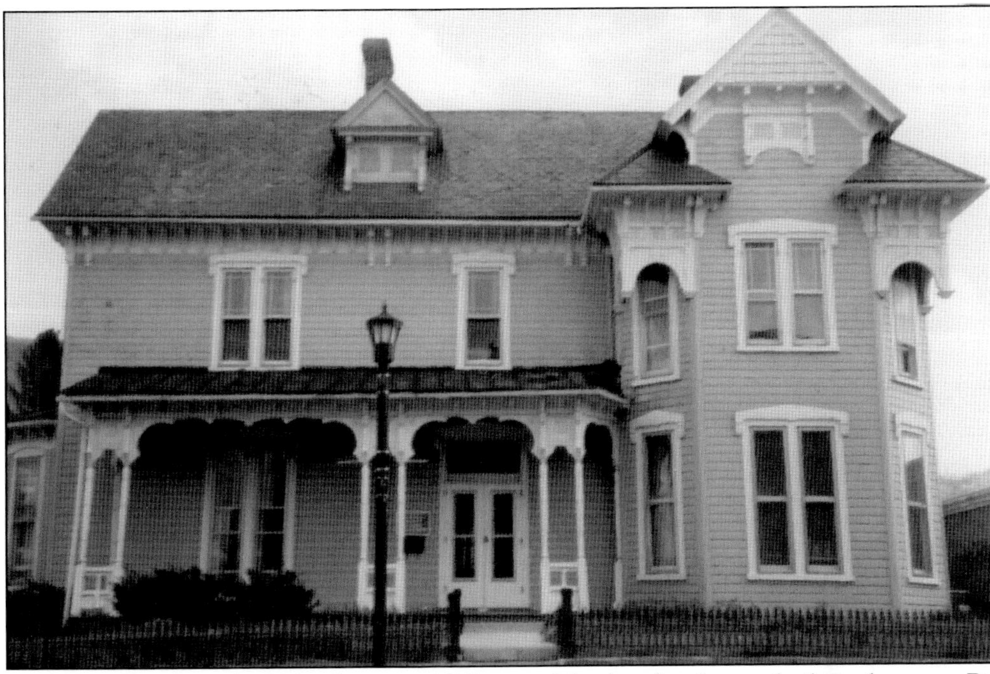

Dr. J. R. Gildersleeve built this house in 1877, one of the first fine houses built in the town. Dr. Gildersleeve, a well-known practicing physician, sold it to W. G. Harrison. From 1911 to 1987, it was owned by Dr. P. D. Johnston and his daughter, Dr. Mary Elizabeth Johnston. It now houses county offices. (Courtesy of Mullins files.)

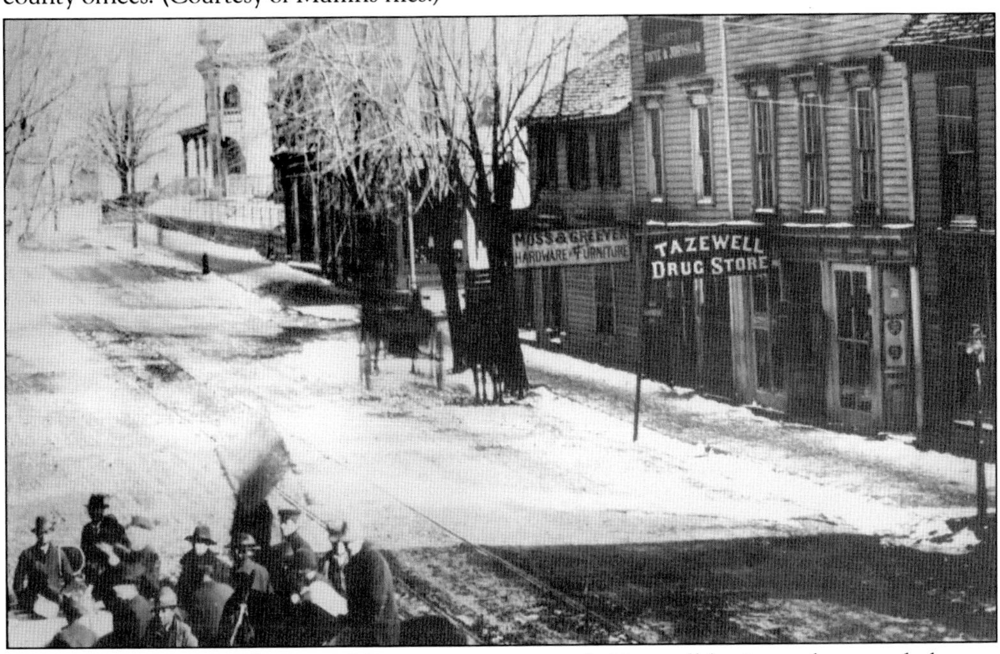

Moss and Greever Hardware and Furniture was an early Tazewell business that stood close to the old Tazewell Drug Store, later Clinch Valley Pharmacy or "Haley's." The successor to their business was Greever Hardware, which was across the street from the old firm. (Courtesy of Cindy Lowe.)

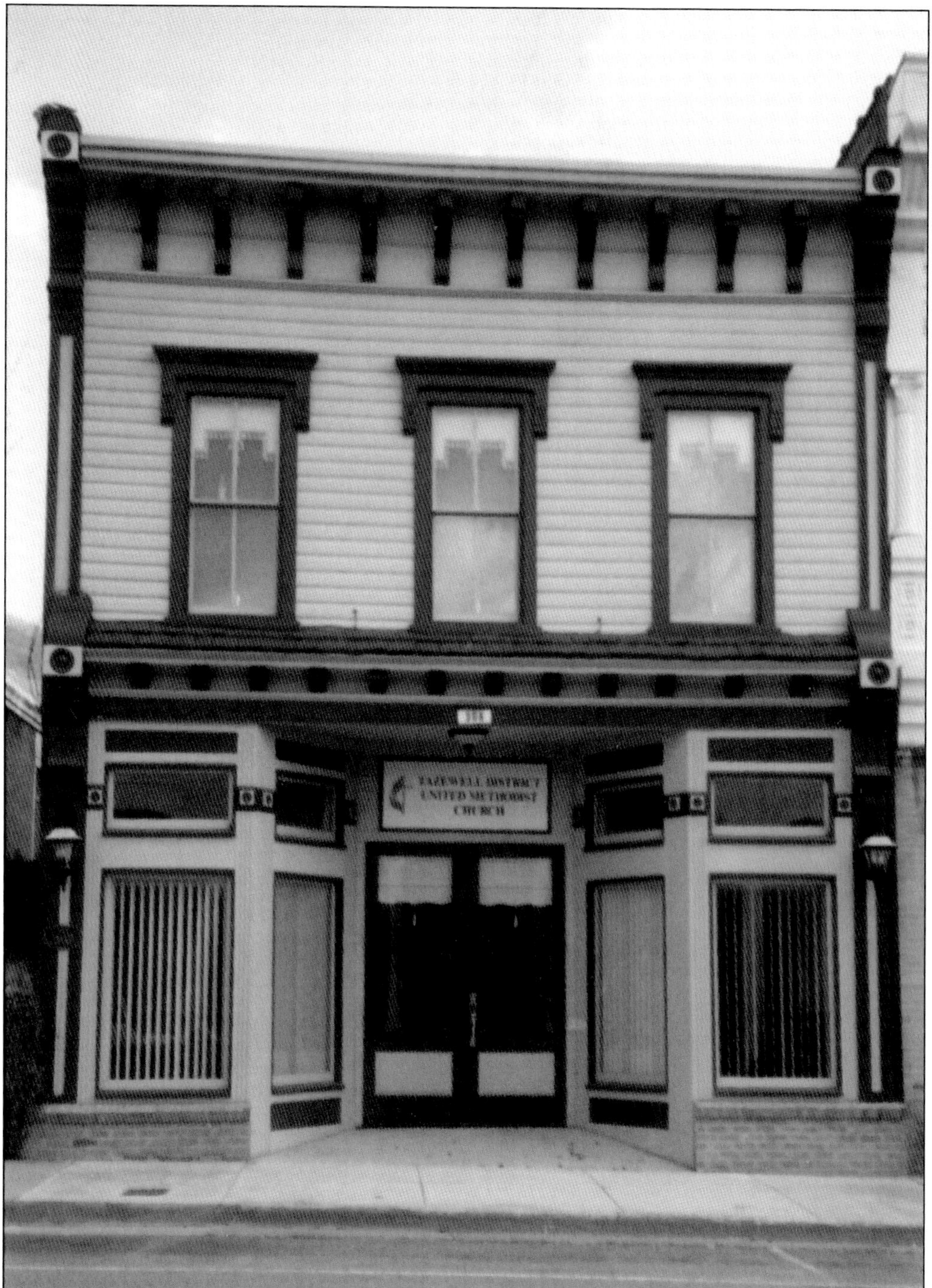

The district offices of the United Methodist Church are located in the renovated *Clinch Valley News* building. The weekly newspaper was published here from 1904 until 1991 by three generations of the Leslie family. It was purchased in 1887 by J. A. Leslie. Upstairs were apartments and the piano studios of Nancy Leslie and Louise Leslie. (Courtesy of Mullins files.)

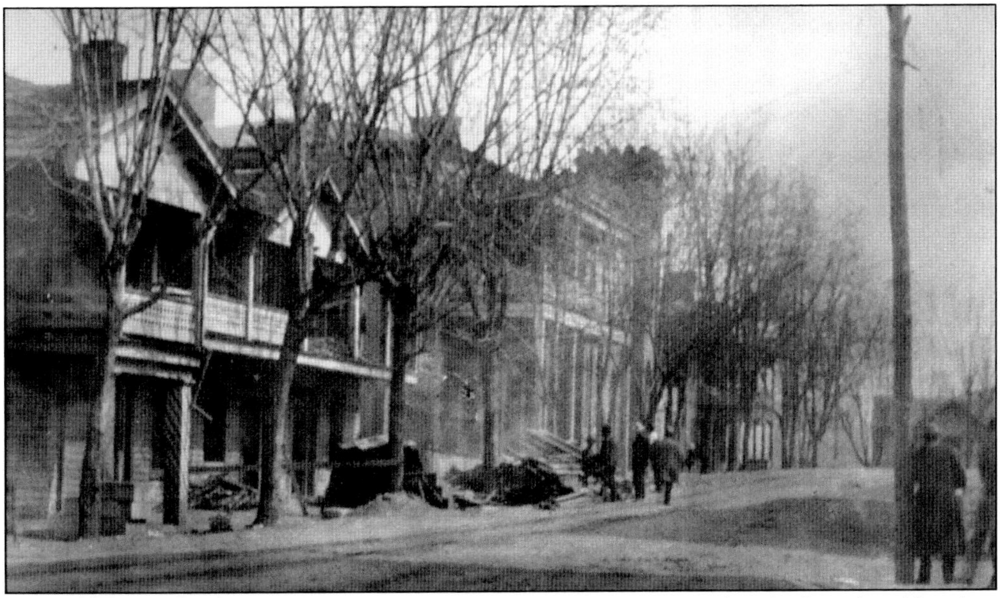

A late-afternoon fog gives Jeffersonville a mystical appearance, a modern look at the olden days through "rose-colored glasses." The location of the county seat was selected by a fistfight. Two men were chosen—one pugilist representing the site at the east end of present Tazewell near Four Way and another combatant representing the site at the western end of town on the present Main Street. They fought for hours, and finally the western site defender won the fight, and Main Street was planned for its present location. (Courtesy of Cindy Lowe.)

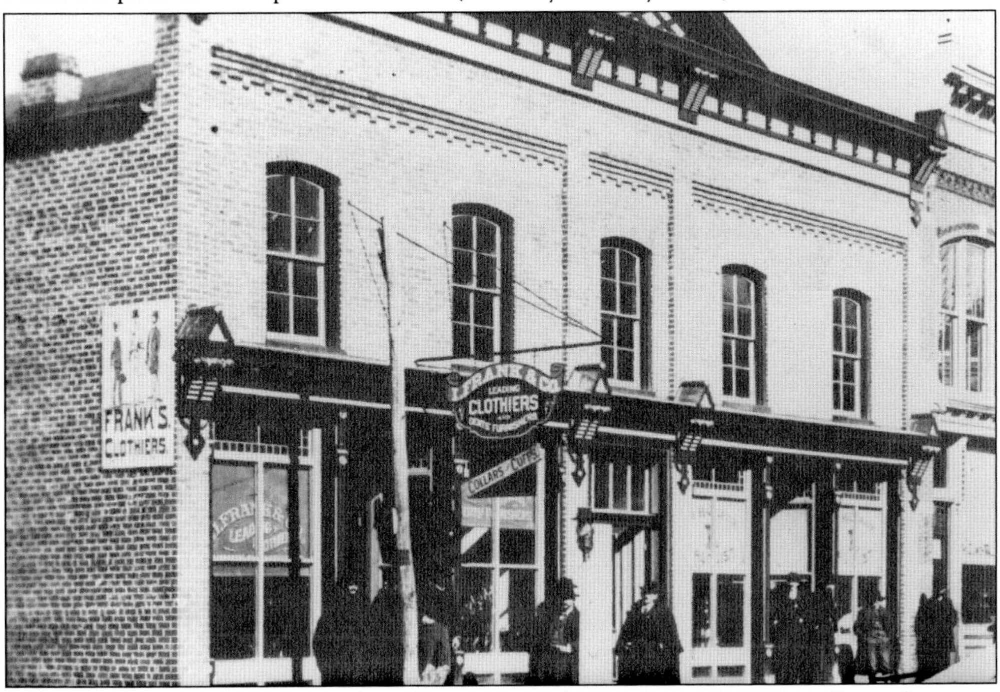

Frank Clothiers was one of a variety of retail establishments located on Main Street during its heyday. People would travel from miles away via railroad, streetcar, and horseback to shop at the many businesses then located on Main Street. (Courtesy of Cindy Lowe.)

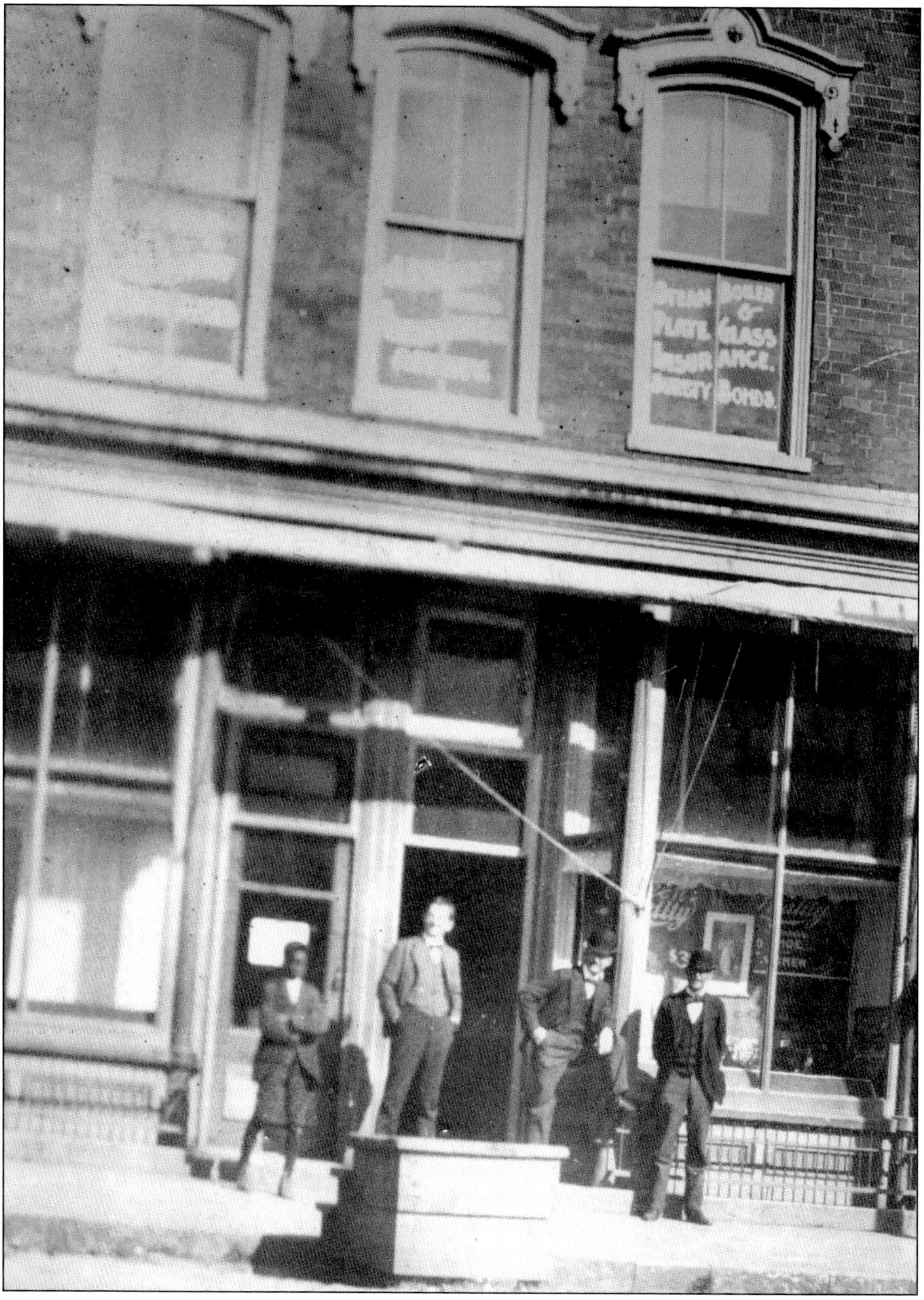

Another retail business on Main Street advertised steam boilers, plate glass, insurance, and security bonds in a smorgasbord of retail offerings in this late-19th-century Tazewell enterprise. (Courtesy of Cindy Lowe.)

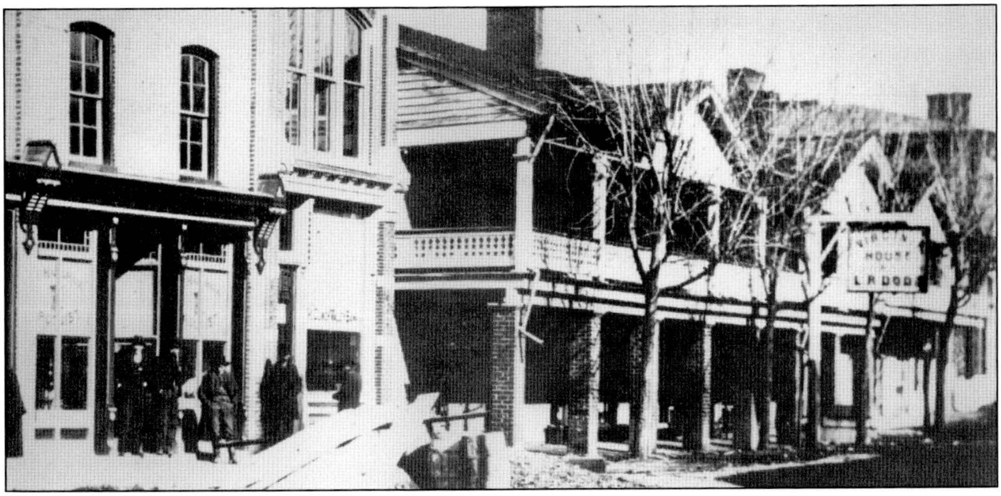

The Central Hotel and other early businesses on Main Street were especially busy on the days when the "drummers" came to town. They were traveling salesmen who rode the train to the Tazewell Depot, caught the hack and later the streetcar to Jeffersonville, and spent a day or two negotiating sales. The Central Hotel was later known as the Virginia House, Dodd Inn, and Virginia Hotel. Hotel Tazewell was later located nearby. (Courtesy of Cindy Lowe.)

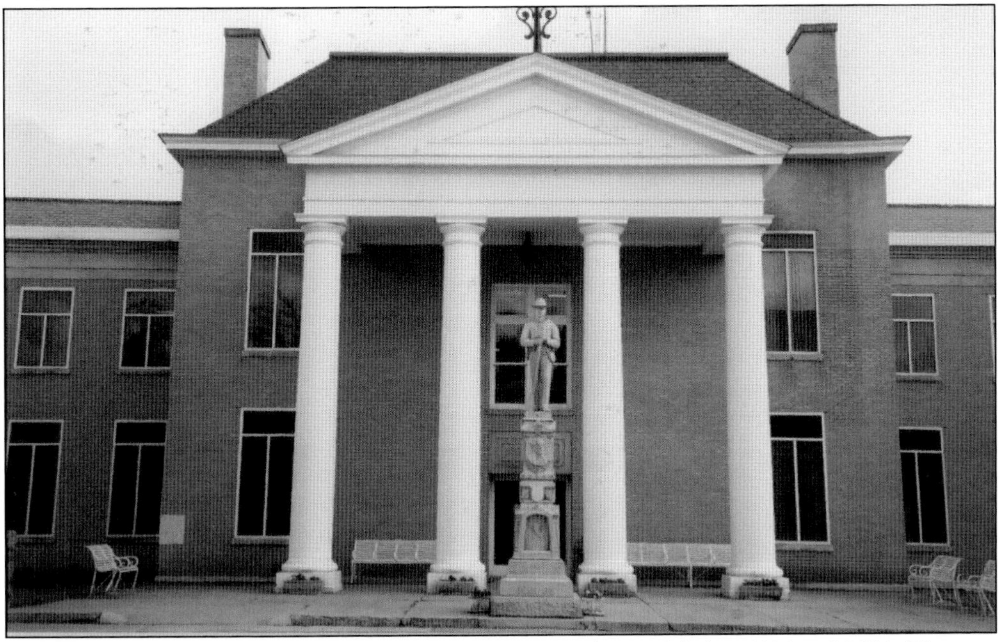
The Tazewell County Court House was built in 1874 and remodeled in 1914 and 2001. The new entrance to the courthouse and jail is on Court Street. The old Main Street entrance is still used. The 2001 additions and remodeling at the courthouse and jail cost approximately $12 million. The weather vane on top of the courthouse was previously on the roof of the Tazewell High School and Elementary School, which was torn down to make room for the Tazewell County Public Library. The town of Tazewell was often called "Tazewell Court House" when the fine 1874 building was erected, and even today it is sometimes still heard. The Confederate monument, standing at the Main Street entrance, was erected by the United Daughters of the Confederacy in 1903. (Courtesy of Mullins files.)

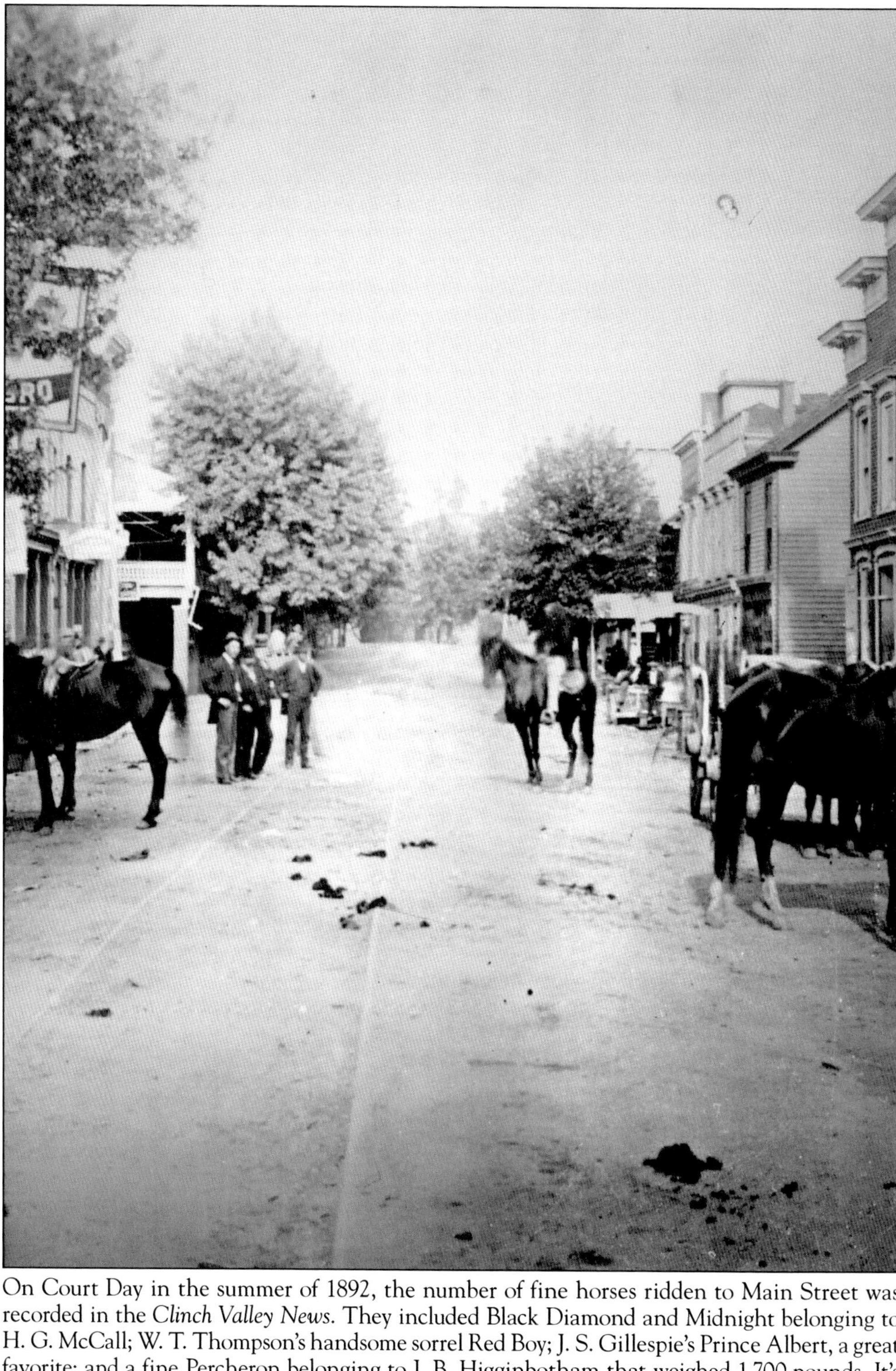

On Court Day in the summer of 1892, the number of fine horses ridden to Main Street was recorded in the *Clinch Valley News*. They included Black Diamond and Midnight belonging to H. G. McCall; W. T. Thompson's handsome sorrel Red Boy; J. S. Gillespie's Prince Albert, a great favorite; and a fine Percheron belonging to J. B. Higginbotham that weighed 1,700 pounds. It's easy to imagine they are pictured here. (Courtesy of Cindy Lowe.)

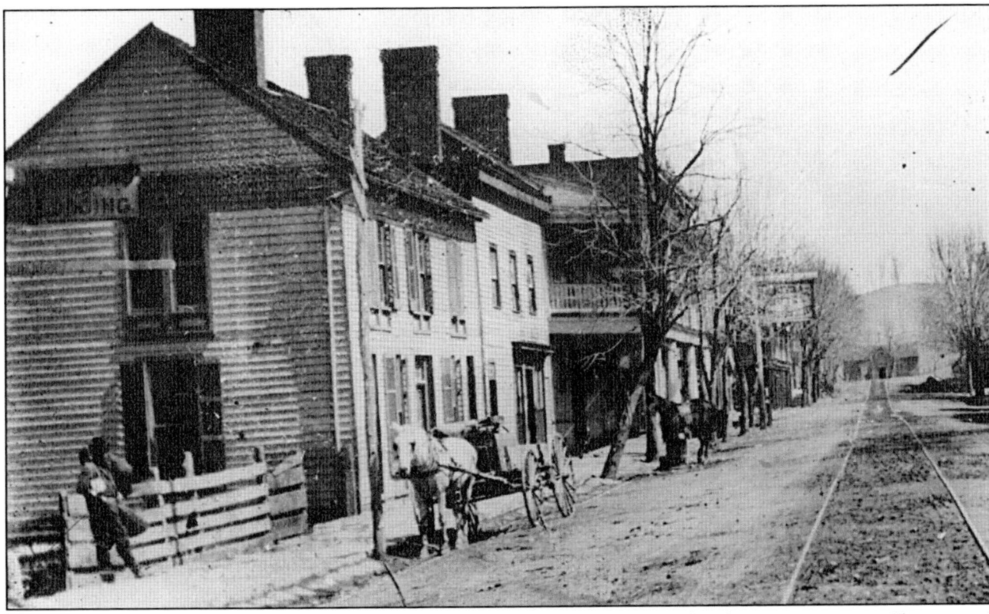

The early streetcar tracks can be seen in this late-1800s picture. The first streetcar or "horsecar" was pulled by horses. When the car reached the top of Fincastle Turnpike (preparing to go around Horseshoe Bend) en route to North Tazewell, the horses were released and allowed to run free down Pine Street to meet the streetcar on Tazewell Avenue after it had coasted around "The Bend." When the car reached the end of the tracks on West Main Street or at the Tazewell Depot, it simply reversed its route with the former back end of the streetcar becoming the new front. (Courtesy of Cindy Lowe.)

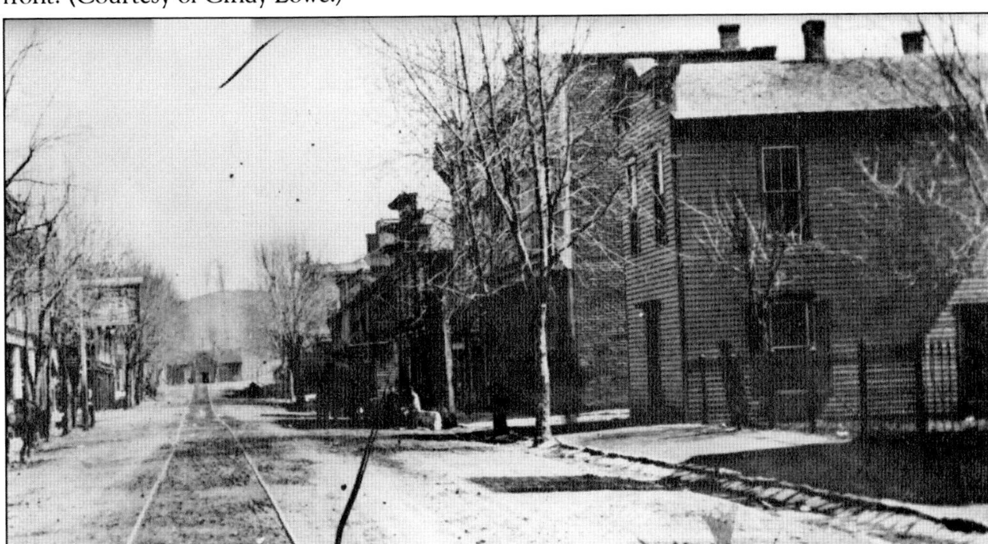

Main Street was divided by the streetcar tracks. These tracks served both the horse-drawn car and the electric trolley as the major means of transportation in the community from 1891 to 1933. Later, years after the streetcar was discontinued, the Main Street rails were paved and an inconvenient "hump" remained in the middle of Main Street, making winter parking hazardous. In the 1970s, the pavement, tracks, and "hump" were removed by town crews in a long, laborious process that disrupted downtown traffic for months. (Courtesy of Cindy Lowe.)

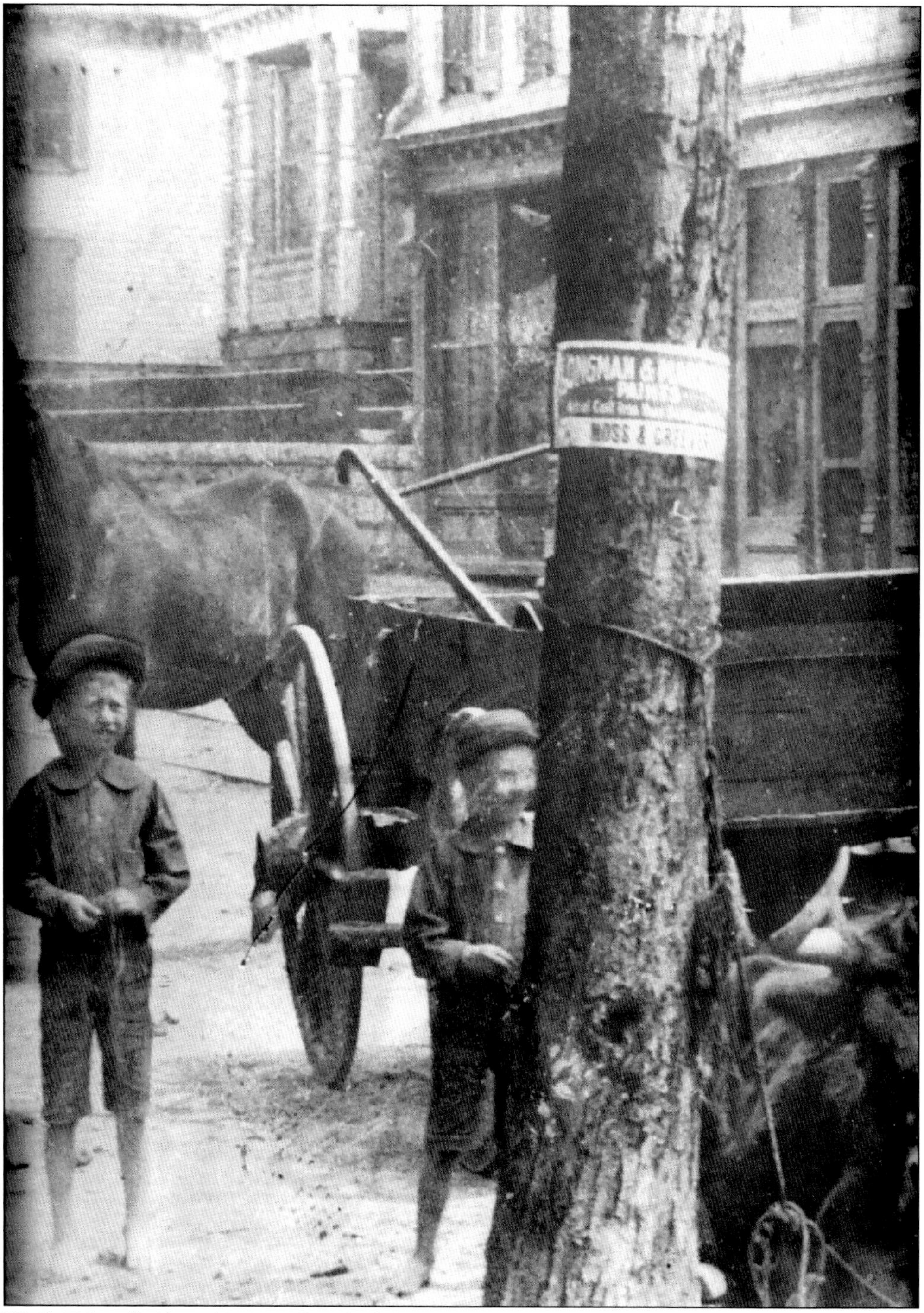

W. E. Tabor (left) and J. A. Tabor (right) are shown standing near a buggy in front of the old Tazewell National Bank building on Main Street. The wall in the background stood in front of the old Tazewell High School and continues today to stand in front of the Tazewell County Public Library. (Courtesy of Tazewell County Public Library.)

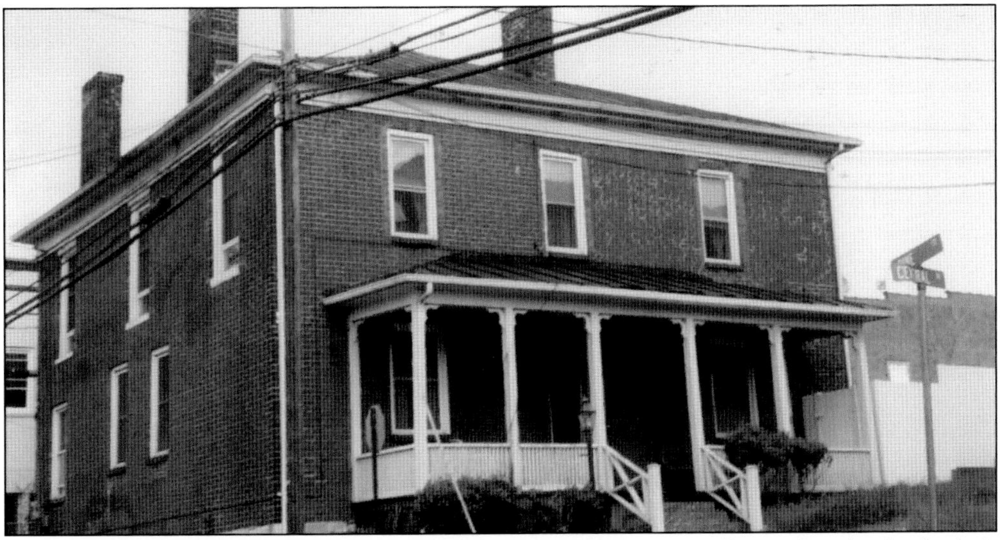

The old jail building, built in 1832, was used as a jail until 1915. Its walls are three bricks thick. It is located behind the site of Jeffersonville's first courthouse. The structure is now used for public services and has in past years been a private dwelling. (Courtesy of Mullins files.)

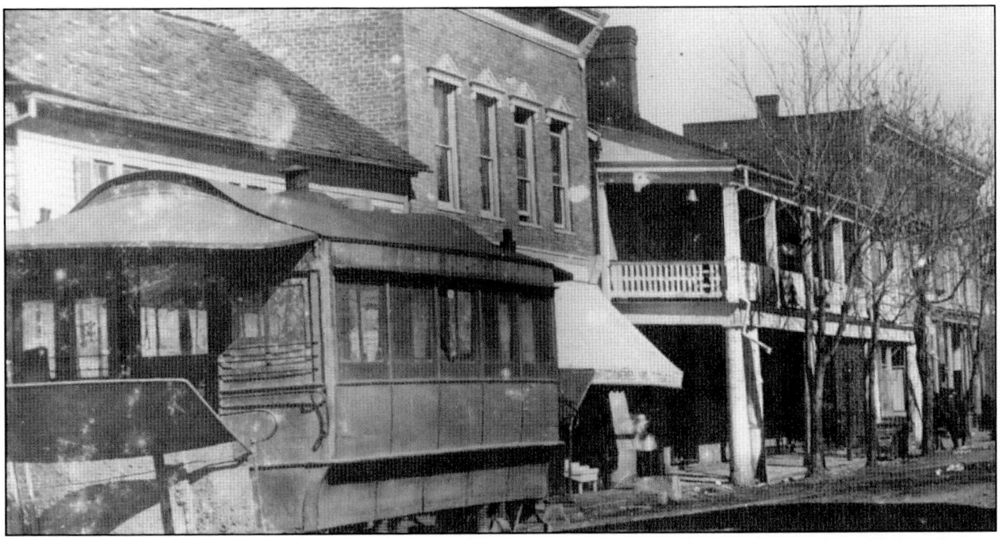

This trolley is believed to be the first Tazewell streetcar. From the 1890s to the 1920s, almost every city of at least 10,000 people acquired an electric streetcar system. Typical fare in Tazewell was 10¢. Open cars were used in warm months, closed ones during winter. The Tazewell trolley was converted from a horsecar to an electric streetcar on Christmas Eve 1902. When it operated by electricity, Tazewell was advertised as "the smallest town in the United States with an electric streetcar." Each streetcar required two workers—a conductor who collected fares and announced the stops and a motorman who operated the car, determined speeds, and kept order. The first conductor was C. M. Linkous, while the first motorman was ? Moore. Later W. D. Corvin and Reece Wimmer held those posts. Businesses advertised on the sides of the car, and often service was suspended so that parties could be held on the traveling vehicle. Tazewell was unique, a community of less than 2,000 people with its own streetcar. In comparison, for example, the smallest town in neighboring North Carolina with an electric streetcar was Salisbury with a population of more than 7,000. (Courtesy of Cindy Lowe.)

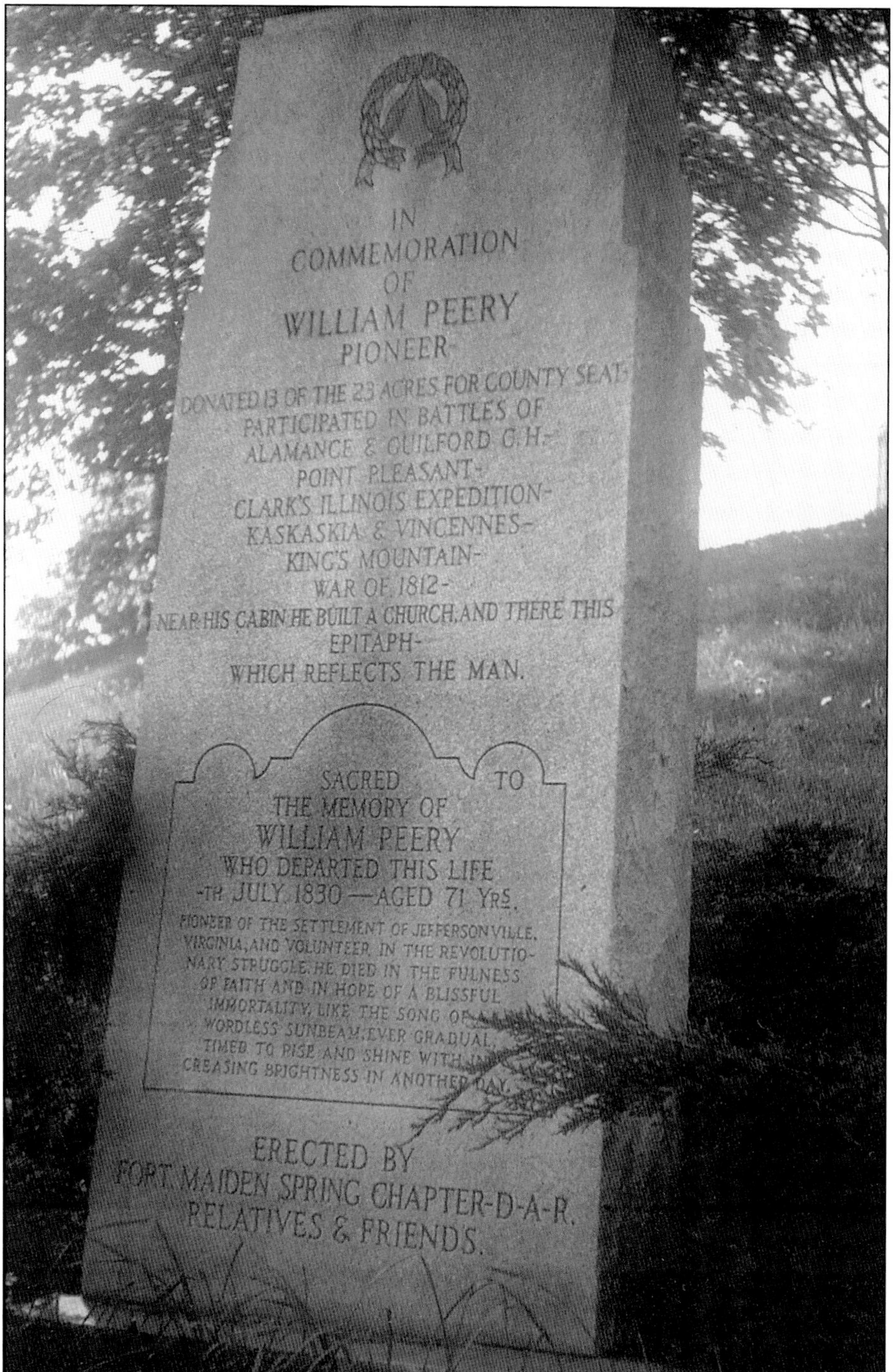

This monument honors William Peery, who gave land for the site of the town of Tazewell. The monument was erected by the Daughters of the American Revolution (DAR) and can still be seen on the grounds of the County Administration Building, which was formerly Tazewell High School. (Courtesy of Nancy Ward files.)

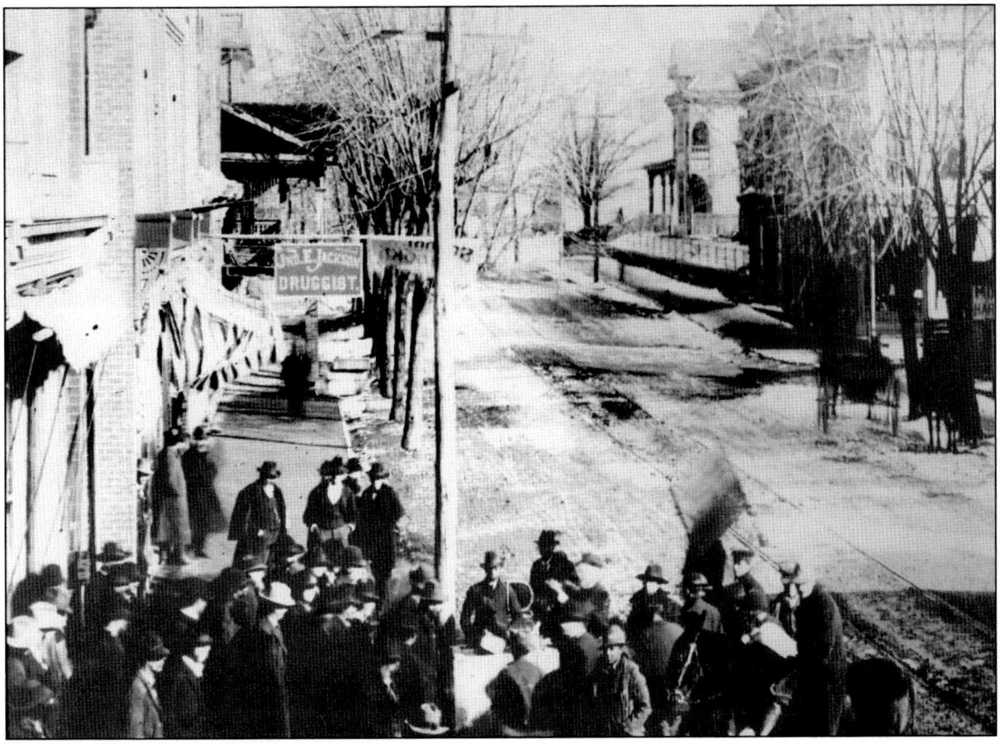

A crowd has gathered at Jackson Drug Company. Maybe it was a special celebration in the early days of this popular Tazewell business. The Jackson family had a drugstore at this location (called the Witten Building at that time) since 1897. The original building burned in a 1913 fire that damaged many Main Street buildings. The structure was rebuilt in 1914. The Opera House was on the second floor of the original building and presented vaudeville shows and local productions. For young people in the Tazewell area, Jackson's was the place to meet and socialize. A 1904 *Clinch Valley News* article stated that "it is getting to be 'the thing' to go to Jackson's for refreshing drinks and creams." (Courtesy of Cindy Lowe.)

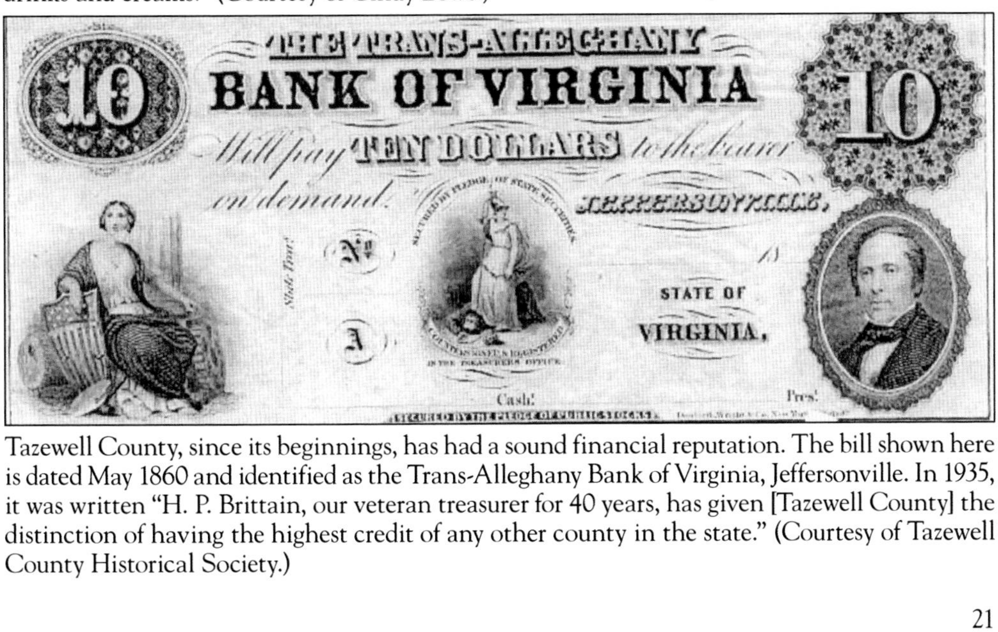

Tazewell County, since its beginnings, has had a sound financial reputation. The bill shown here is dated May 1860 and identified as the Trans-Alleghany Bank of Virginia, Jeffersonville. In 1935, it was written "H. P. Brittain, our veteran treasurer for 40 years, has given [Tazewell County] the distinction of having the highest credit of any other county in the state." (Courtesy of Tazewell County Historical Society.)

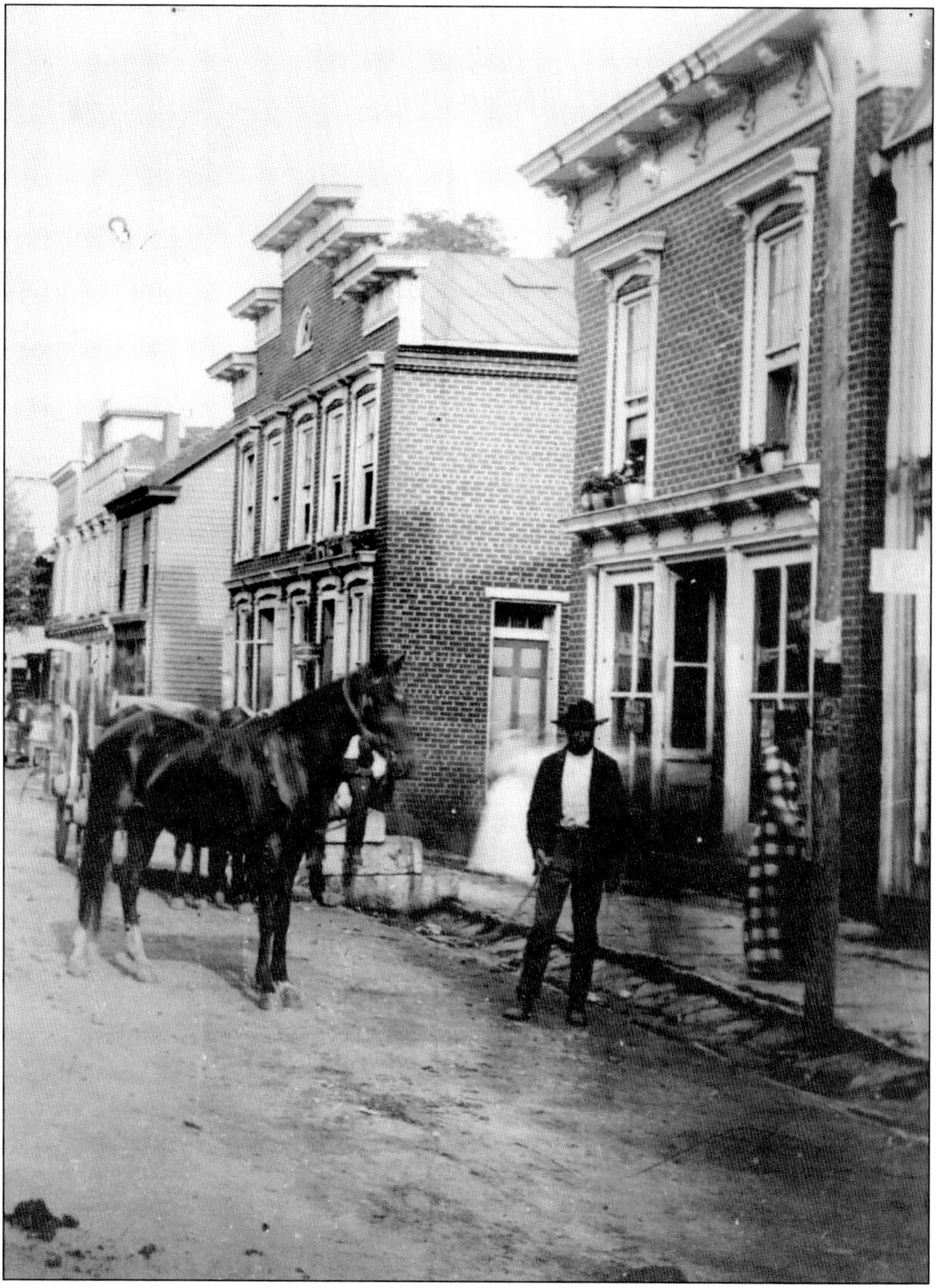

Horses, on a hot summer day, enjoyed the shade of the Main Street trees as much as the people did. The major mode of transportation in the early days of Jeffersonville was by horseback or by horse and buggy. The coming of the streetcar in the late 1800s and the automobile in the 1900s altered the landscape of Main Street forever. The trees were removed when automobiles took the place of horses and more space was needed for parking and increased traffic. (Courtesy of Cindy Lowe.)

The original buildings in Lawyer's Row date back to the early days of Jeffersonville. These buildings have been occupied by lawyers throughout the history of the county seat. They continue to serve that function today. In fact, this is the place where the tales of Tazewell, true and fictional, have been told and retold as the citizens and the legal communities have and continue to come together. (Courtesy of G. Michael Alford.)

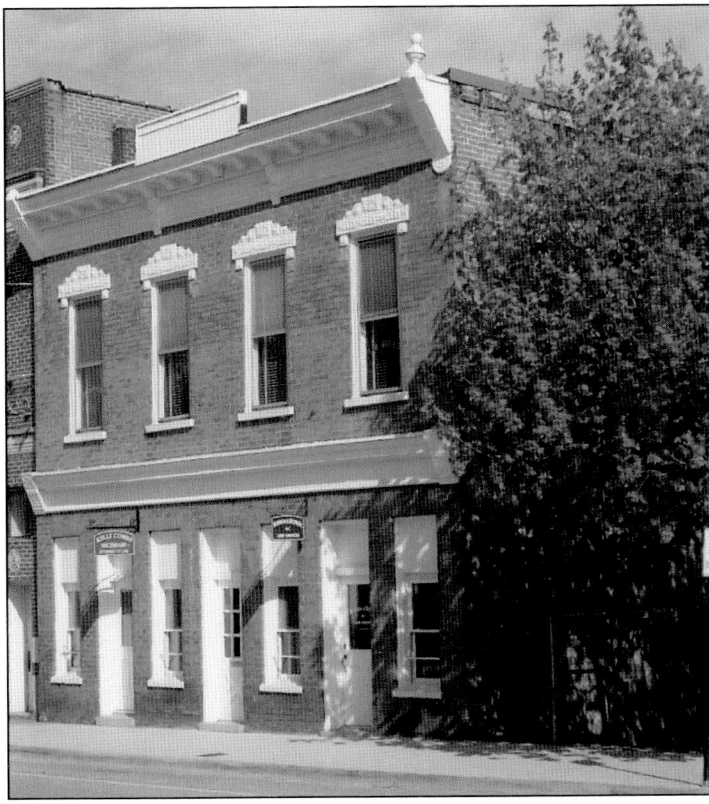

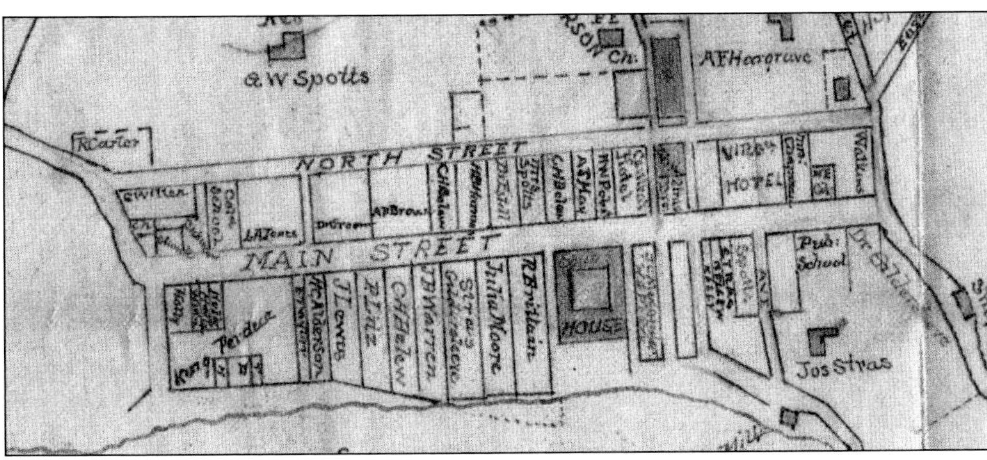

This 1888 map of Jeffersonville shows many of the business and other landowners on Main Street. Paralleling Main Street then was North Street, now known as Pine Street. Also shown on the map is the Virginian Hotel, a "colored" public school, and a "white" public school. (Courtesy of Mullins files.)

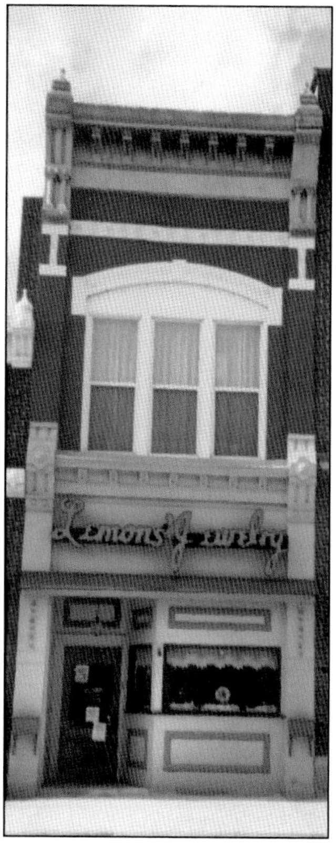

This unique narrow building on Main Street has been the site of jewelry stores since 1904, when H. W. Pobst moved into the quarters vacated by the Bank of Tazewell County. The Pobst family business continued until the 1960s, when John K. Crawford bought the store. Now it is operated by Lemon's Jewelry. The building is believed to be the original facade constructed in 1889. (Courtesy of Mullins files.)

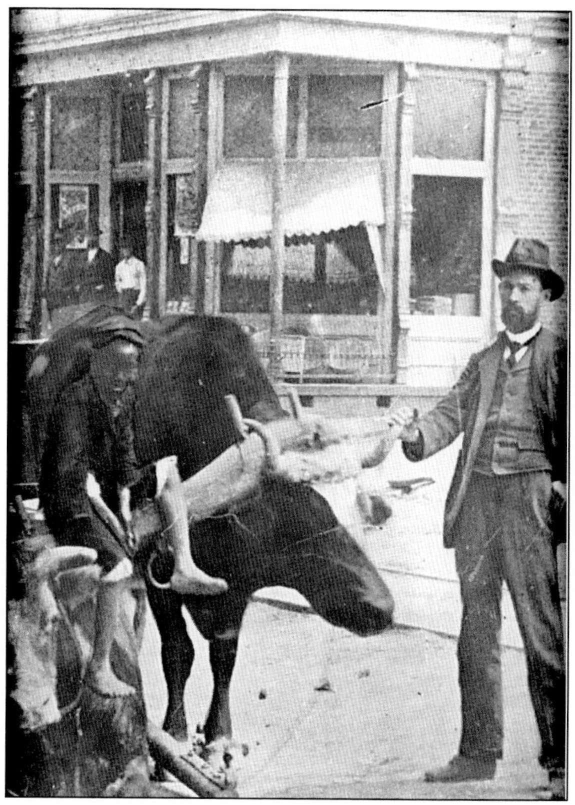

L. B. Tabor (left), Buck the ox, and H. P. Brittain (right) stand at the intersection of Main Street and Marion Avenue. The old Tazewell National Bank provides the backdrop. (Courtesy of Tazewell County Public Library.)

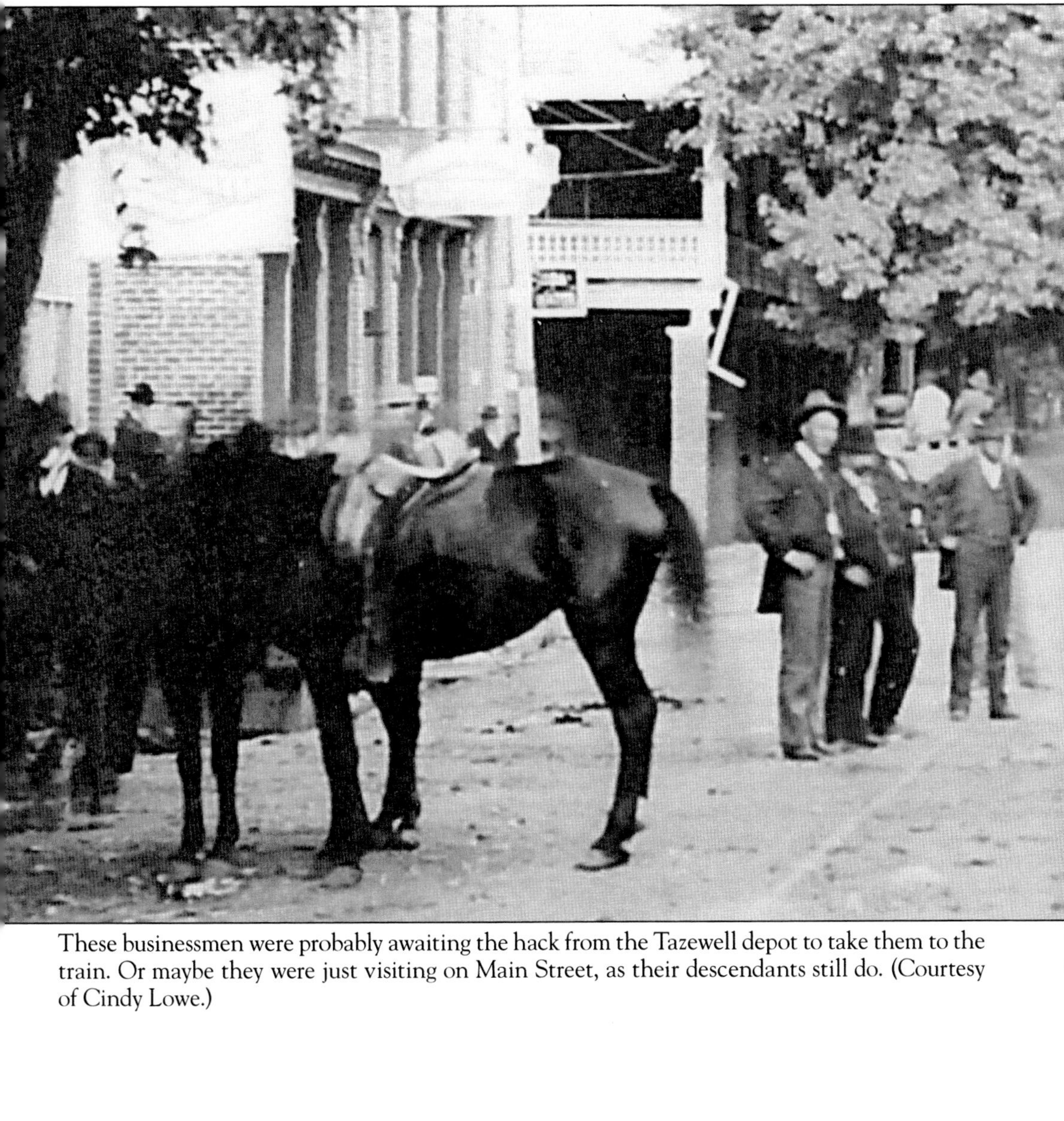

These businessmen were probably awaiting the hack from the Tazewell depot to take them to the train. Or maybe they were just visiting on Main Street, as their descendants still do. (Courtesy of Cindy Lowe.)

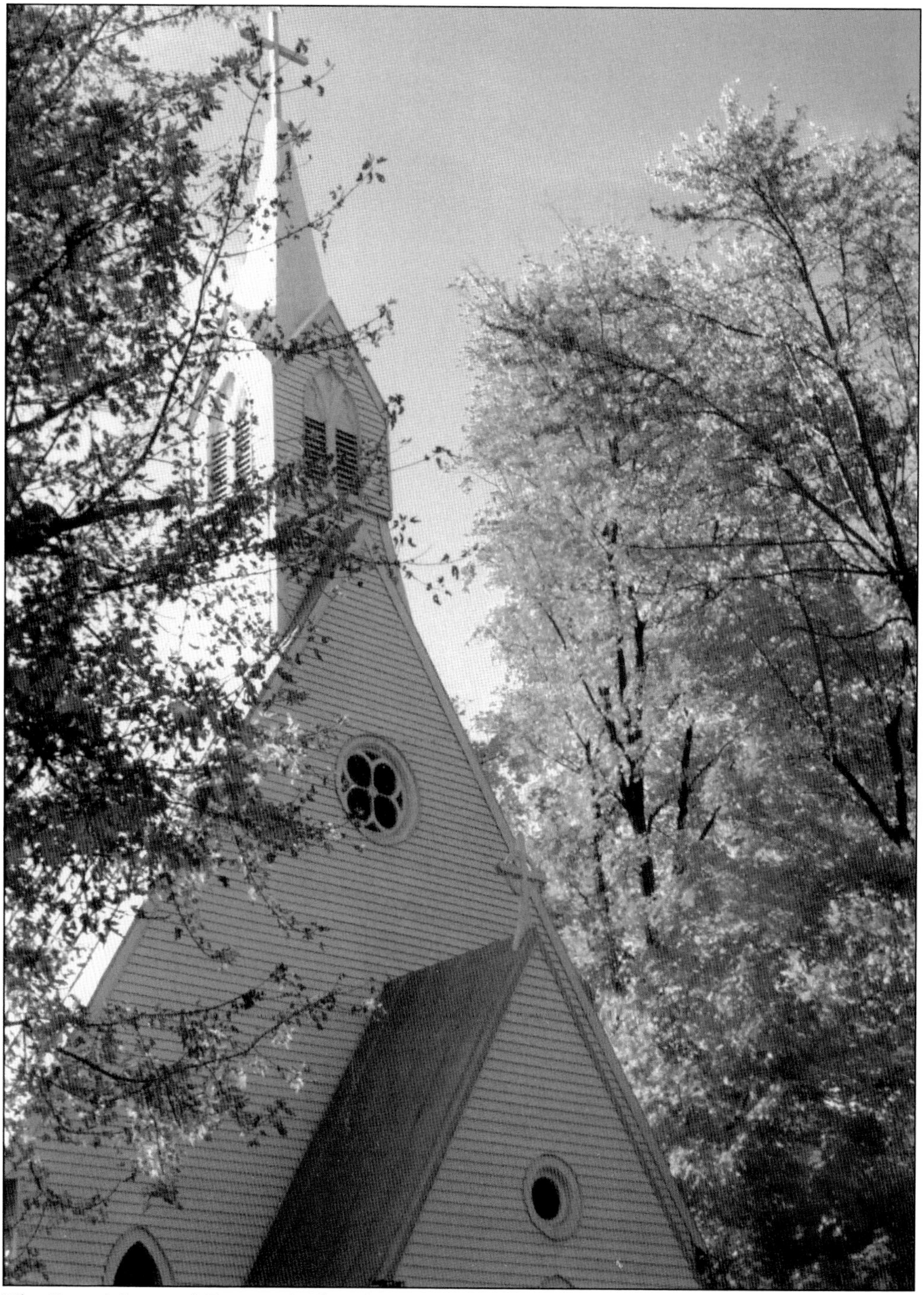

The Stras Memorial Episcopal Church, named for the Stras family, was built in 1886. Its first member was Joseph Stras, a lawyer who moved to Tazewell from Wytheville. The Stras family continues to be active in the church. The church was completely rebuilt in 2005 due to structural problems with the original building. The red door and the unique steeple add to its charm. (Courtesy of Rusty Hatfield.)

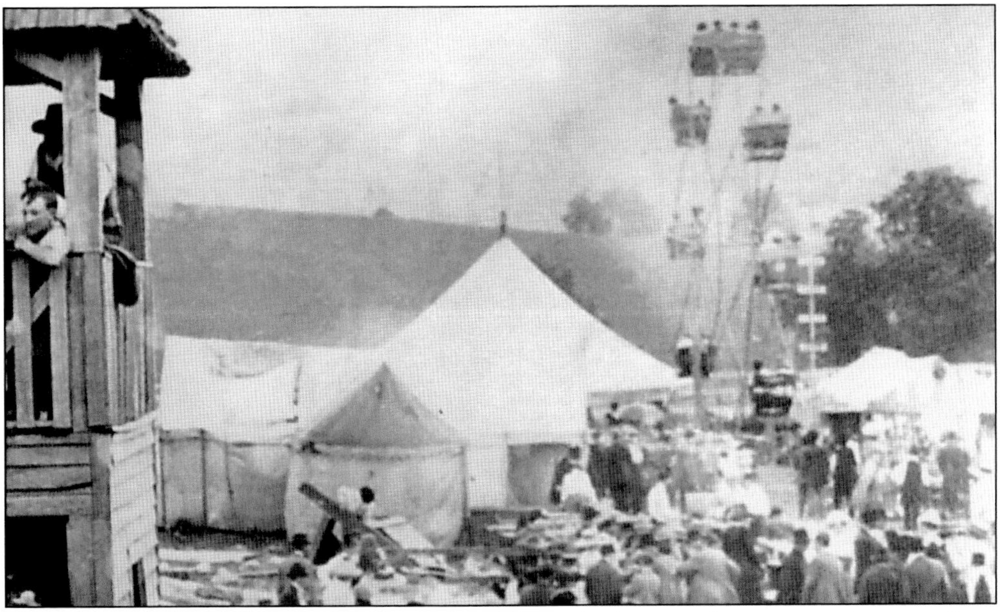

The Tazewell County Fair began in 1882 and through the years has remained an excellent showcase for local products. Nothing at the fair was more memorable, however, than the Ferris wheel, which first appeared around 1900. The original Ferris wheel had been constructed just a few years before for the 1893 World's Fair in Chicago. The Ferris wheel pictured here is, therefore, almost as old as the fair itself. Thousands have attended the fair throughout the years, and the high interest and the big crowds continue to the present time. (Courtesy of Cindy Lowe.)

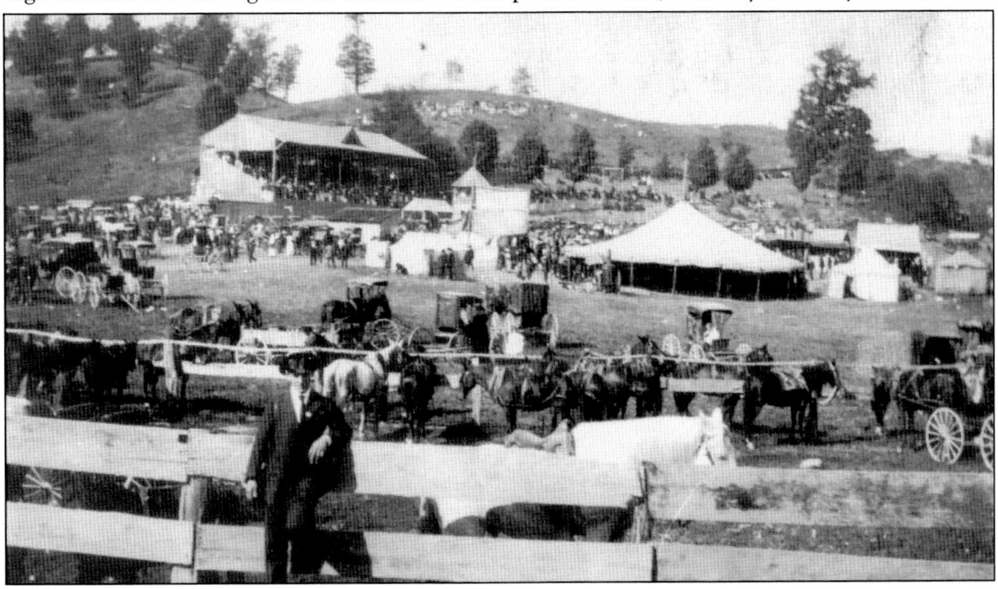

Early Tazewell fairs were noted for their fine agricultural products. The judging was very strict, and the winners displayed their championship ribbons and trophies proudly for years. The crowd that gathers at the annual event is often the largest single gathering in the county during the year. This 1897 event brought people in horses and buggies from a wide area to the fairgrounds. The popular event continues today with a full-time director, Betty Monk Melvin of Burkes Garden. (Courtesy of Cindy Lowe.)

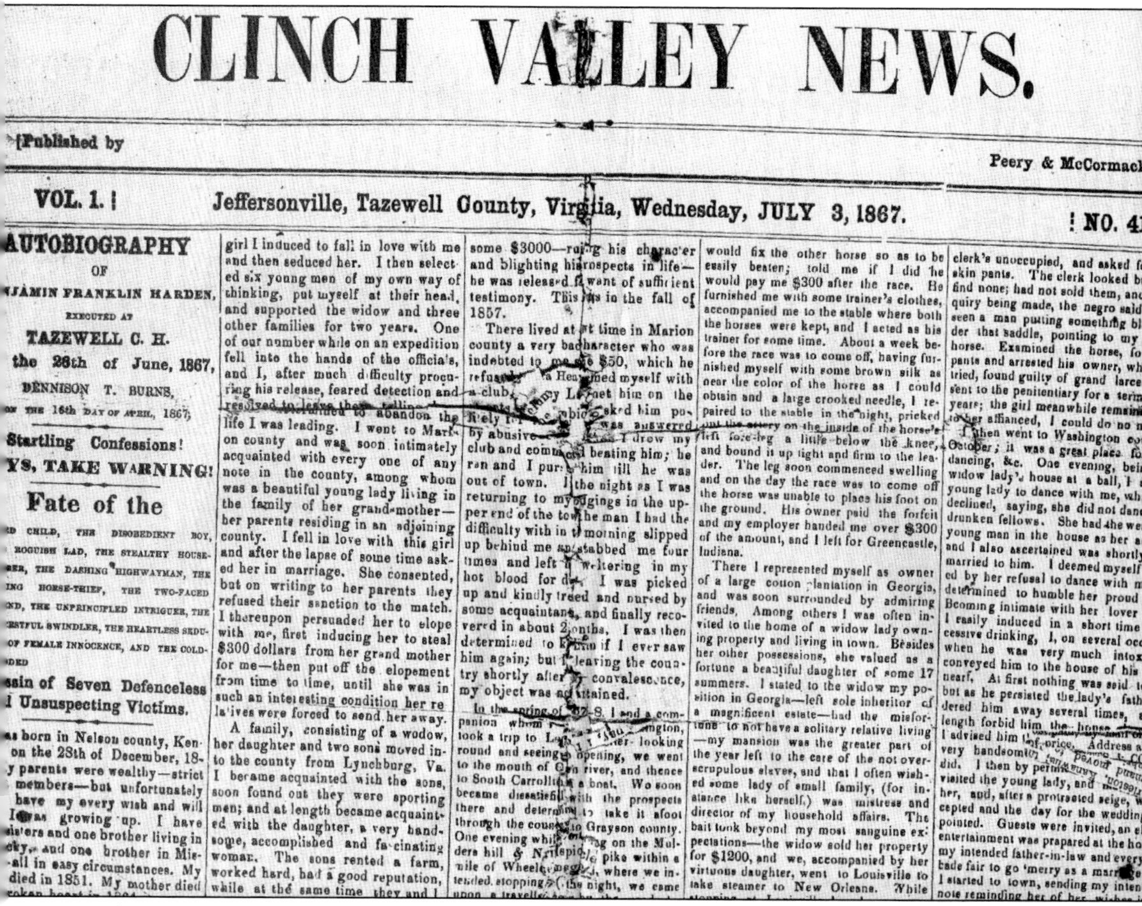

CLINCH VALLEY NEWS.

Published by — Peery & McCormack

VOL. 1. | Jeffersonville, Tazewell County, Virginia, Wednesday, JULY 3, 1867. | NO. 4

AUTOBIOGRAPHY OF [illegible]JAMIN FRANKLIN HARDEN, EXECUTED AT TAZEWELL C. H. the 26th of June, 1867, DENNISON T. BURNS, ON THE 16th DAY OF APRIL, 1867.

Startling Confessions! [illegible]YS, TAKE WARNING! Fate of the [illegible]D CHILD, THE DISOBEDIENT BOY, ROGUISH LAD, THE STEALTHY HOUSE-[illegible]ER, THE DASHING HIGHWAYMAN, THE [illegible]ING HORSE-THIEF, THE TWO-FACED [illegible]ND, THE UNPRINCIPLED INTRIGUER, THE [illegible]TFUL SWINDLER, THE HEARTLESS SEDUCER OF FEMALE INNOCENCE, AND THE COLD-[illegible]DED [illegible]ssin of Seven Defenceless [illegible] Unsuspecting Victims.

[illegible] born in Nelson county, Ken[illegible] on the 28th of December, 18-. [illegible]y parents were wealthy—strict members—but unfortunately have my every wish and will [illegible] growing up. I have sisters and one brother living in [illegible]cky, and one brother in Mis[illegible] all in easy circumstances. My [illegible] died in 1851. My mother died [illegible]

girl I induced to fall in love with me and then seduced her. I then selected six young men of my own way of thinking, put myself at their head, and supported the widow and three other families for two years. One of our number while on an expedition fell into the hands of the officials, and I, after much difficulty procuring his release, feared detection and resolved to leave them, telling [illegible] to abandon the life I was leading. I went to Mar[illegible] on county and was soon intimately acquainted with every one of any note in the county, among whom was a beautiful young lady living in the family of her grand-mother—her parents residing in an adjoining county. I fell in love with this girl and after the lapse of some time asked her in marriage. She consented, but on writing to her parents they refused their sanction to the match. I thereupon persuaded her to elope with me, first inducing her to steal $300 dollars from her grand mother for me—then put off the elopement from time to time, until she was in such an interesting condition her relatives were forced to send her away.

A family, consisting of a widow, her daughter and two sons moved into the county from Lynchburg, Va. I became acquainted with the sons, soon found out they were sporting men; and at length became acquainted with the daughter, a very handsome, accomplished and fascinating woman. The sons rented a farm, worked hard, had a good reputation, while at the same time they and I [illegible]

some $3000—ru[illegible] his character and blighting his prospects in life—he was released [illegible] want of sufficient testimony. This [illegible] in the fall of 1857.

There lived at [illegible] time in Marion county a very bad character who was indebted to me [illegible] $50, which he refused [illegible] Hea[illegible] myself with a club, [illegible] L[illegible] met him on the [illegible] asked him po[illegible] was answered by abusive [illegible] I drew my club and commenced beating him; he ran and I pur[illegible] him till he was out of town. [illegible] the night as I was returning to my lodgings in the upper end of the to[illegible] the man I had the difficulty with in the morning slipped up behind me and stabbed me four times and left [illegible] weltering in my hot blood for d[illegible]. I was picked up and kindly treed and nursed by some acquaintance, and finally recovered in about 2 months. I was then determined to [illegible] if I ever saw him again; but [illegible] leaving the country shortly after my convalescence, my object was not attained.

In the spring of '57-8, I and a companion whom [illegible] ington, took a trip to L[illegible] looking round and seeing [illegible] opening, we went to the mouth of G[illegible] river, and thence to South Carrollt[illegible] a boat. We soon became dissatisfied with the prospects there and determined to take it afoot through the country to Grayson county. One evening whil[illegible] on the Mulders hill & N[illegible] pike within a mile of Wheel[illegible], where we intended stopping [illegible] the night, we came upon a travell[illegible]

would fix the other horse so as to be easily beaten; told me if I did he would pay me $300 after the race. He furnished me with some trainer's clothes, accompanied me to the stable where both the horses were kept, and I acted as his trainer for some time. About a week before the race was to come off, having furnished myself with some brown silk as near the color of the horse as I could obtain and a large crooked needle, I repaired to the stable in the night, pricked [illegible] on the inside of the horse's left fore-leg a little below the knee, and bound it up tight and firm to the leader. The leg soon commenced swelling and on the day the race was to come off the horse was unable to place his foot on the ground. His owner paid the forfeit and my employer handed me over $300 of the amount, and I left for Greencastle, Indiana.

There I represented myself as owner of a large cotton plantation in Georgia, and was soon surrounded by admiring friends. Among others I was often invited to the home of a widow lady owning property and living in town. Besides her other possessions, she valued as a fortune a beautiful daughter of some 17 summers. I stated to the widow my position in Georgia—left sole inheritor of a magnificent estate—had the misfortune to not have a solitary relative living—my mansion was the greater part of the year left to the care of the not over-scrupulous slaves, and that I often wished some lady of small family, (for instance like herself,) was mistress and director of my household affairs. The bait took beyond my most sanguine expectations—the widow sold her property for $1200, and we, accompanied by her virtuous daughter, went to Louisville to take steamer to New Orleans. While [illegible]

clerk's unoccupied, and asked f[illegible] skin pants. The clerk looked b[illegible] find none; had not sold them, and [illegible] quiry being made, the negro said [illegible] seen a man putting something bl[illegible] der that saddle, pointing to my horse. Examined the horse, fo[illegible] pants and arrested his owner, wh[illegible] tried, found guilty of grand larce[illegible] sent to the penitentiary for a term [illegible] years; the girl meanwhile remain[illegible] to her affianced, I could do no [illegible] I then went to Washington c[illegible] October; it was a great place fo[illegible] dancing, &c. One evening, bei[illegible] widow lady's house at a ball, I [illegible] young lady to dance with me, wh[illegible] declined, saying, she did not danc[illegible] drunken fellows. She had the we[illegible] young man in the house as her a[illegible] and I also ascertained was shortly married to him. I deemed myself [illegible] ed by her refusal to dance with m[illegible] determined to humble her proud [illegible] Becoming intimate with her lover I easily induced in a short time [illegible] cessive drinking, I, on several occ[illegible] when he was very much intox[illegible] conveyed him to the house of his [illegible] neart. At first nothing was said t[illegible] but as he persisted the lady's fath[illegible] dered him away several times, [illegible] length forbid him the house [illegible] I advised him [illegible] very handsom[illegible] did. I then by per[illegible] visited the young lady, and [illegible] her, and, after a protracted seige, [illegible] cepted and the day for the wedding [illegible] pointed. Guests were invited, an el[illegible] entertainment was prepared at the ho[illegible] my intended father-in-law and every [illegible] bade fair to go 'merry as a marri[illegible] I started to town, sending my inten[illegible] note reminding her of her wishes [illegible]

This 1867 copy of the *Clinch Valley News* is the oldest edition of the county weekly in existence. This front page is labeled Jeffersonville, Tazewell County, Virginia, Wednesday, July 3, 1867. The newspaper began in 1845 and is believed to have run continuously, although many early editions have been lost. Most of the copies since 1886 are on microfilm at the Tazewell County Library and at other state libraries, including Virginia Tech and the University of Virginia. The microfilmed copies are in constant use by historians and genealogists. The *Clinch Valley News* is one of the oldest newspapers in Virginia. Its first editor and publisher was Henry M. Smyth. Other newspapers have been published in Tazewell at various times. Those newspapers include the *Tazewell Index*, the *Tazewell Times*, the *Tazewell Democrat*, the *Jeffersonville Advocate*, and the *Tazewell Republican*. (Courtesy Vertical Files, Tazewell High School.)

Two

Down on the Clinch

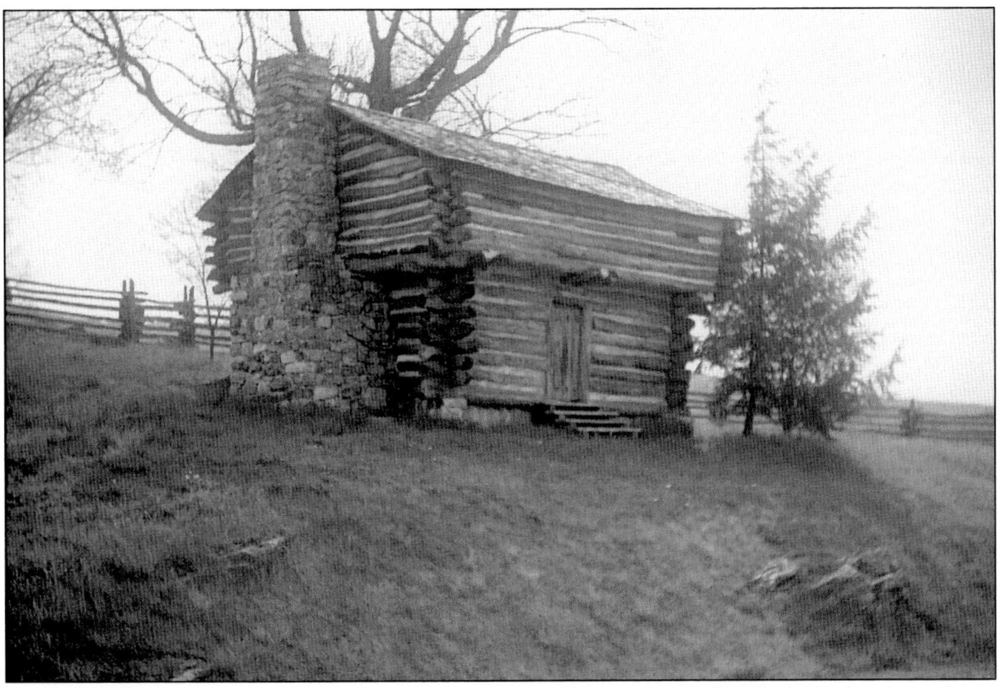

The first permanent settlement by pioneers in Tazewell County was the Crab Orchard site down on the Clinch River. The community, also known as Pisgah due to the location of the oldest church in Tazewell County, was settled by Thomas Witten and his family in the late 1760s or early 1770s. Fort Witten stands guard over a growing Tazewell, and especially the Pisgah area, as a reminder that the world is sometimes "too much with us." (Courtesy of Mullins files.)

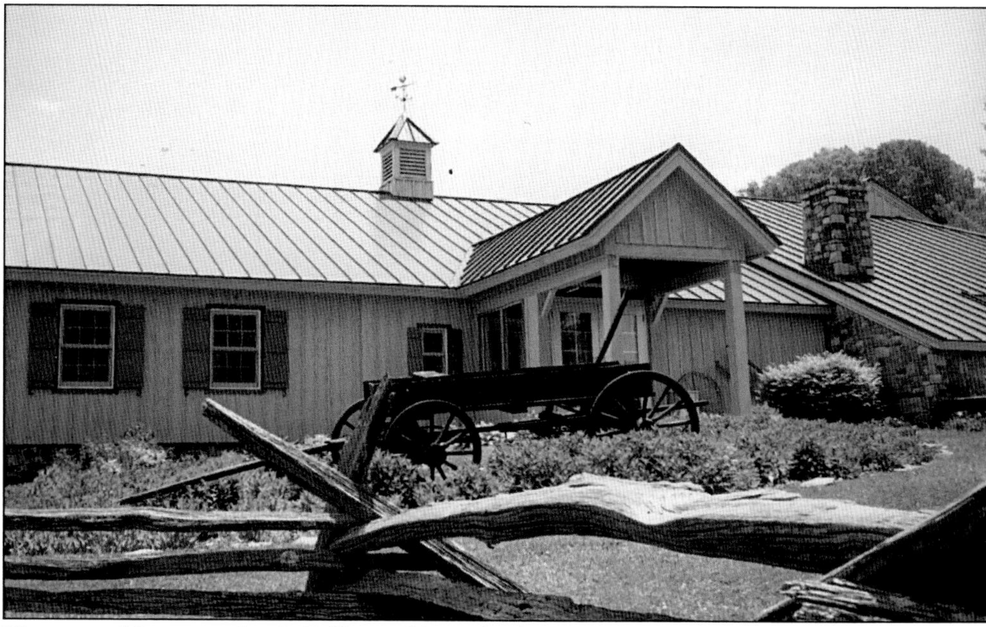

The new addition to the A. Jefferson Higginbotham Jr. Museum Center was opened in May 2006. This renovation was the most extensive building and remodeling at the Historic Crab Orchard Museum since it first opened in 1982. The first director was Nellie White Bundy, who is remembered for her persistence in seeing her dream come true. She literally pushed a wheelbarrow up and down Main Street collecting the museum's first items. (Courtesy of Mullins files.)

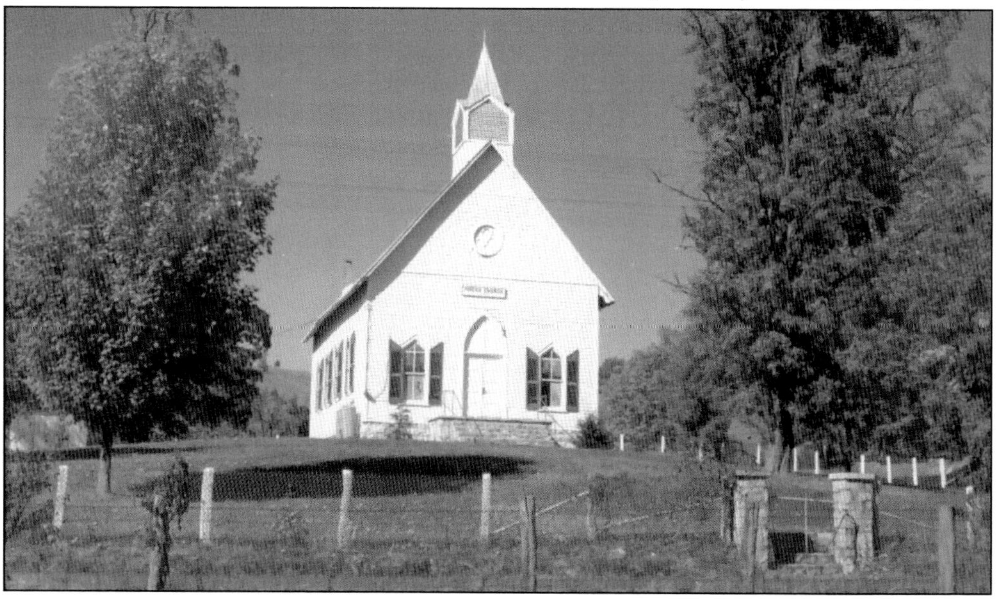

The grounds of the Pisgah United Methodist Church (UMC) have served as a gathering for picnics, family reunions, and school classes for many years. The church was organized in 1793, the first congregation in the newly settled Tazewell area. The church was actually organized six years before the creation of Tazewell County. The Pisgah Church now occupies its third building. The present structure was built in 1889 as a result of the location of the new Clinch Valley Line of the Norfolk and Western Railway on the church's earlier property. (Courtesy of Mullins files.)

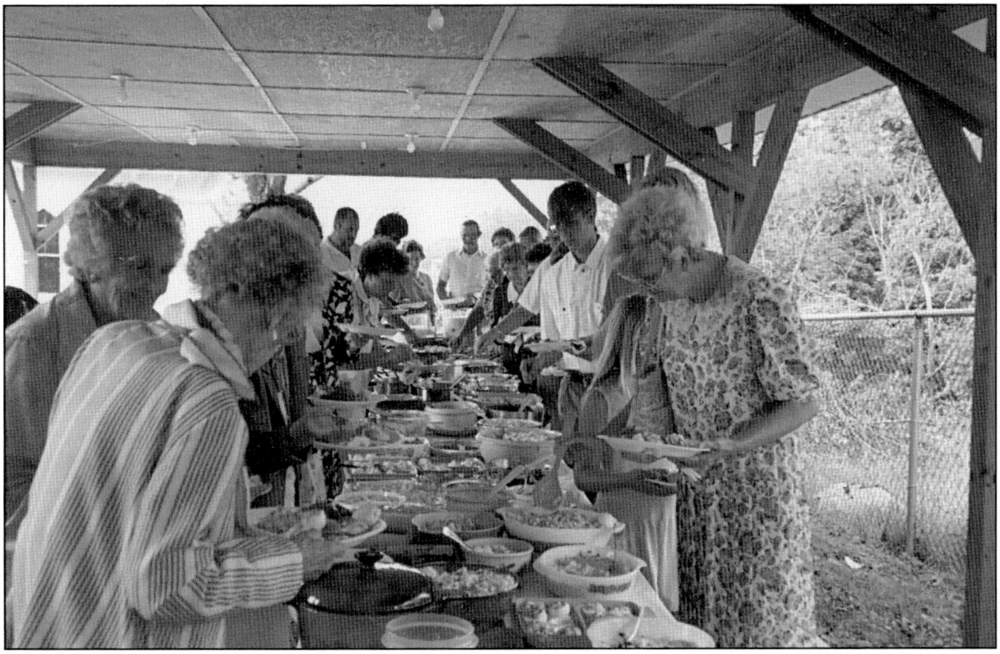

Homecomings and dinners on the grounds are common summer and fall gatherings throughout the Tazewell area. A large crowd enjoys a wide variety of local cuisine choices at the Pisgah Church's annual homecoming gathering. In fact, the picnic shelter at the Pisgah Church is a popular spot on hot summer days. For many years, a picnic at Pisgah, close to the Clinch River, has been an enjoyable Tazewell custom. (Courtesy of Mullins files.)

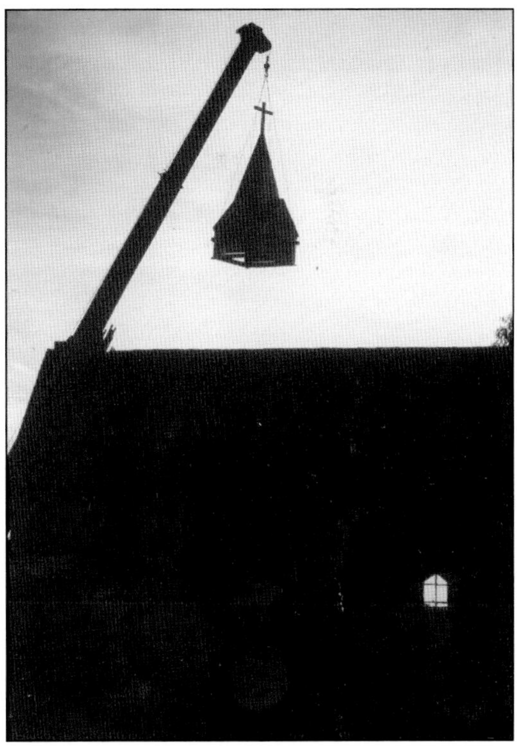

In 1975, the original steeple at Pisgah Church, including its heavy cast-iron bell, was rebuilt to correct an ominous and increasingly apparent leaning to the left. The new steeple was raised into place by a crane operated by Reece Witt. The steeple was reconstructed at Federal Supply Company in North Tazewell. Interestingly the original church was built by Federal Supply's predecessor, T. K. Hall and Sons Planing Company, at the same location in 1889. The 1975 steeple was lifted to occupy its position of prominence atop Tazewell's oldest house of worship. (Courtesy of Pisgah UMC.)

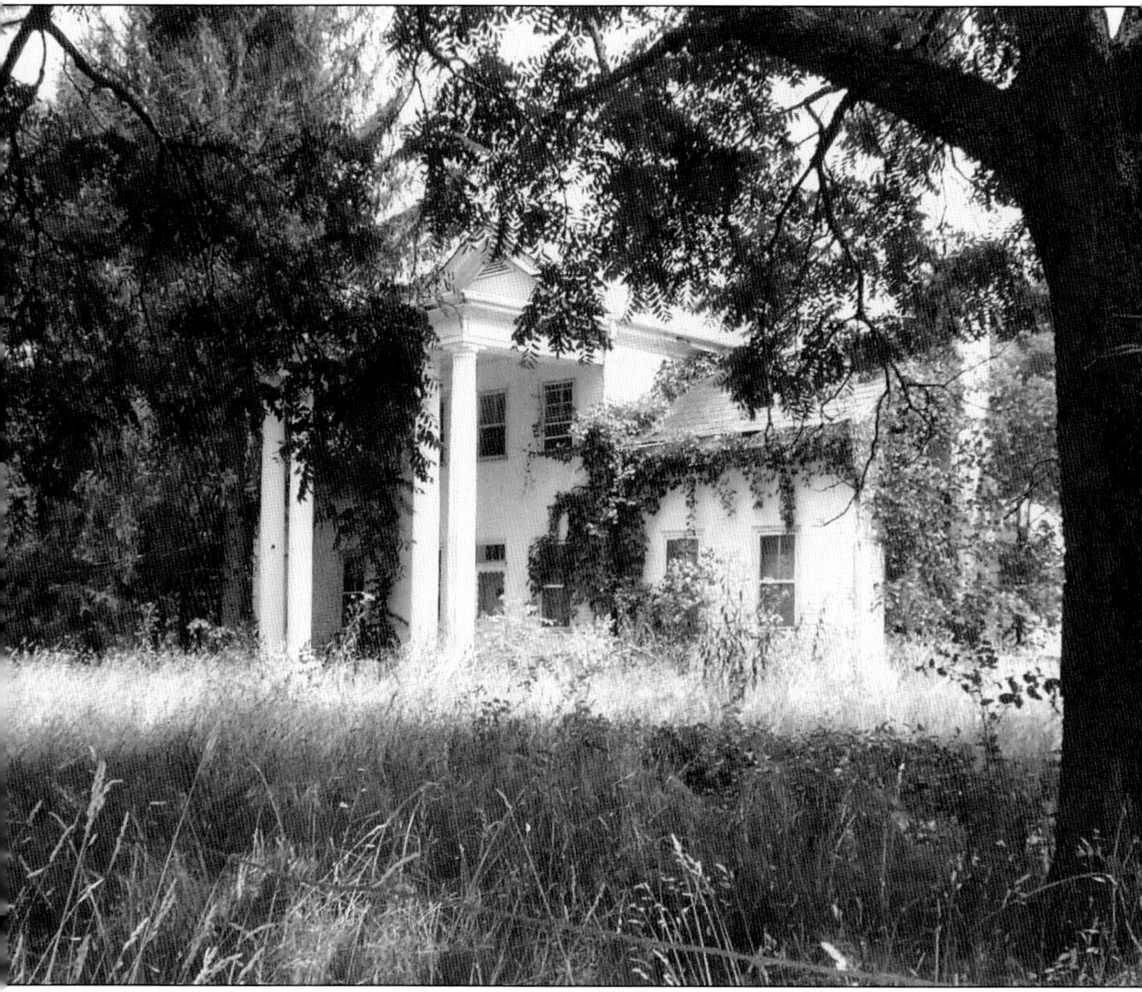

The Wilkerson Witten house was built in 1830 by brick masons Langston Shelton and Pleasant Murphy from Bedford. It has been extensively remodeled by subsequent owners, including the Olmsted family. (Courtesy of Nancy Ward files.)

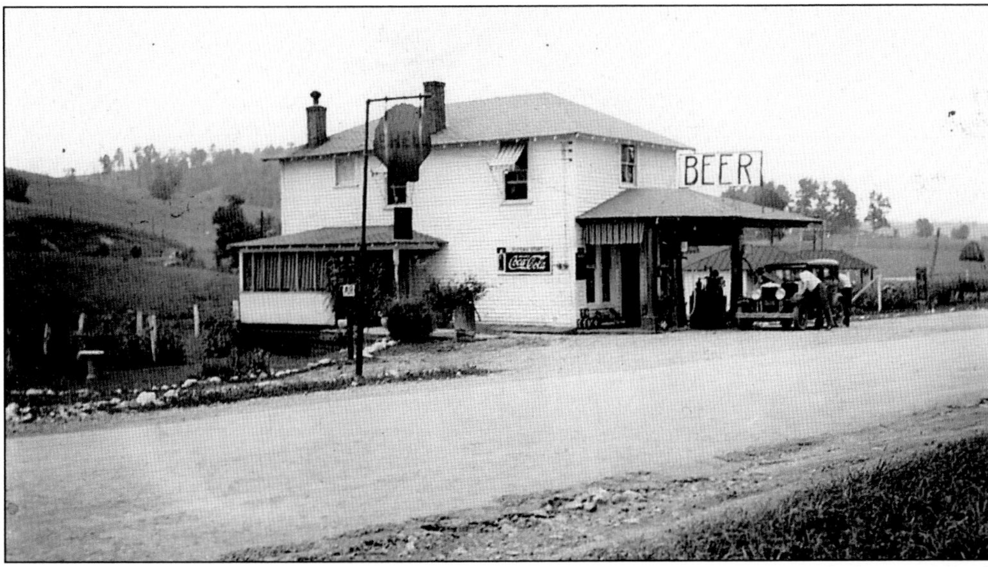

The Old Fort Inn, owned and operated by the Blanchard Keister family, stood close to Pisgah on Highway 19/460. It was originally called the Pisgah Store and served as a tourist stop and general store. This picture was taken in 1936. The building is not standing today, but many people remember visiting the popular store. (Courtesy of Emmy Keister Dennison.)

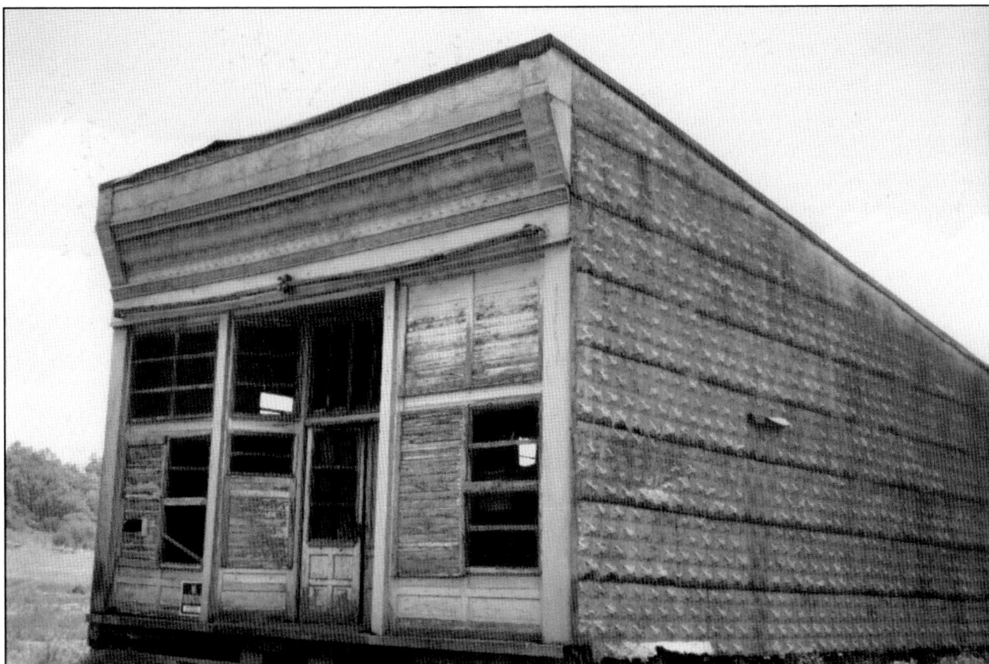

The old Pisgah Store stood by the railroad tracks close to the home of Jeff Higginbotham and family. In 2005, it was moved intact to the site adjacent to Highway 19/460 belonging to the Historic Crab Orchard Museum. It will be renovated as a typical "country store" in the near future and will be part of a historic complex planned to represent a *c.* 1900 Southwestern Virginia community. The surrounding fields were the site of a Native American village excavated when the four-lane highway was built. (Courtesy of Mullins files.)

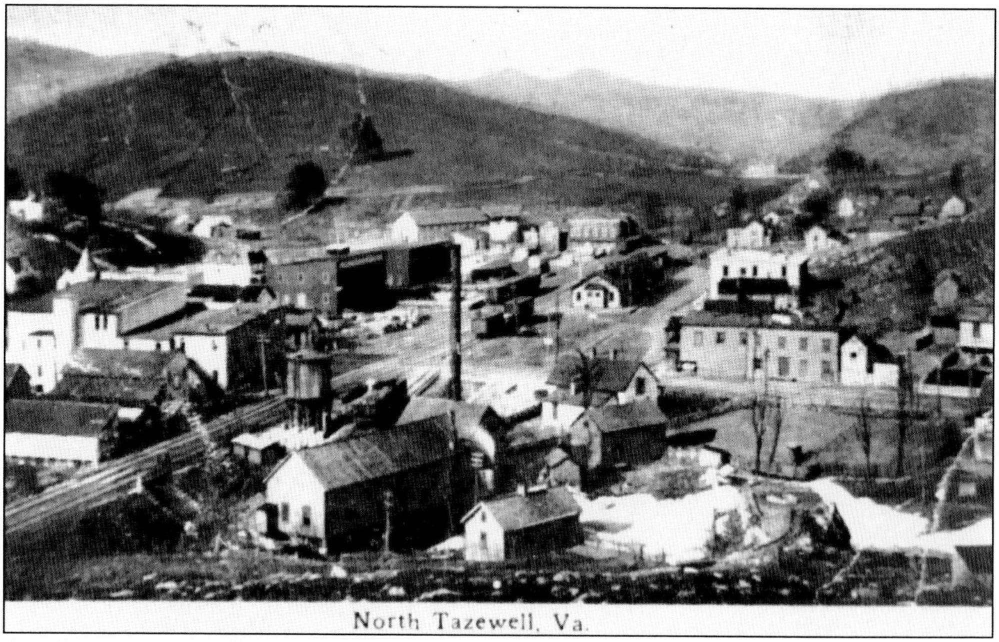

Another community that grew up "down on the Clinch" was the village of Kelly. Soon after the arrival of the railroad in 1888, Kelly, the location of the Tazewell Train Station, dubbed itself North Tazewell. (Courtesy of Jack Repass.)

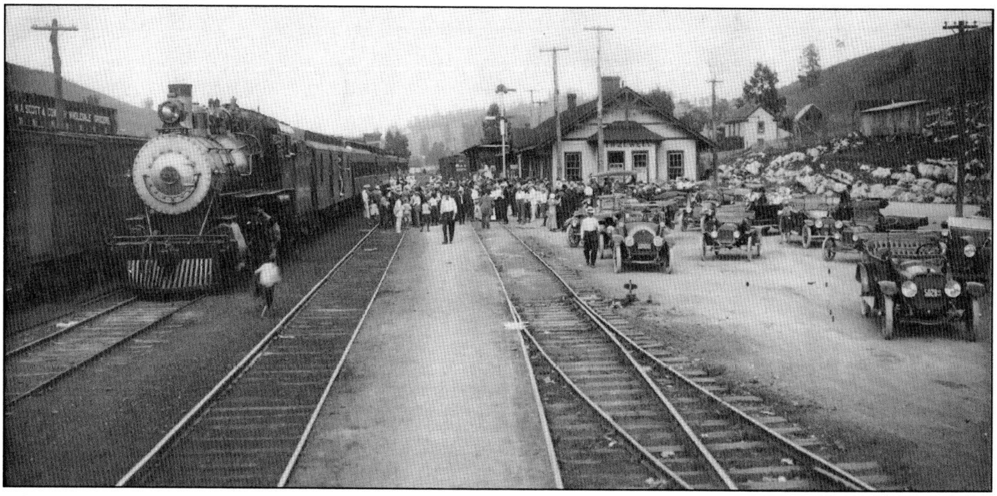

The building of the depot at North Tazewell awakened this riverside community and led to a commercial revolution. This depot is one of the many stations opened when the early days of coal shipments meant prosperity to Southwestern Virginia. Freight trains loaded with coal still pass through on their way to Norfolk and shipment overseas. In fact, North Tazewell grew up around the depot. The Norfolk and Western Railroad was instrumental in opening up the coalfields in the 1880s, and towns and businesses grew along the tracks. Among the well-remembered station agents at North Tazewell were L. L. Dickenson and Major Hatfield. Passengers can no longer board the train at North Tazewell, but a half century ago, the passenger train was an important part of the daily routine. Often people drove to the depot at 7:00 in the evening to watch the passengers get on and off. It was also possible to meet the train and mail last-minute letters. (Courtesy of Mullins files.)

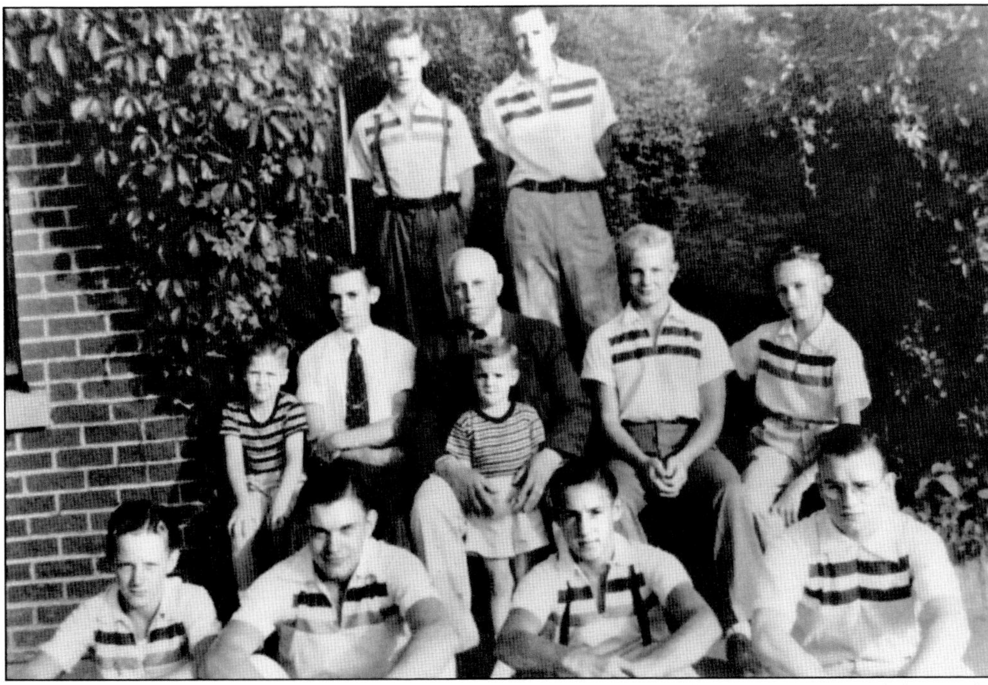

Dr. Jack Walter Witten of North Tazewell gave a home to scores of foster sons. From left to right in this 1940s picture are (first row) Bill Waldron, Harry Smith, George Grimes, and Fred Ireson; (second row) Jack Hawks, Marcus Crockett, Dr. Witten, Donny Mann, Tom Hurst, and Ashby Mahon; (third row) Morris Ferrell and Don Watson. Dr. Witten sheltered his first "son" in 1907, a seven-year-old whose mother asked him before she died to care for her young son. After World War I, Dr. Witten began the lifetime work of providing a home and education to more than 150 boys. Along with his medical practice, he served 30 years in the Virginia General Assembly. (Courtesy of Jack Repass.)

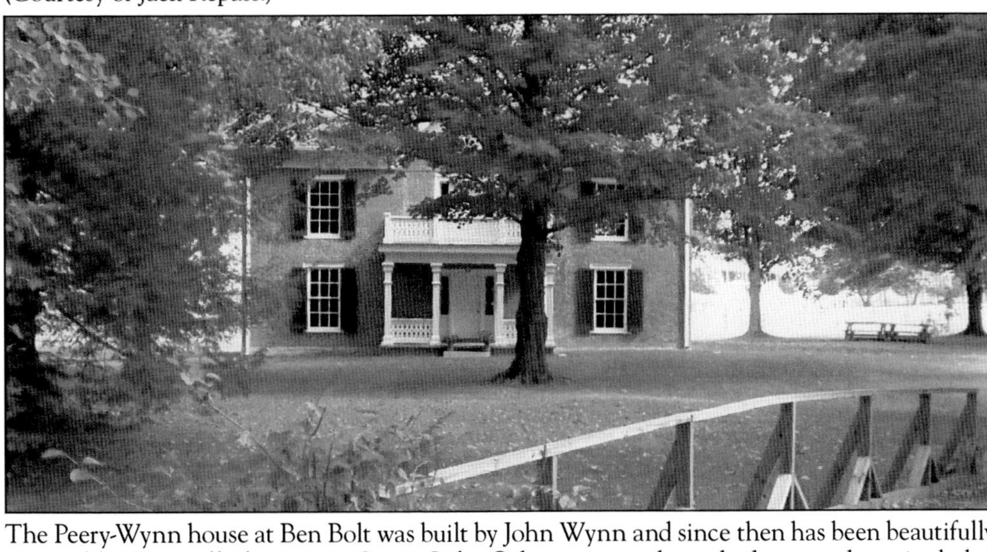

The Peery-Wynn house at Ben Bolt was built by John Wynn and since then has been beautifully restored by Tazewell pharmacist Scott Cole. Other owners through the years have included Squire Thomas Peery, Capt. William E. Peery, Harman Peery, and Robert Peery. (Courtesy of Nancy Ward files.)

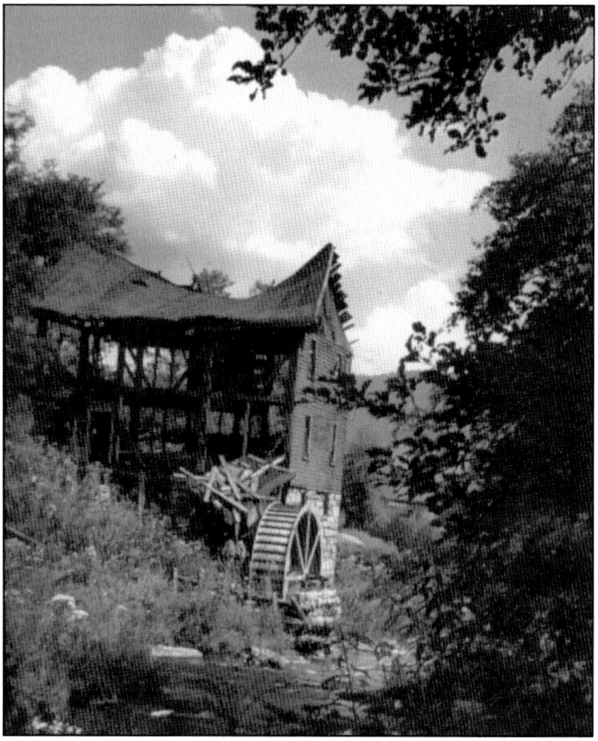

Farther up the Clinch, Witten's Mill, even in the dilapidated stage of later years, was a romantic reminder of the days when the community was thriving and the mill was an important business enterprise. The mill, often photographed, was built in 1870 by Thomas W. Witten and Richard Smoot. Only a few stones remain at the site. (Courtesy of Joe Evans.)

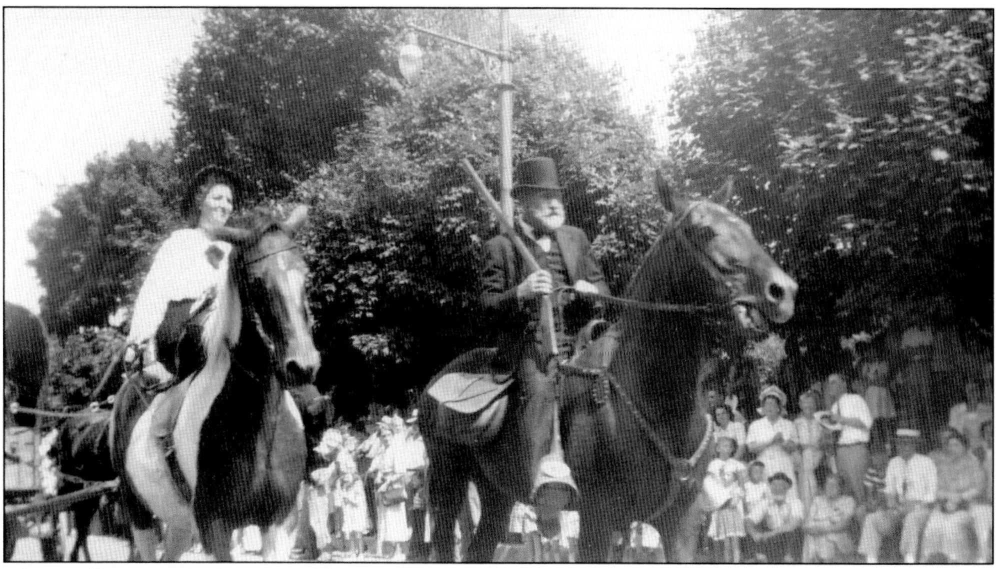

The Molly Tynes Ride, started by the Tazewell Horseman's Club in July 1963, followed the trail from Tazewell to Wytheville that Molly took 100 years earlier during the War Between the States. Due to her warning of the advancing troops, Wytheville, Fort Chiswell, and Saltville were able to successfully defend themselves. The first reenactment began at the Tyneses' home at Rocky Dell on the Gratton Road. Later the ride originated at the Tazewell Livestock Market, then located at Four Way or Burkes Garden Siding. Molly Tynes (Davidson) is buried at the Jeffersonville Cemetery. The United Daughters of the Confederacy placed a memorial at her grave. She has often been called "Paul Revere in Petticoats." (Courtesy of Nancy Ward files.)

Three

Jeffersonville Becomes Tazewell

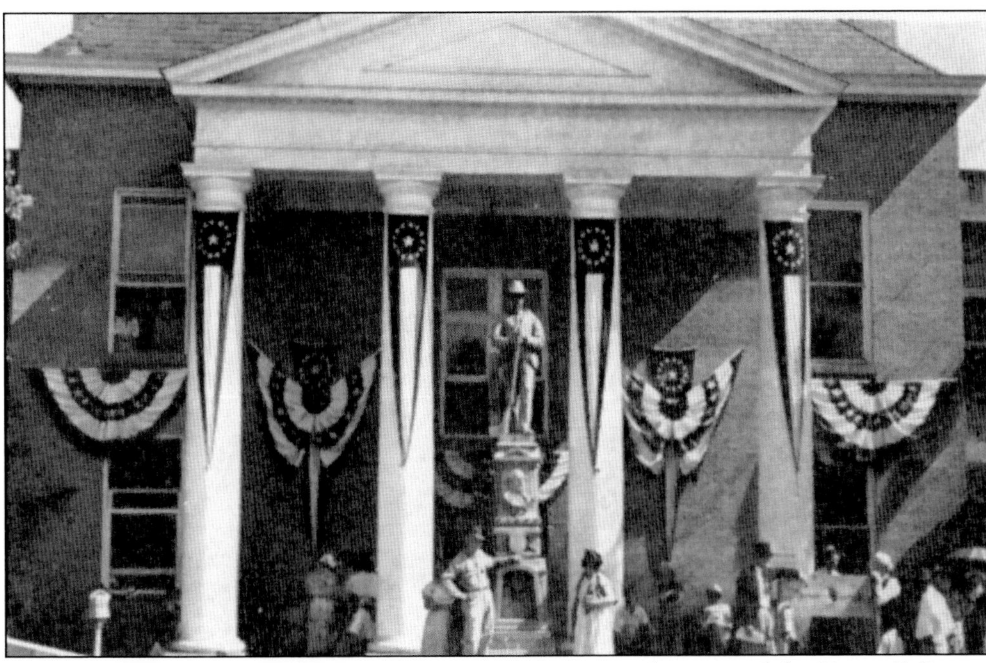

The very dignified Tazewell County Court House got into the spirit of the Tazewell County Sesquicentennial in June 1950 like many of the people who attended the big event. The columns and windows were all decked out in red, white, and blue banners. (Courtesy of June Friedl.)

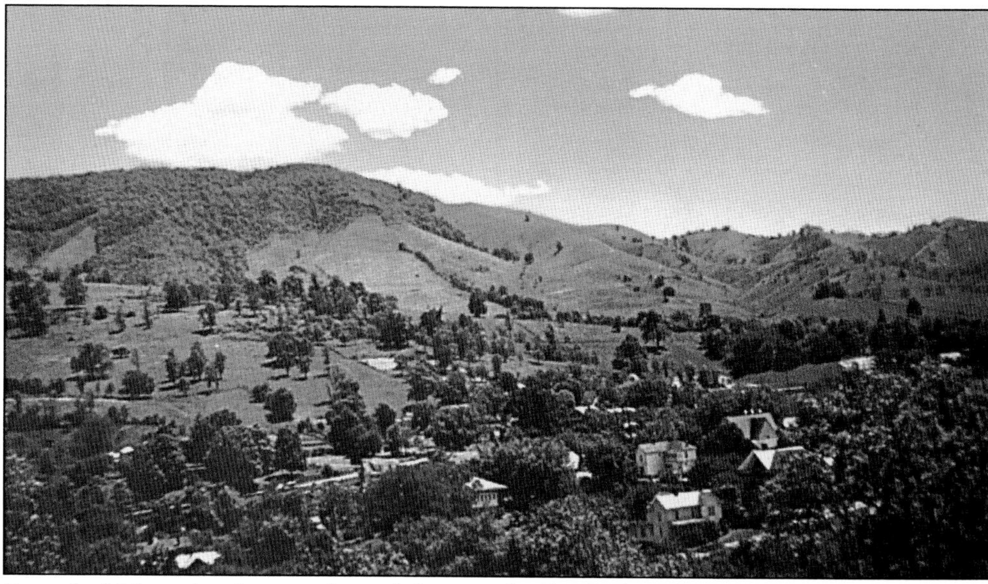

From the high peaks where modern subdivision dwellers look at the town of Tazewell, it appears to be the typical Southwestern Virginia hometown. Jeffersonville, later Tazewell, is nestled among the mountains and guarded by the beautiful Rich Mountain range. The latest census report lists 4,800 people in the town of Tazewell. (Courtesy of Tazewell County Historical Society.)

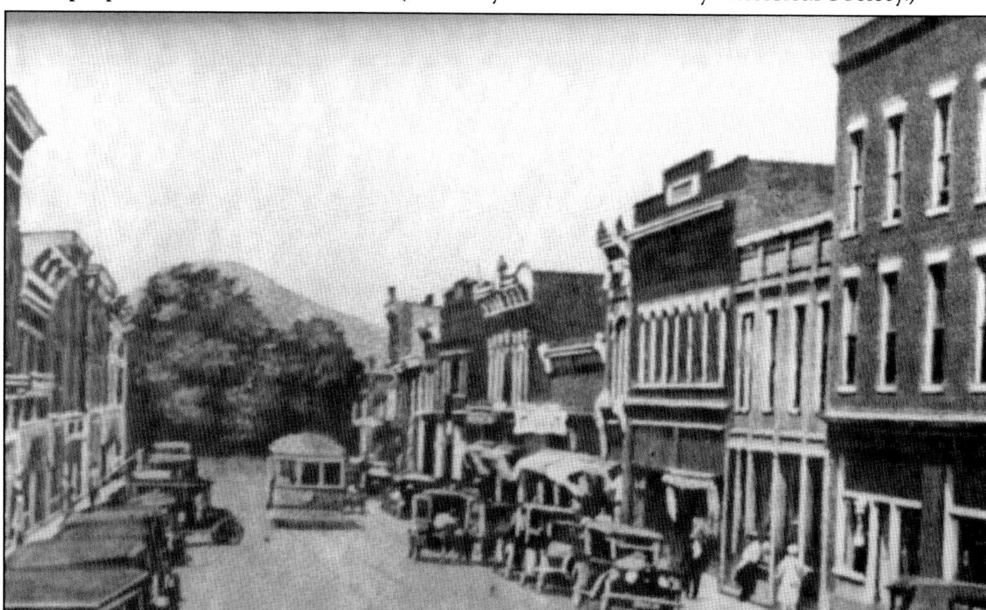

The fact that early Tazewell had a streetcar has become a unique part of the town's history. The biggest and at first unrecognized threat to streetcars during the 1920s was the rapid expansion of the use of automobiles, buses, and paved highways. After trolley service was discontinued in 1933, the original Tazewell trolley was placed in storage. Tazewell native Douglas Fleet recalls that the streetcar was sold to a Bastian, Virginia, businessman who used it for a hotdog stand in Bland County for many years. In this image, the car travels west down a Main Street lined with vintage automobiles. (Courtesy of Jeff Higginbotham.)

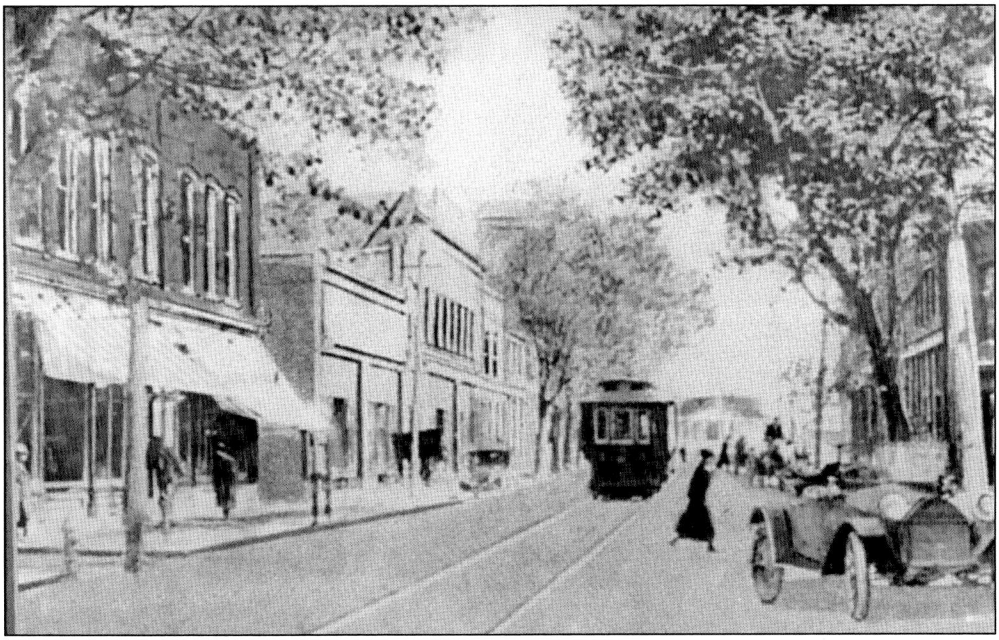

With the streetcar and a horse-drawn wagon coming, this woman made a quick run to safety across Main Street. The streetcar was tan colored with a bright red stripe running along the side of the car. The car was parked on a "Y" track in the car barn on Tazewell Avenue, also known as "Carline." The streetcar left Main Street on the hour and half past the hour. It left North Tazewell and the depot at a quarter past and three quarters past each hour. Note the trees on Main Street, which were a casualty to modern traffic in later years. (Courtesy of Jeff Higginbotham.)

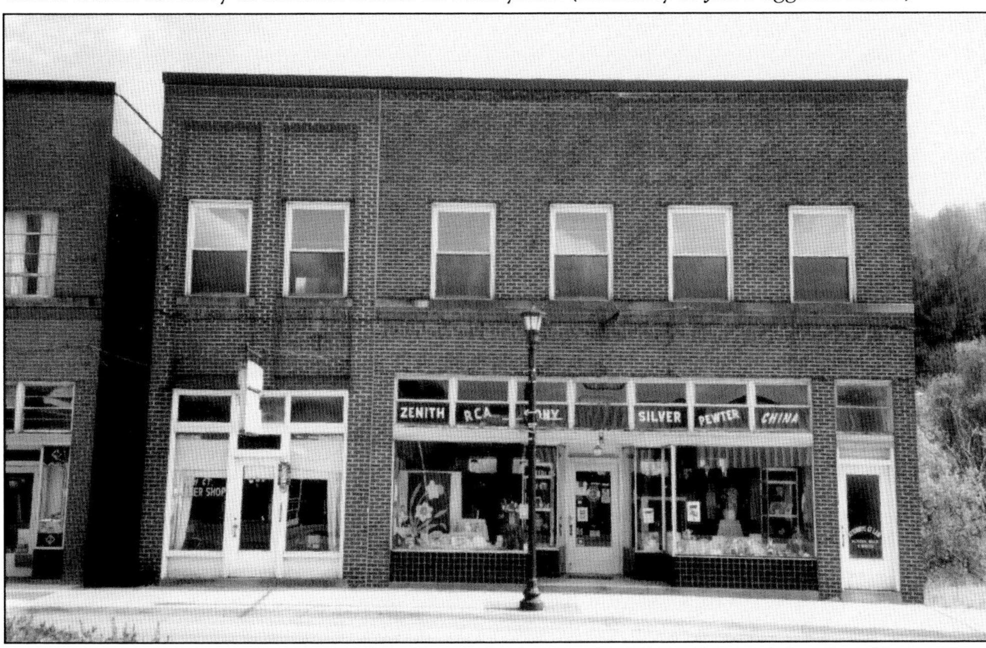

Van's TV and Gift Shop is owned by the VanDyke family. The offices of the Candlewax Coal Company, owned by the same family, are located upstairs. To the left is Fred McFarland's Barber Shop, a longtime establishment on Main Street. (Courtesy of Mullins files.)

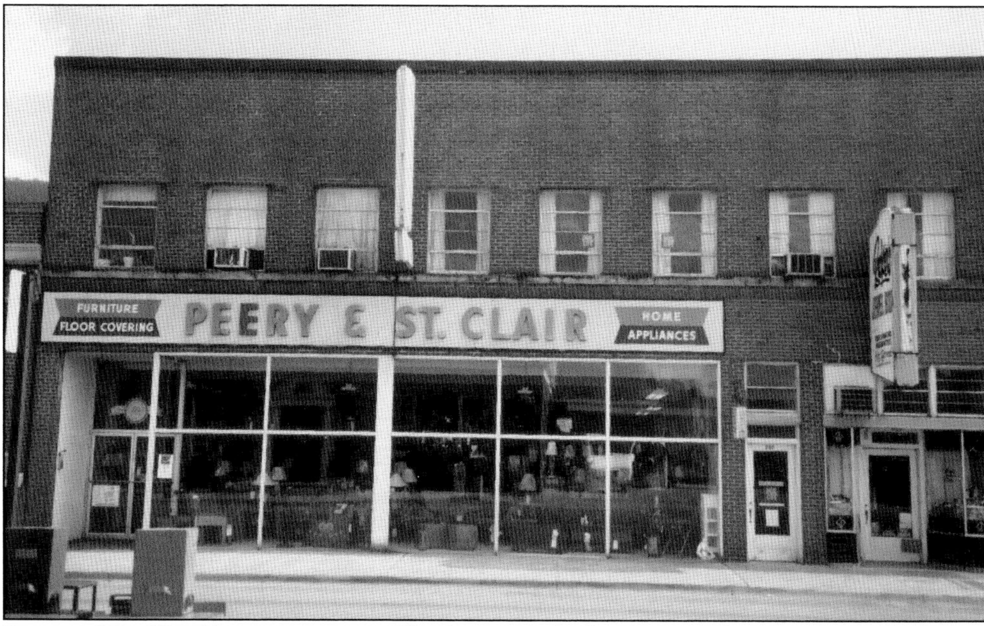

Peery and St. Clair Furniture, operated by the VanDyke family, moved to this location in recent years after being a block east on Main Street. Earlier this building was the site of the Federated Store, an important clothing business. Peery and St. Clair Funeral Home is located on Ben Bolt Avenue. Peery and St. Clair, Inc., was founded in the 1800s by the prominent Peery and St. Clair families. To the right is Becker's Jewel Box, owned and operated by Luther and Cynthia Becker. (Courtesy of Mullins files.)

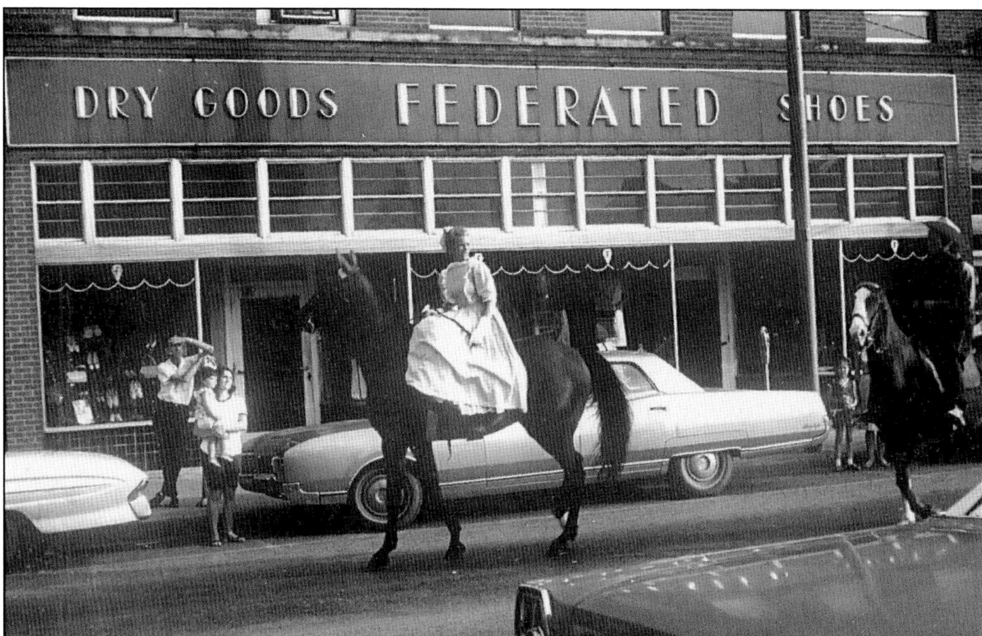

The Federated Store, pictured in 1959, was a popular clothing store. Business offices were upstairs. It stood at the present site of Van's TV and Gift Shop and was operated by the VanDyke family. This building is now occupied by Peery and St. Clair Furniture. (Courtesy of Mullins files.)

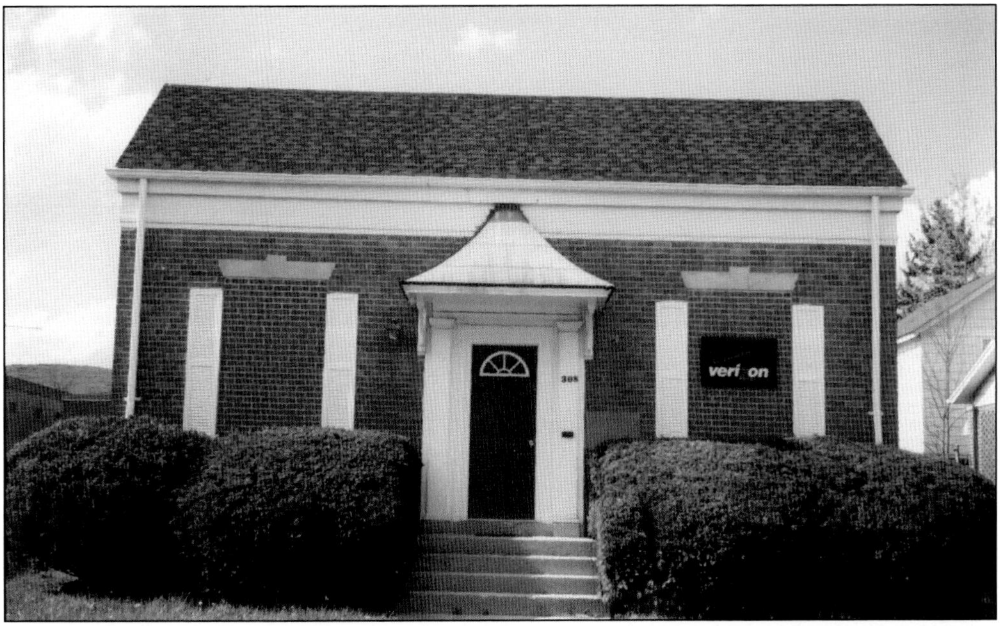

The telephone company building now serves Verizon and prior to that the General Telephone Company. Until 1941, the telephone company was located on Elk Street. This telephone office on West Main Street has undergone many changes through the years, from the friendly local operator who answered all calls to the modern system. (Courtesy of Mullins files.)

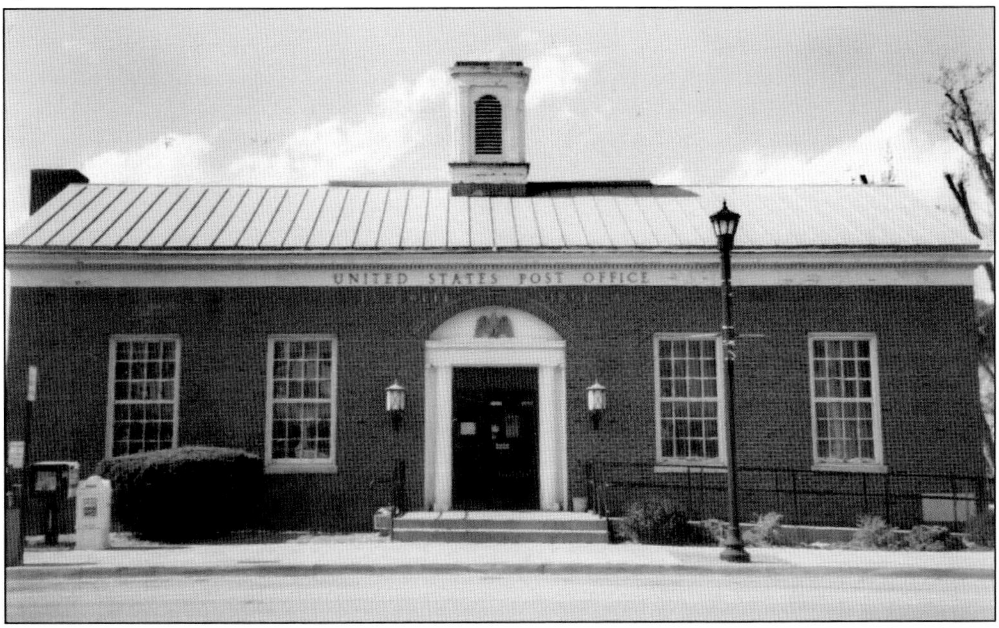

The Tazewell Post Office is located on the western end of Main Street. Two examples of New Deal–era mural art are found on the walls of the post office. The Tazewell murals were painted by a 30-year-old artist, William H. Calfee of Washington, D.C., between July 1939 and July 1940. Calfee also painted murals in Virginia at Harrisonburg, Petersburg, and Phoebus, as well as Shelbyville, Delaware, and Bel Air, Maryland. His Phoebus mural was selected as the best in Virginia in a competition sponsored by *Life* magazine. (Courtesy of Mullins files.)

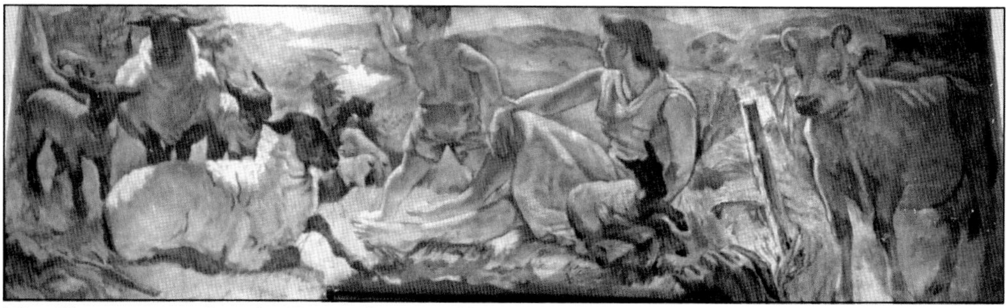

The "depression art" at the Tazewell Post Office is recognized as valuable folk art. Costing $900, the murals are oil paintings described in an inventory completed in 1972 by Prof. Dean Carter of Virginia Tech as "realistic with emphasis on line, rather light tonalities, light greens, blues, and earth colors, very thinly painted." This mural, *Sheep—Mother and Child—Cow*, represents the significant impact that agriculture has had on Tazewell's history. A woman and a child are seen sitting on a hill, typical of Southwestern Virginia. To their right and left are sheep and cows, also typical of this region. (Courtesy of Mullins files.)

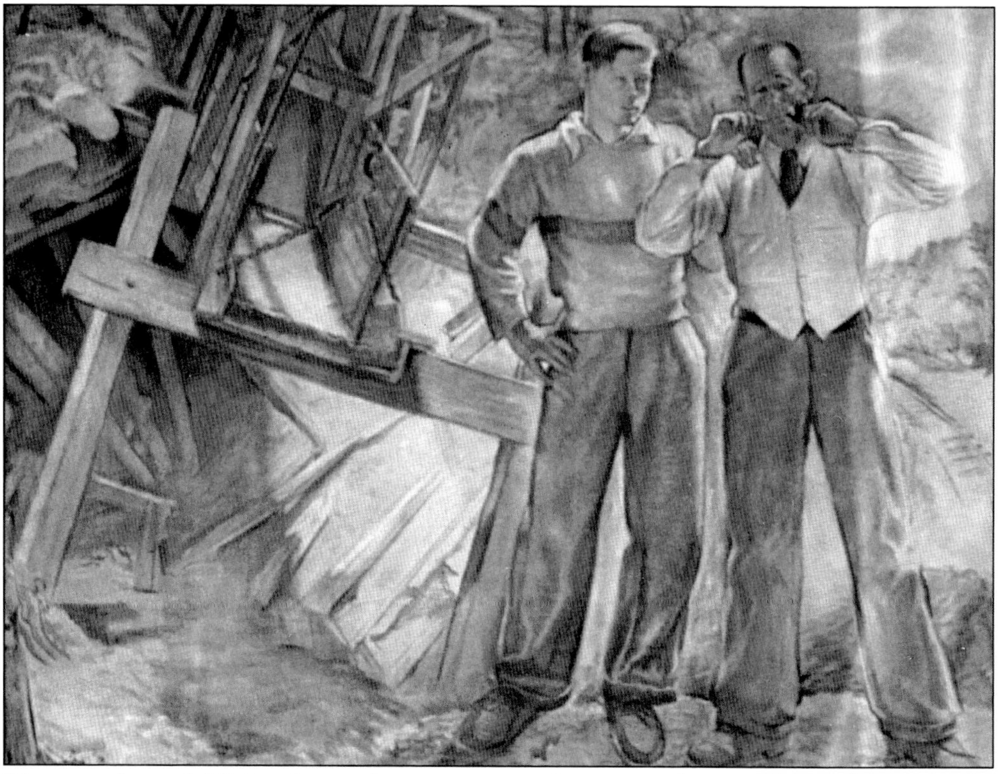

The second mural, *Mining*, depicts the important coal mining industry and its influence on the Tazewell area. In this mural, a man and a boy are shown standing in front of a small mine from which coal is moved by sliding it down a shaft. Unemployment was a big problem in the 1930s. During the nationwide Depression, the government commissioned artists to decorate many of the nation's public buildings as a way of providing jobs. More than just decorations and often mistaken as WPA projects, these murals were actually the Treasury Department Section of Painting and Sculpture's effort to restore confidence in people during the Great Depression. Post offices were chosen as places to display the art since many ordinary citizens conduct business there routinely. (Courtesy of Mullins files.)

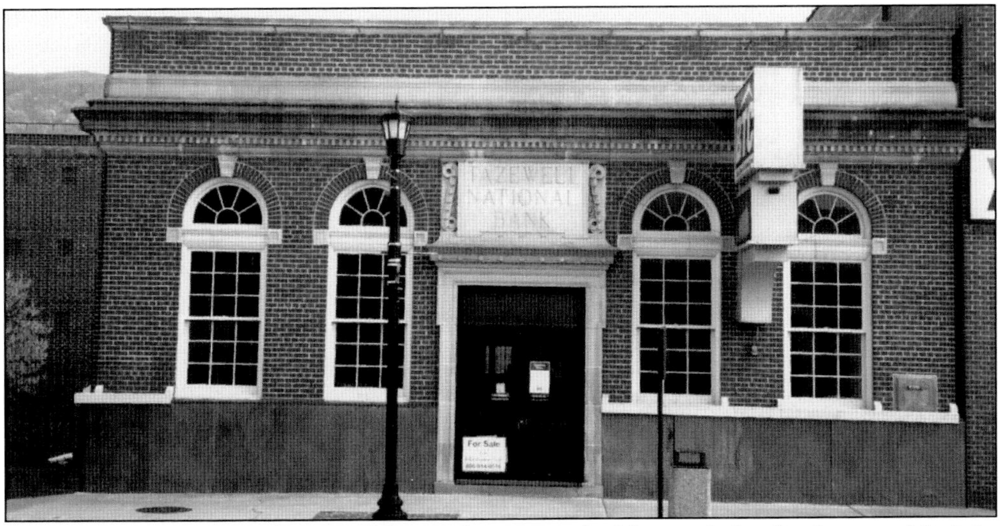

The Tazewell National Bank, a sound financial institution highly regarded in Southwestern Virginia, was organized in 1902 with George W. Gillespie as president. In recent years, the main office was at the new building in the Four Way area. Changes in ownership have brought the bank under the auspices of Premier Bank, North America, First Virginia Bank–Clinch Valley, and the present BB&T Corporation. For a short time, the branch bank at the earlier headquarters on Main Street was operated by Planters Bank. In 2006, this bank was sold to National Bank and joined the former Bank of Tazewell County under the National Bank name. (Courtesy of Mullins files.)

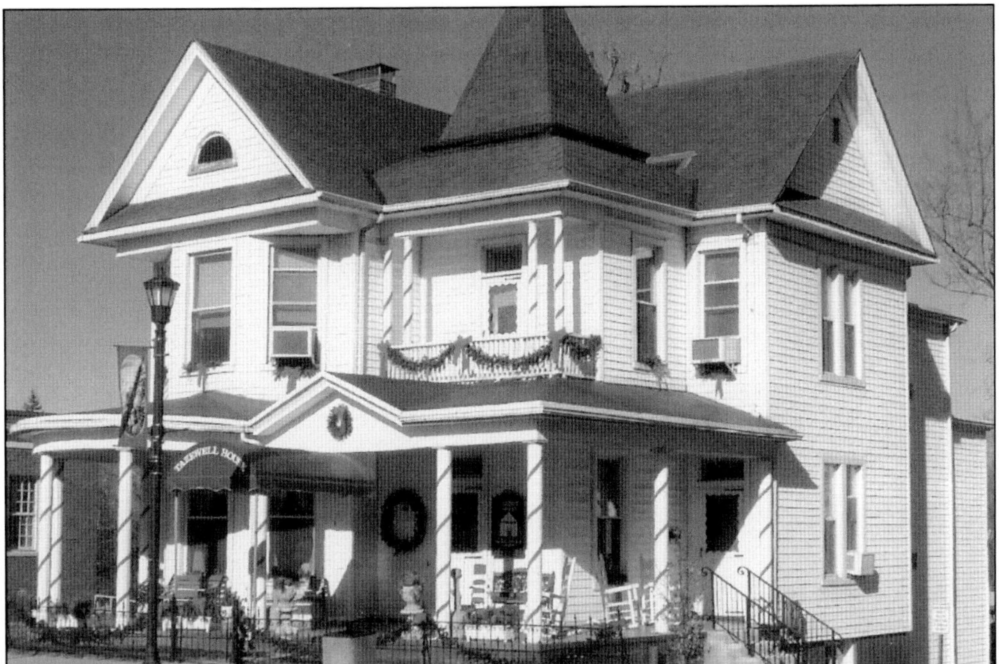

Tazewell House has stood silently as many Tazewell parades have passed by since it was built on Main Street in 1899. Before it was Tazewell House, it served as a private residence and later the Peery and St. Clair Funeral Home. Tazewell House is now maintained by the Cumberland Mountain Community Services. (Courtesy of G. Michael Alford.)

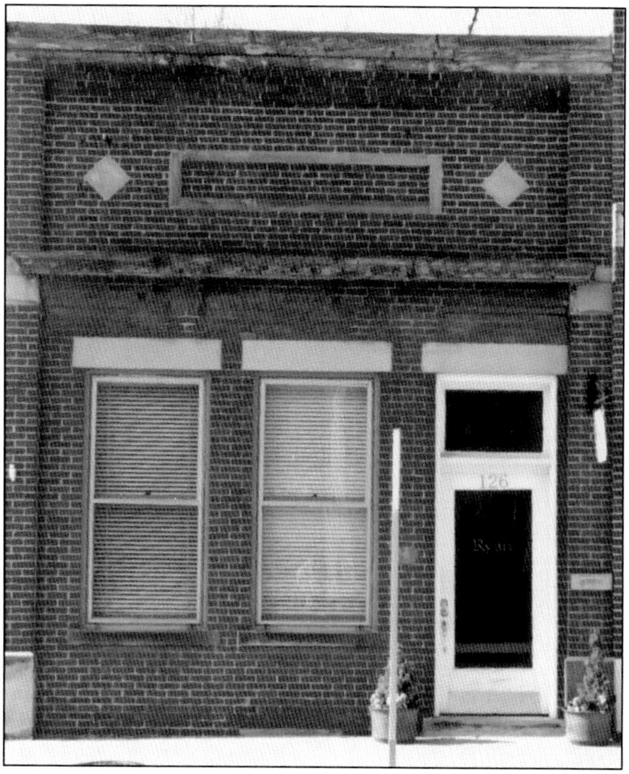

Number 126 Main Street is a special address in Tazewell's legal community. At different times, the offices of Gov. George C. Peery and Supreme Court Justice A. C. Buchanan were located there. These two outstanding state leaders were both Tazewell County natives. The Ryan Law Firm now occupies this building. (Courtesy of Mullins files.)

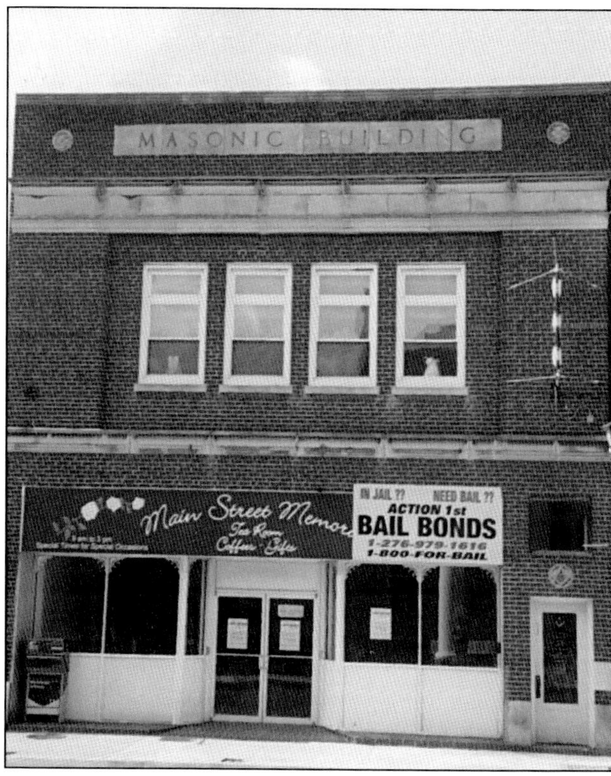

Tazewell Masonic Lodge Number 62 was chartered in Jeffersonville in 1852. William P. Cecil was designated as worshipful master. The meeting place for the lodge was originally in the Tazewell County Court House. The original lodge, constructed around 1891, was over the store of James P. Kelly on Main Street. The worshipful master at that time was T. R. Peery. The Clinch Valley Commandery of Knights Templar was organized in Tazewell in 1892. James O'Keeffe was eminent commander. The present building was constructed in 1931. J. S. Bottimore was the first grand master of Masons in Virginia from the Tazewell Lodge around 1900. Earl S. Wallace was the second grand master of Virginia Masons from the Tazewell Lodge in 1958. (Courtesy of Mullins files.)

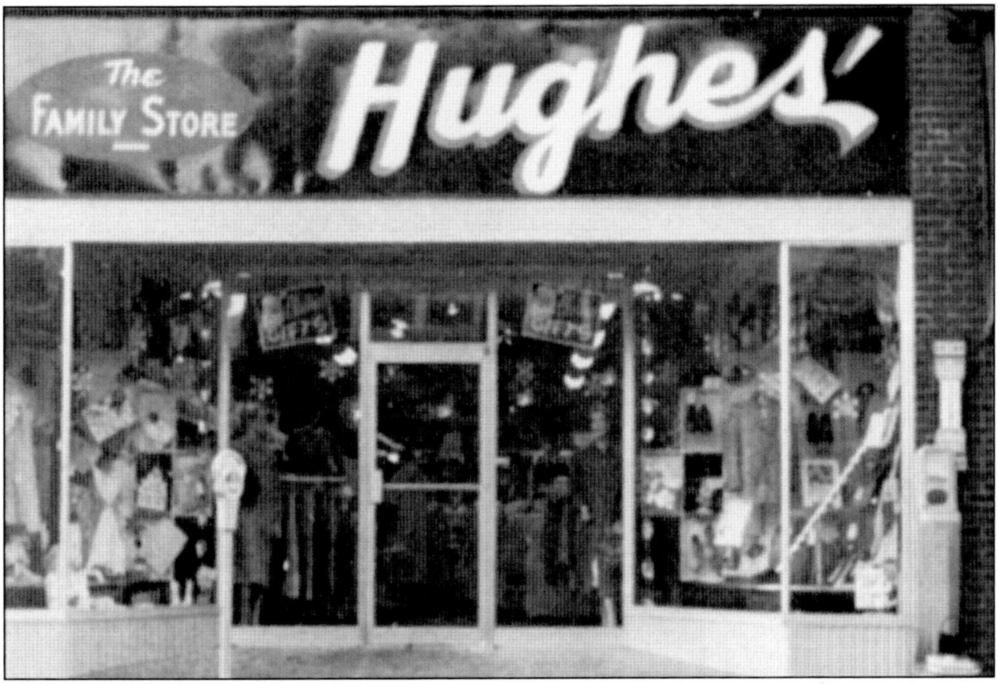

Hughes Shoe Store was owned and operated by Bill Hughes and his wife, Katherine, for many years. Bill Hughes and his brother, Jim, were recognized for their artistry in creating the Christmas decorations on Main Street. The decorations were acclaimed statewide for their unique beauty. The post office was once in this location. (Courtesy of Mullins files.)

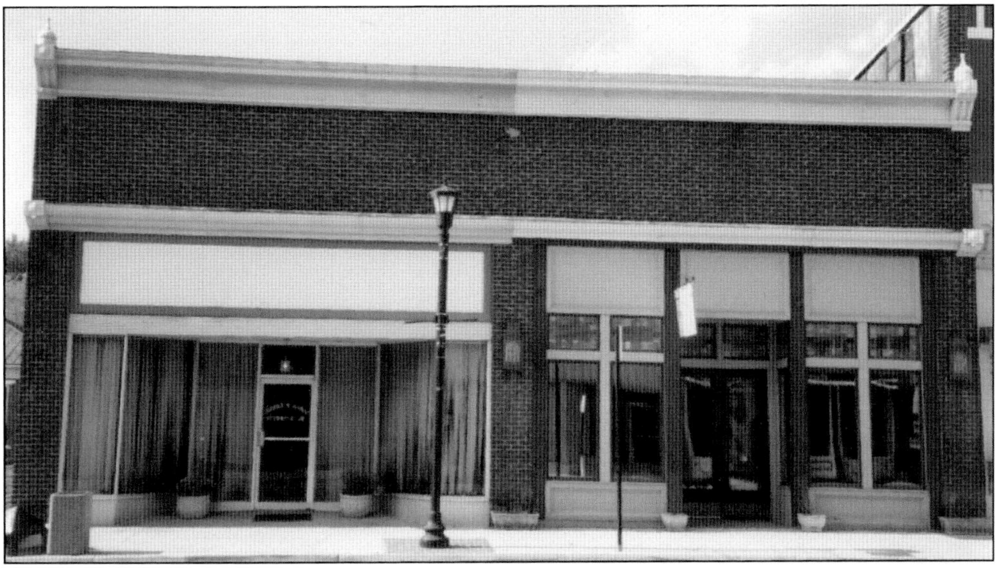

Adjoining the Hughes Shoe Store was the Jackson Drug Company, organized in 1897. These two buildings were once owned by the Witten family and were often called by that family name. Jackson's was known throughout the county for its fountain and good food, as well as its medicines and notions. The law offices of Frederick W. Harman and Felicia de Courcy occupy the former Main Street businesses of Hughes Shoe Store and Jackson Drug Company. (Courtesy of Mullins files.)

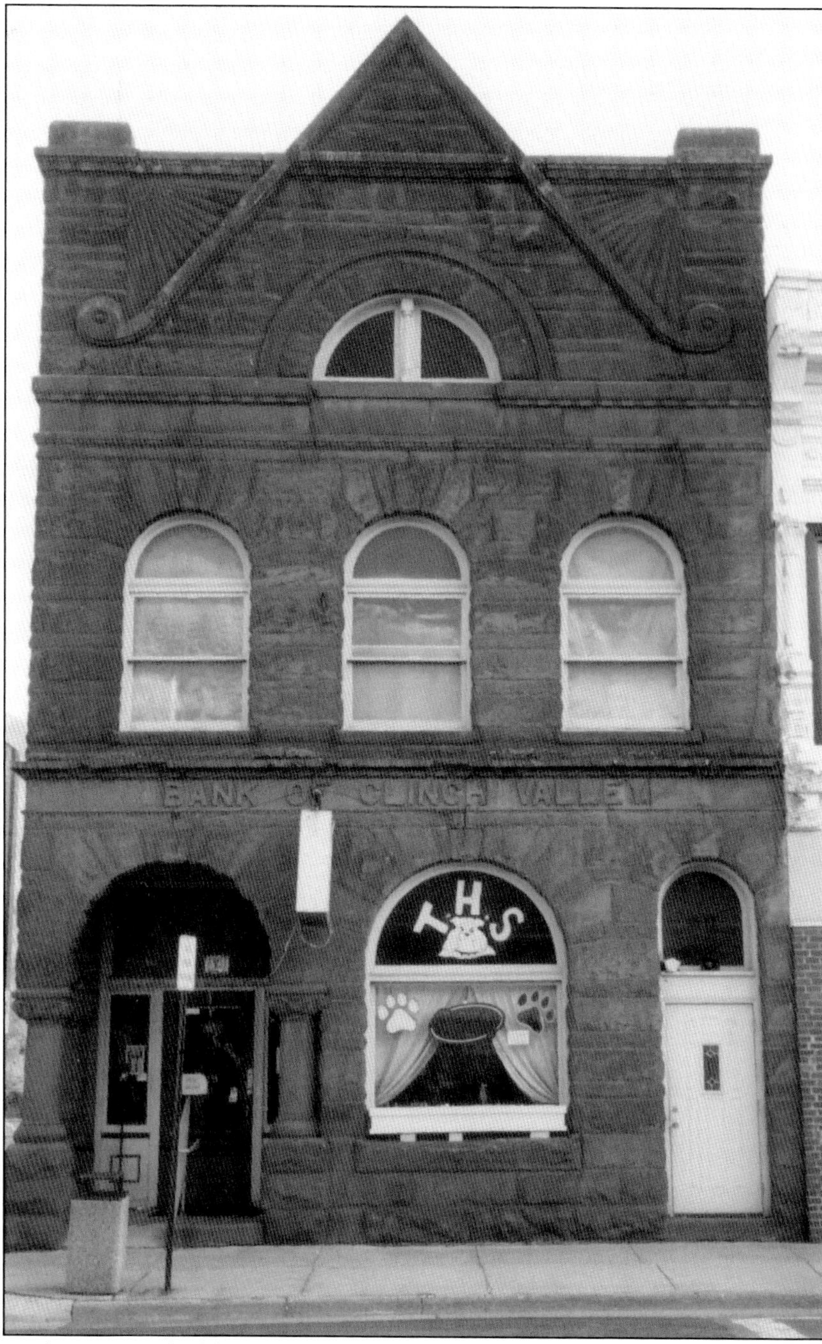

This ornate brownstone building was built about 1900 for the Bank of Clinch Valley. The original name is still visible on the top front. Before that time, the bank was in the small building that is now Lemon's Jewelry. The stone for the facade was shipped from a quarry in Hummelstown, Pennsylvania. In fact, Tazewell is the site of the only Hummelstown brownstone in Virginia and the southernmost example of that type of structure. The present occupant is a Korean restaurant, Yong's Cuisine. For many years, the building served as Britts Restaurant and was also used several other years as offices of the Tazewell County School Board. (Courtesy of Mullins files.)

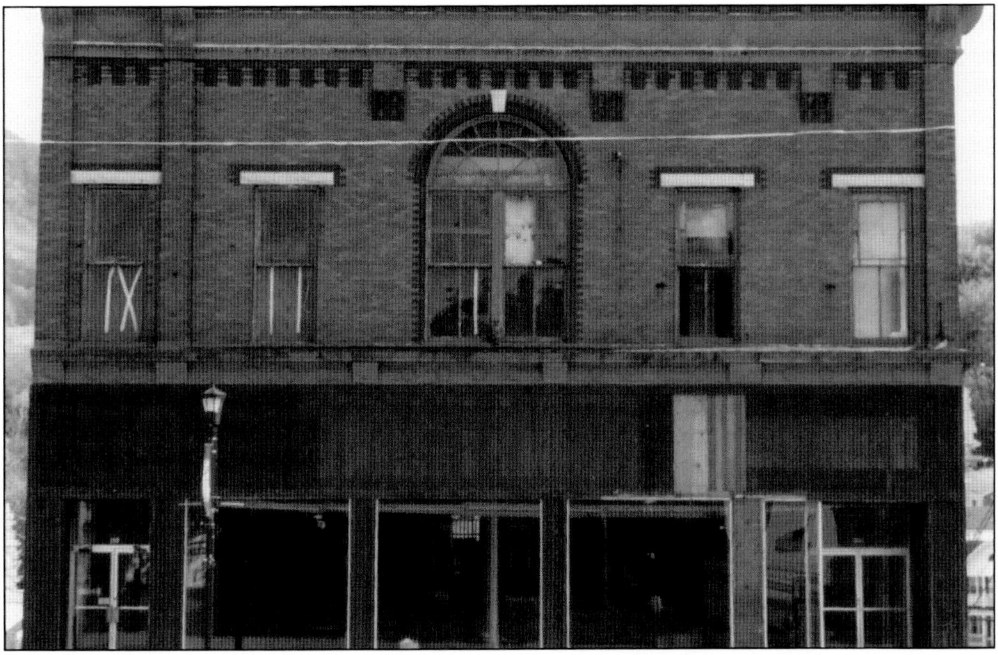

The original Peery and St. Clair building was constructed in 1903 for Will Ed Peery and Alexander St. Clair. It was noted for its fine furniture and hardware supplies. The business moved down the street in the 1960s. Also in the 1960s, Peery and St. Clair acquired the Dr. W. I. Painter house for use as a funeral home. Dr. Painter was a prominent Tazewell physician who started his practice in 1897. Since that time, the funeral home has moved to a new facility on Ben Bolt Avenue. County offices will soon occupy the former hardware and furniture building. Business offices, including a dentist, have occupied the upstairs rooms at various times. (Courtesy of Mullins files.)

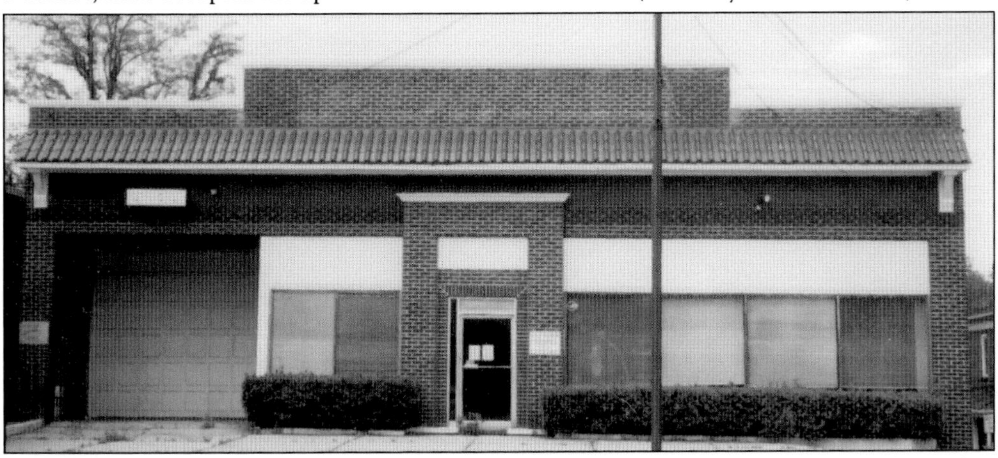

The Western Auto Store, operated by Dave Davenport and, later, John Glavaris, was located in this building for many years. In earlier days, it was the home of Tazewell Motor Company, owned by Henry Preston Jr., and Kilgore Motor Sales, owned by Emory Kilgore. Kilgore's Ford was one of several major car dealerships on Main Street in the mid-1900s. Other dealers on or near Main Street Tazewell around 1950 included Walkers Chevrolet, Oldsmobile and Buick; Cregar Brothers Motor Service Pontiac and GMC; Painter Motor and Machinery Company Dodge and Plymouth; Jones Motors Studebaker; Cruise Motor Company Hudson and International Trucks; and Eldreth Motors Rambler. (Courtesy of Mullins files.)

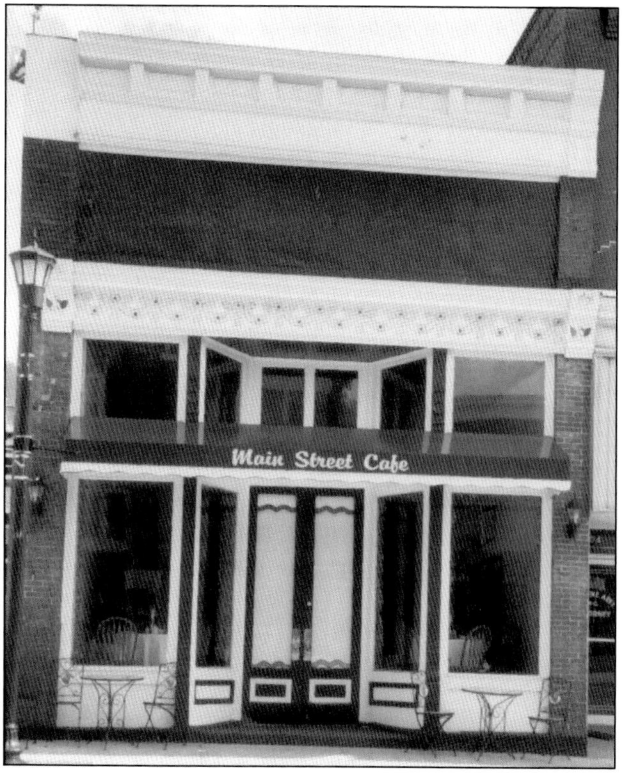

The old Spotts/Stras Building was called the C. T. Peery and Sons Grocery for at least two generations on Main Street. The grocery store is especially remembered for its daily delivery service to the kitchens of Tazewell customers. Now the remodeled building is the popular Main Street Café. The original building was constructed in 1899. The basement was the location of Tazewell's first electric power plant and later the town's first ice plant. (Courtesy of Mullins files.)

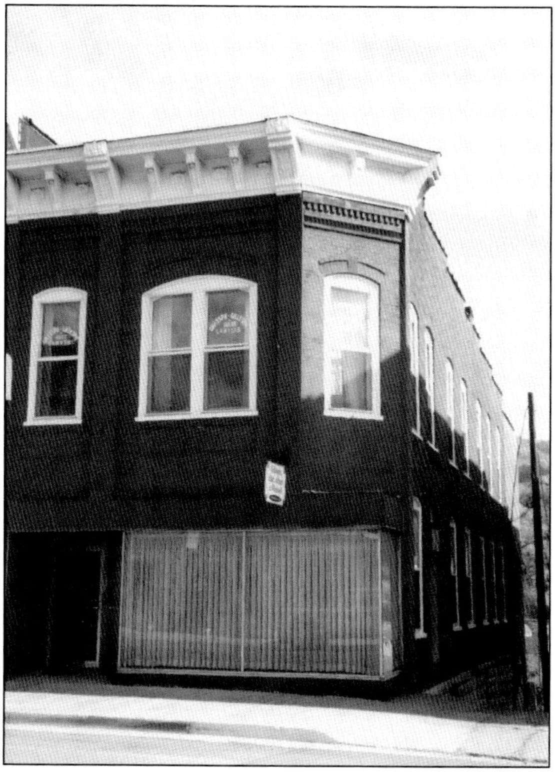

The present law offices of Gillespie, Hart, Altizer, and Whitesell occupy the same site as the law office of the legendary Maj. Henry and Samuel C. Graham, who practiced in Tazewell following the War Between the States. Their comments and abilities in the courtroom are still discussed when attorneys get together. Upstairs early editions of the *Clinch Valley News* were published in the days of hand-set type and harsh partisan political opinions. (Courtesy of Mullins files.)

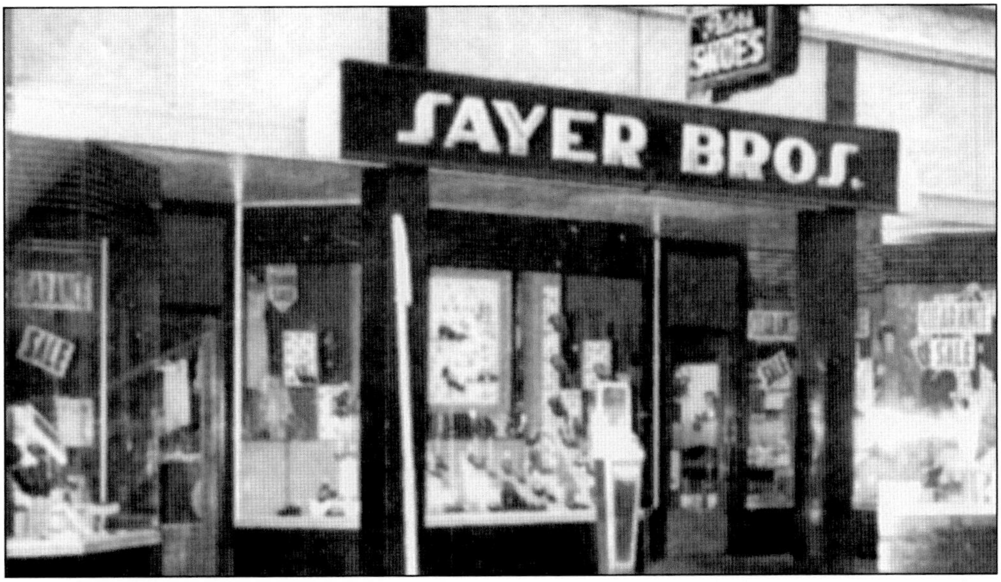

Sayers Brothers Department Store, a clothing business, stood where the present Town Park is located. The manager was Bill Hughes. Upstairs at one time were the offices of Dr. J. W. Shawver and the Tazewell County Health Department. In the basement, there was once a popular bowling alley. (Courtesy of Mullins files.)

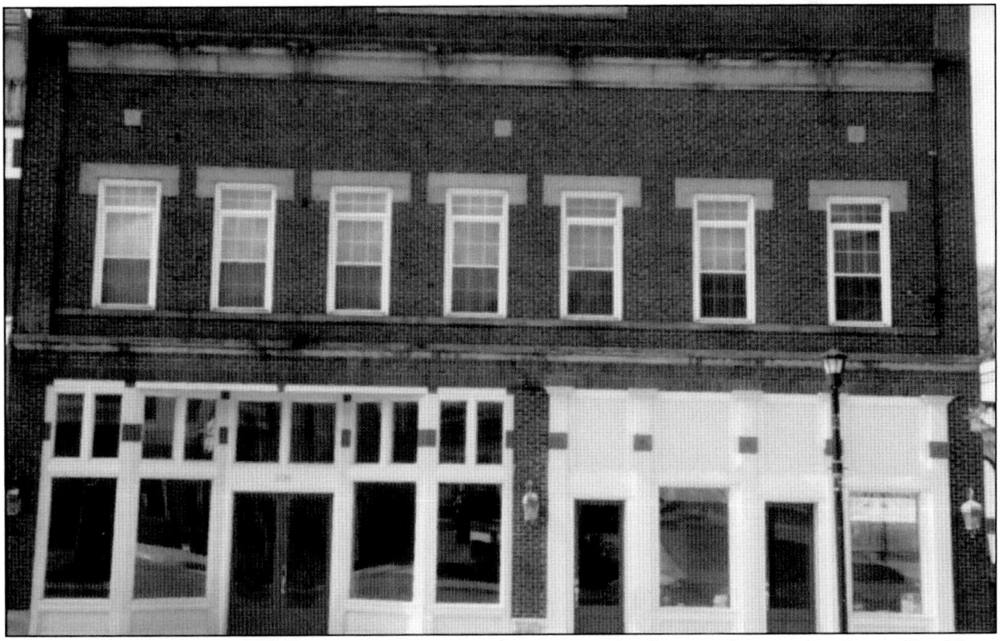

The J. A. Greever Building dates back to 1889. The sign on the front indicates the date of building and the 1914 remodeling date following the Main Street fire of 1913. The business closed in 1980. J. J. Greever, a son of the founder, was the last Greever family member to own the establishment. The rocking chairs in the front window were a meeting place for farmers who came to town to visit late in the afternoons. The Greever Funeral Home was for many years located next door before it was moved to the Royall home on Fincastle Turnpike. Now the beautifully remodeled building is the location of the law firm of Altizer, Walk and White. (Courtesy of Mullins files.)

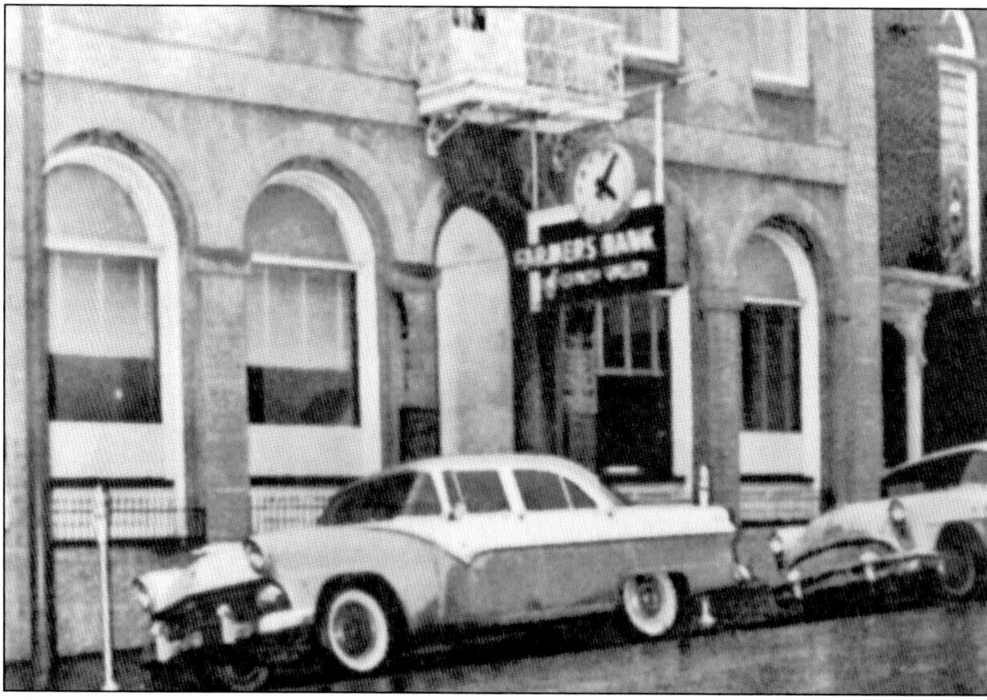

The Farmers Bank of Clinch Valley is pictured here in 1959. Not long after this picture, the old building was demolished to make room for the new bank building, which was later the Bank of Tazewell County and is now the National Bank. (Courtesy of the *Peak*, Tazewell High School.)

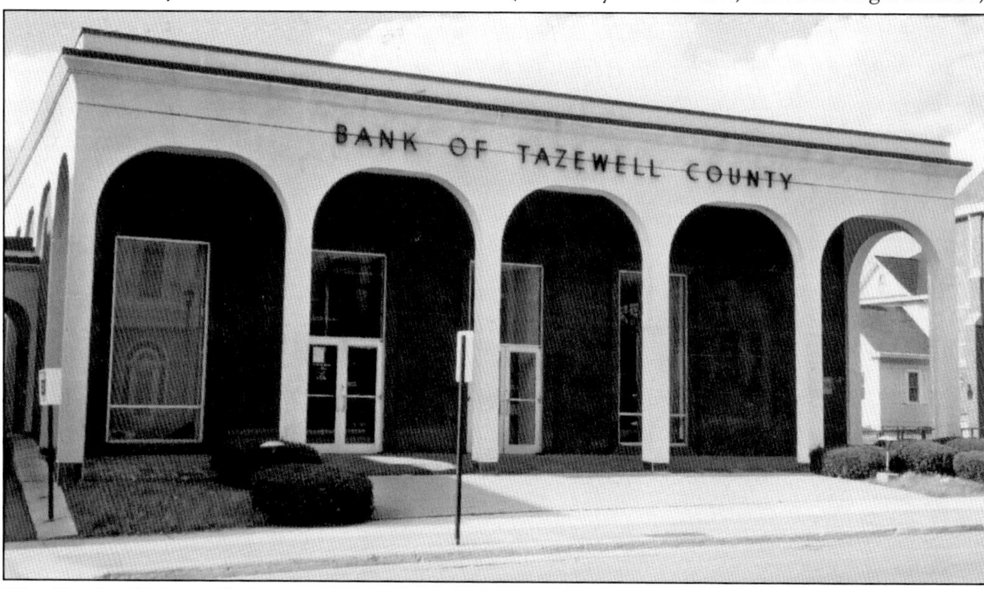

The Bank of Tazewell County merged with the National Bank of Blacksburg to become the National Bank. The new building is located on what was the site of the Farmers Bank of Clinch Valley, the Hotel Tazewell, the Shamrock Grill and Bowling Alley, the Barnes Moore Barber Shop, and an army-navy store. Among many of the outstanding officers through the years were Aaron Russ, Walter Baugh, Ray Dodson, Bill Woodall, Alonzo Crouse, and C. E. Hankla, who all contributed to Tazewell's development. (Courtesy of Mullins files.)

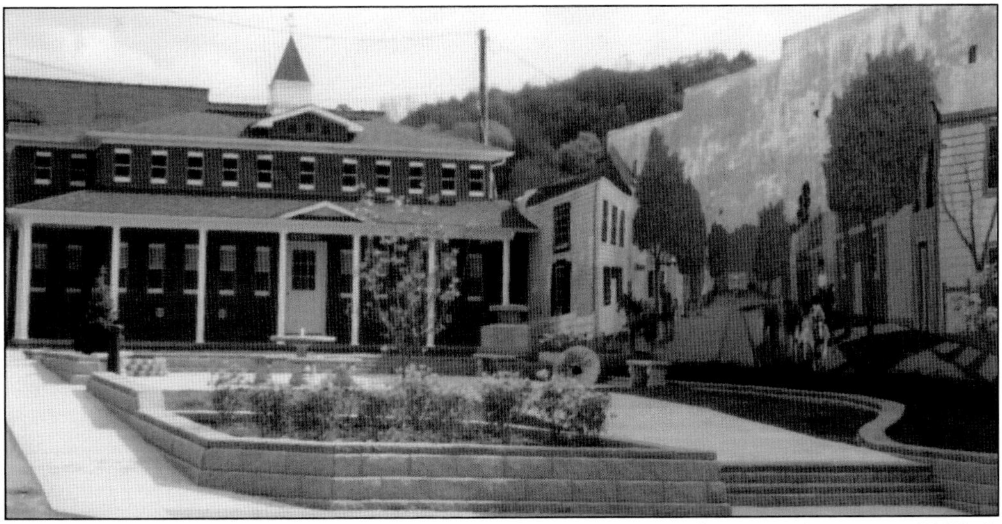

The Town Park was constructed at the corner of Main Street and Marion Avenue in 2005. A replica of the first Tazewell High School building adds to the park, with its front porch used as a stage for public programs each week of the summer. Often office workers on Main Street eat their lunch in the park. The cornerstone, laid by the Tazewell Lodge in 1995, contains a vault with Tazewell memorabilia enclosed. The time capsule is to be opened in 2045. The mural at the Town Park tells the story of early Main Street, when horses and buggies were the primary mode of transportation. The realistic mural was painted by Johnny Hagerman; a later touch-up was completed by Jess Bailey. The beautiful flowers in summer and the decorations at Christmas make the park a focal point for the community. (Courtesy of Mullins files.)

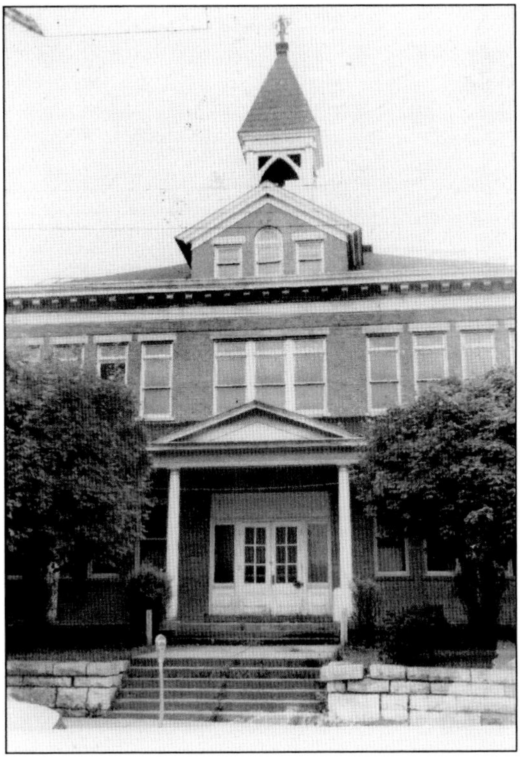

This school building on Main Street served both elementary and high school students throughout the years. It was razed to make room for the Tazewell County Library in the 1960s. The weather vane on the roof now stands atop the Tazewell County Court House. The steps and stone wall remain the same for the modern library, which was built in 1967. (Courtesy of Leslie files.)

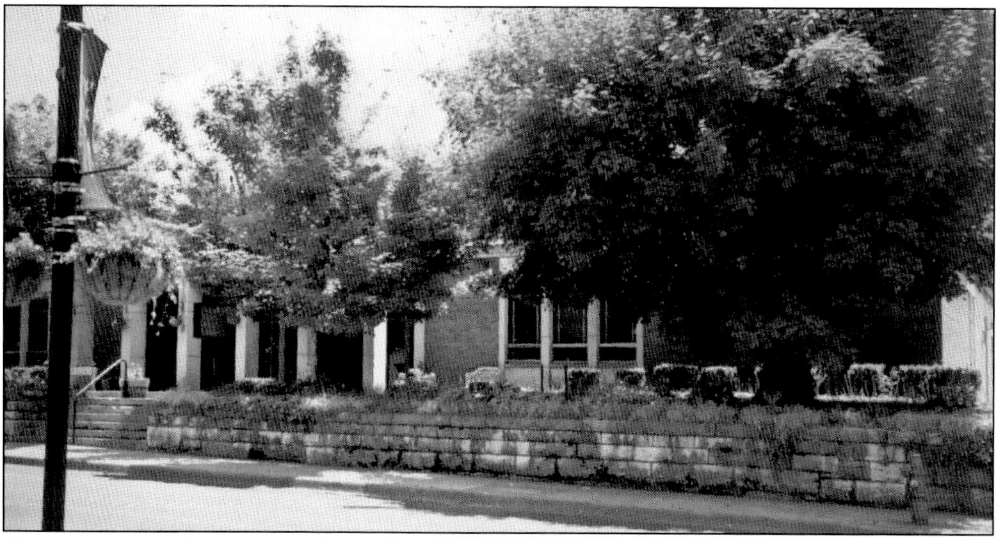

The new Tazewell County Public Library was opened in 1967 on the Main Street site once occupied by Tazewell High and Elementary Schools. The county supervisors who approved the important project were Jim Bailey, Emory Kilgore, and Graham Hedrick. The first members of the library board were Mrs. W. B. Leslie, Cora Lee Philpott, Garnett Shufflebarger, Mrs. J. K. Sult, and Lester Jones. (Courtesy of Mullins files.)

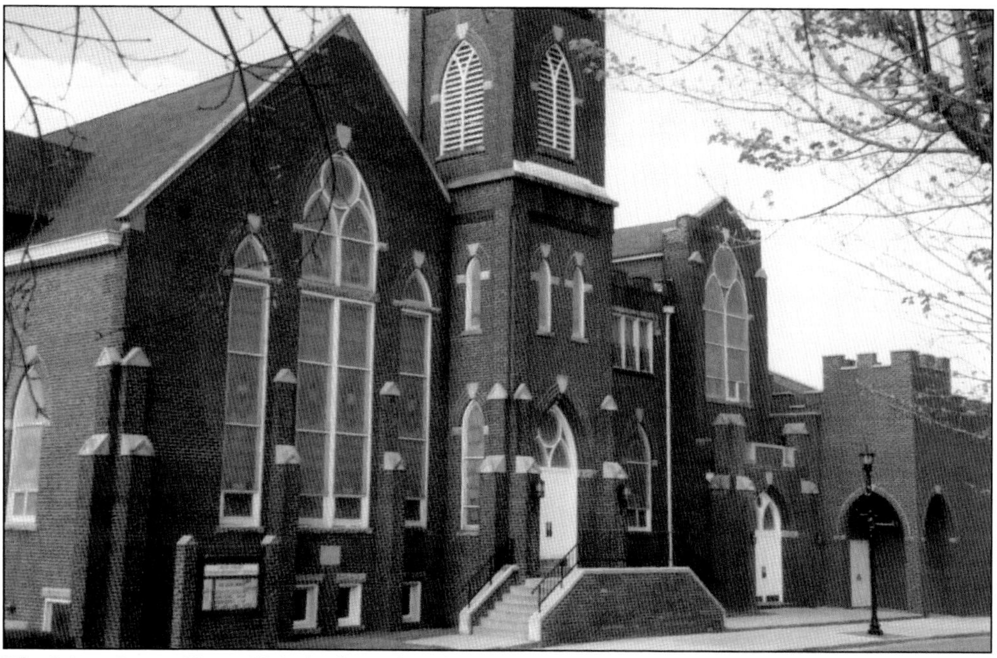

The Main Street United Methodist Church was built in 1913, succeeding a building that dated back to 1861. The adjoining property, formerly the Clinch Theatre, was bought by the church in recent years, and a recreational facility and fellowship hall were added. Another addition to the church building was the Chapman House, which is used for church offices and Sunday school rooms. The beautiful stained-glass windows add to the beauty of the church. The Clinch Theatre building was constructed in 1916 by Frank T. and E. F. Witten and replaced the Old Inn, built about 1820 by Capt. Robert Crockett. (Courtesy of Mullins files.)

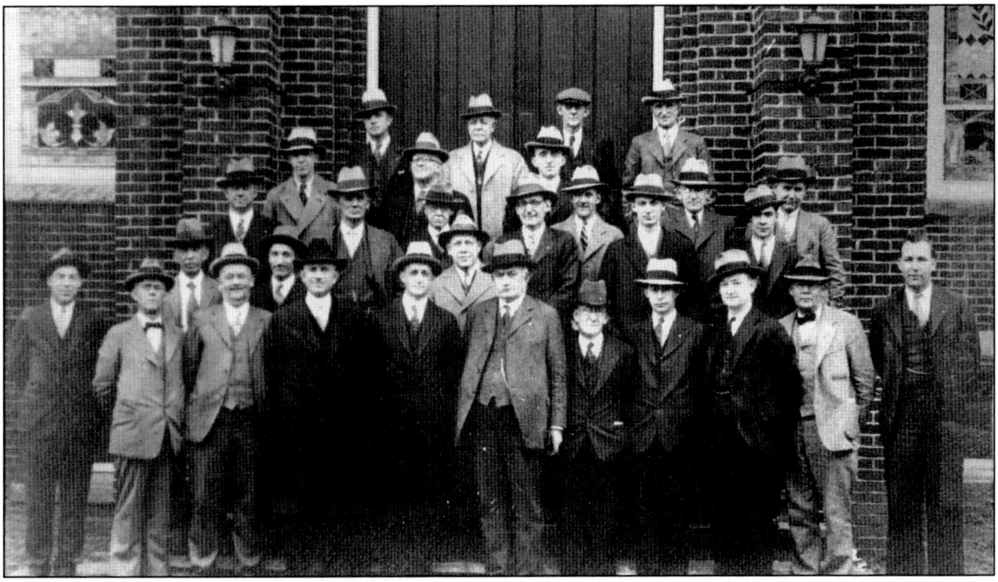

In the 1940s, the members of the Tazewell Rotary Club were pictured on the steps of the Main Street Methodist Church. The membership included most of the area businessmen. They were, from left to right, (first row) Dr. H. T. Haley, Will Tom Gillespie, Jeff Ward, Dr. W. W. Arrowood, Judge A. C. Buchanan, H. E. Harman, W. Bland Leslie, Franklin Leslie, Barnes Moore, Dr. P. D. Johnston, and Jack Kyle; (second row) J. A. Greever, T. A. Pobst, and B. W. Stras; (third row) R. O. Crockett, Sen. S. J. Thompson, Dr. E. L. Jackson, Aaron Russ, Joe S. Gillespie, C. P. Gillespie, Noel Walker, unidentified, Dick Kelly, W. M. Gillespie, Dr. Rufus Copenhaver, R. O. VanDyke, unidentified, J. B. Boyer, Bill Painter, and Lacy Tynes. (Courtesy of Leslie files.)

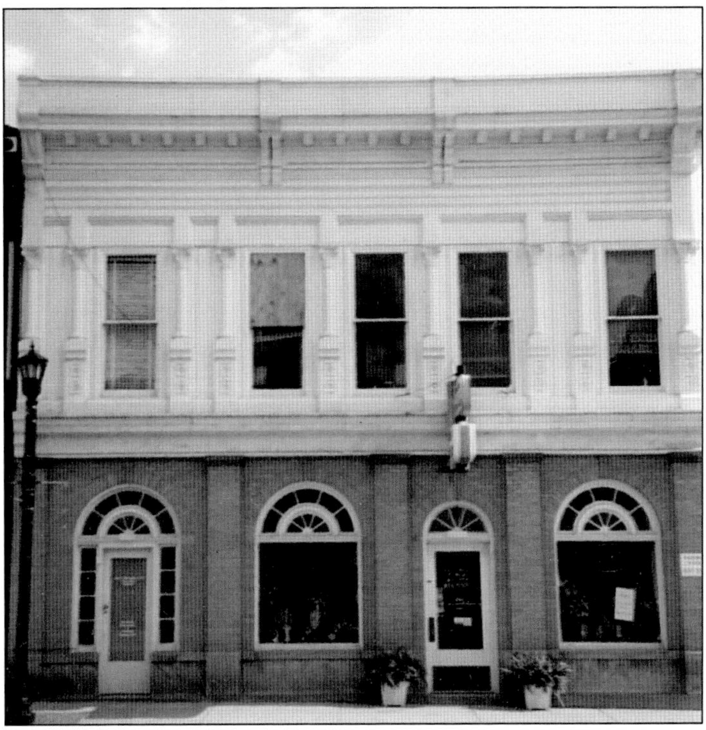

The Tazewell National Bank was originally at this location. The building is now occupied by Tazewell Florist and Gifts. Built in 1901, the vault now serves as a repository for flowers. The bank president's office was in the adjoining small building, which has been occupied by various business offices and Barnes Moore's barbershop. The second floor, typical of the early buildings on Main Street, was formerly private apartments. Now there are business offices there, including those of local attorneys. (Courtesy of Mullins files.)

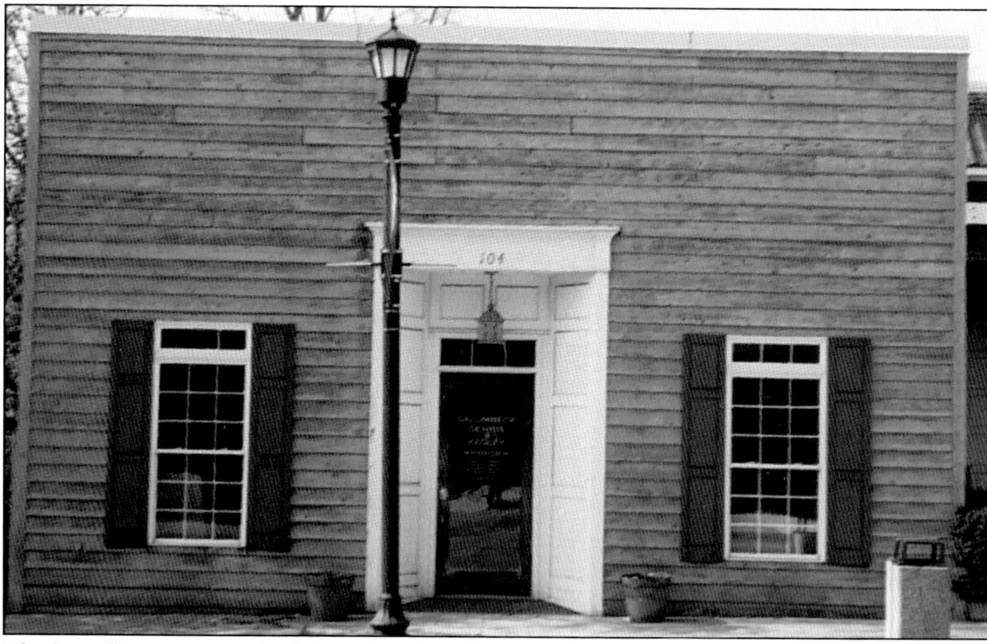

The law offices of Galumbeck, Dennis, and Kegley occupy this renovated building. At one time, the Neighborhood Market was at this locale. On the upper floor was the office of Robert Harman, a well-known photographer. (Courtesy of Mullins files.)

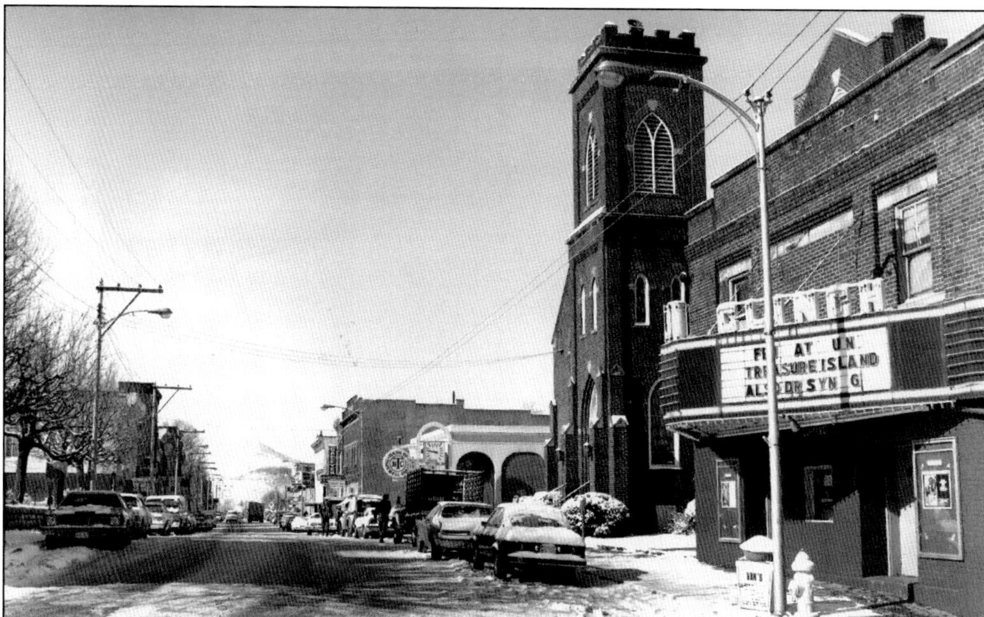

The Clinch Theatre was opened in 1916 by Frank T. Witten and E. F. Witten, and the first talking picture, *Happy Days*, was shown in 1930. Before that, silent films were shown and vaudeville acts were booked for the stage. Before the theater was built, the Old Inn, built in 1820, occupied the site. The building was dismantled in 1990 to make room for the annex to the Main Street United Methodist Church. The Clinch Theatre in Tazewell and the Valley Theatre in North Tazewell were popular places for moviegoers of all ages. (Courtesy of Leslie files.)

The law offices of Stephen Arey occupy the old site of Haley's Drug Company, operated in the early years of the 1900s by H. T. Haley and the St. Clair family. Along with its reputation for fine service and good food, Haley's became the popular location of "Haley's Retreat," a bench in front of the store where businessmen (and others) gathered each day and early evening to catch up on the day's news. It is said that more business was conducted at the "Retreat" than in the Main Street offices and more news was discussed than could be found in the area newspapers. Upstairs were private apartments. Before Haley's drugstore, the building held Hawkins Pharmacy, named for the owner and druggist. It was built about 1902. (Courtesy of Mullins files.)

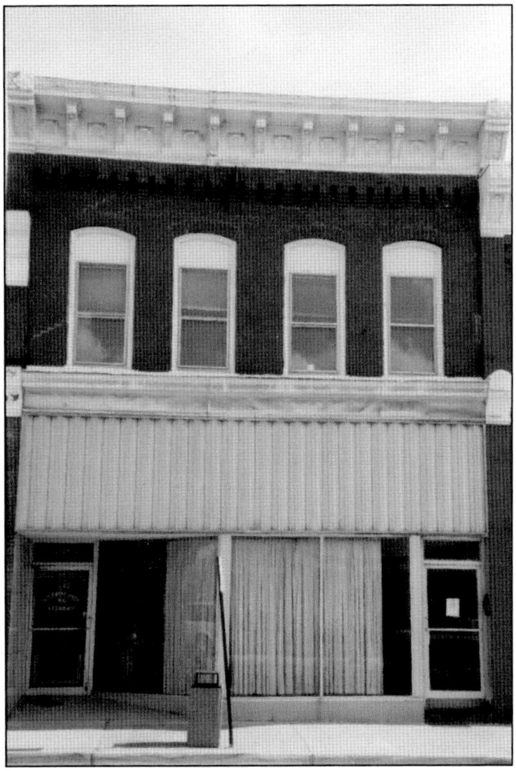

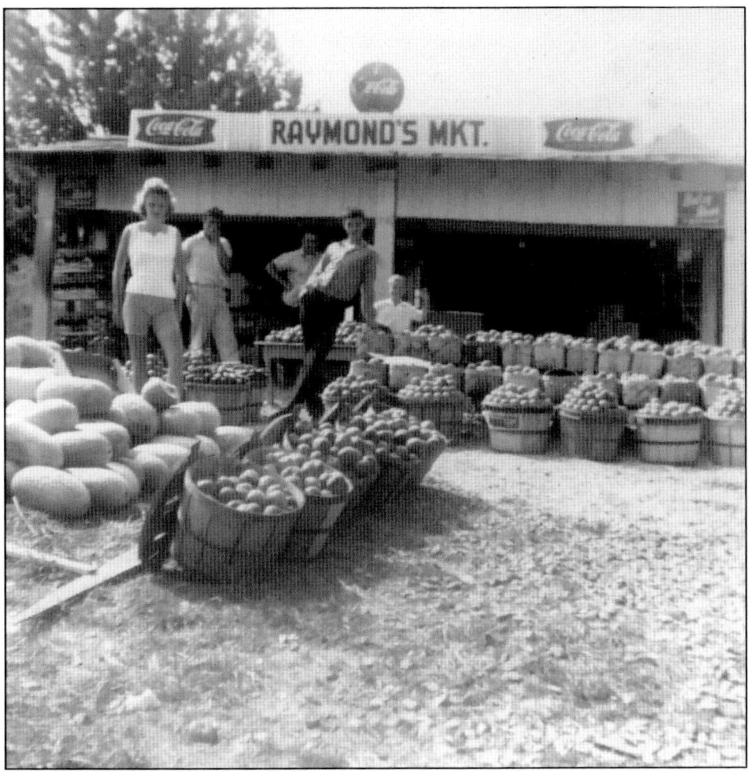

Raymond's Market, operated by Raymond Kinder, was a favorite meeting place for those seeking fresh produce in the 1950s and 1960s. From left to right, Etta Kinder (Matney), Raymond Kinder, and two unidentified men examine the fine melons and fresh fruit at this market located east of Tazewell. (Courtesy of Brandon Matney.)

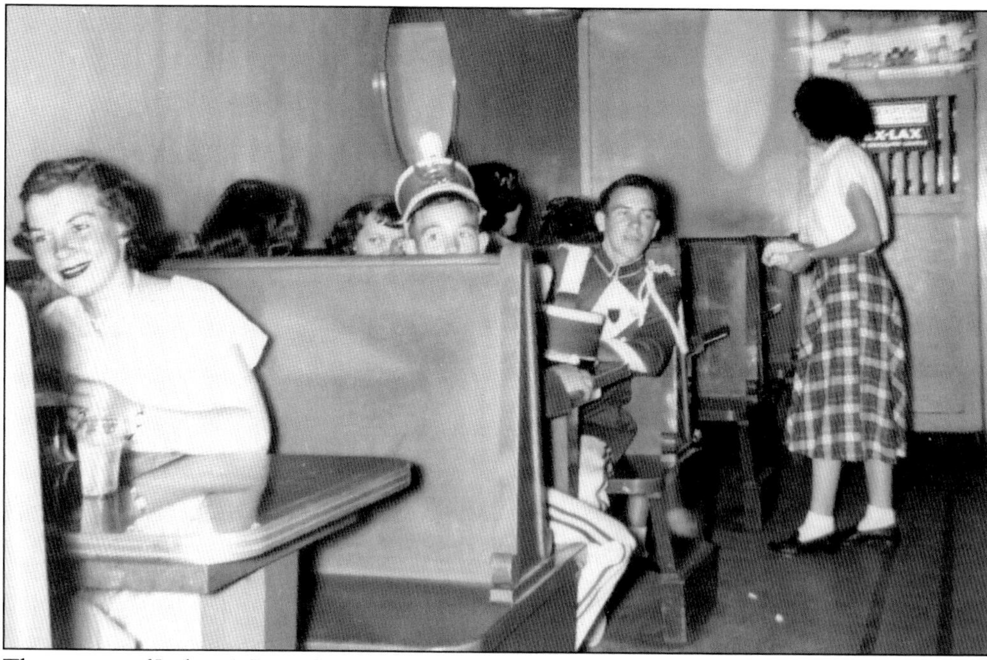

The interior of Jackson's Drug Company served as a favorite hangout for Tazewell teenagers during the 1940s and 1950s. Among other things, Jackson's fountain was renowned for its tin-roofs—an ice cream, chocolate, and peanut concoction eaten with a wooden spoon. Bill Phillips is in the back booth with no hat, while Betty Jo Davis is in the front booth. The waitress is Peggy Pruett (Lawson). Main Street Jackson's sister drugstore, Jackson-Fleet, was also known far and wide for its delicious milkshakes at its Tazewell Depot location. (Courtesy of Ralph Mullins.)

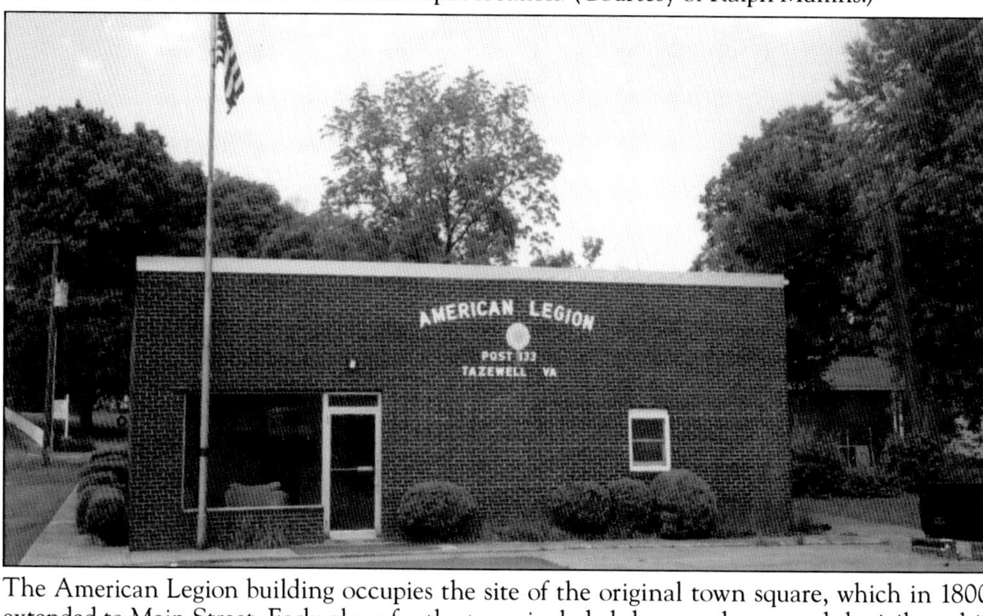

The American Legion building occupies the site of the original town square, which in 1800 extended to Main Street. Early plans for the town included the courthouse and the jail on this property. It has almost become a "town square" again, since the Town of Tazewell Municipal Offices and the town police offices join the American Legion building on this property. (Courtesy of Mullins files.)

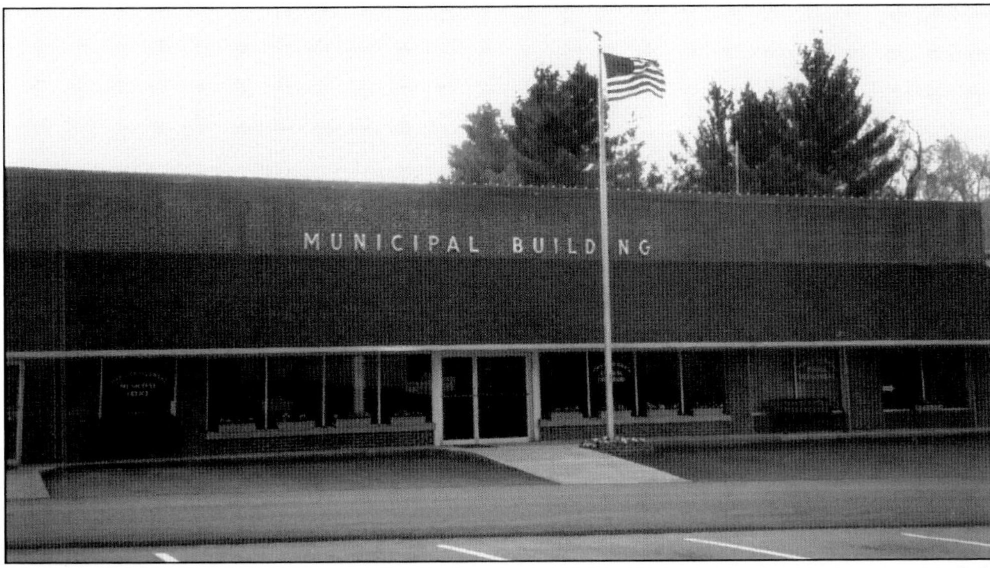

The Municipal Building, before extensive remodeling, was originally the Cruise Automobile Dealership. Here are the offices of Mayor Jack Harry and Town Manager Jerry Wood. Harry followed longtime mayor Charles Green, who retired in 2006 after many years of service. His term is well remembered for many improvements made within the town's corporate limits. (Courtesy of Mullins files.)

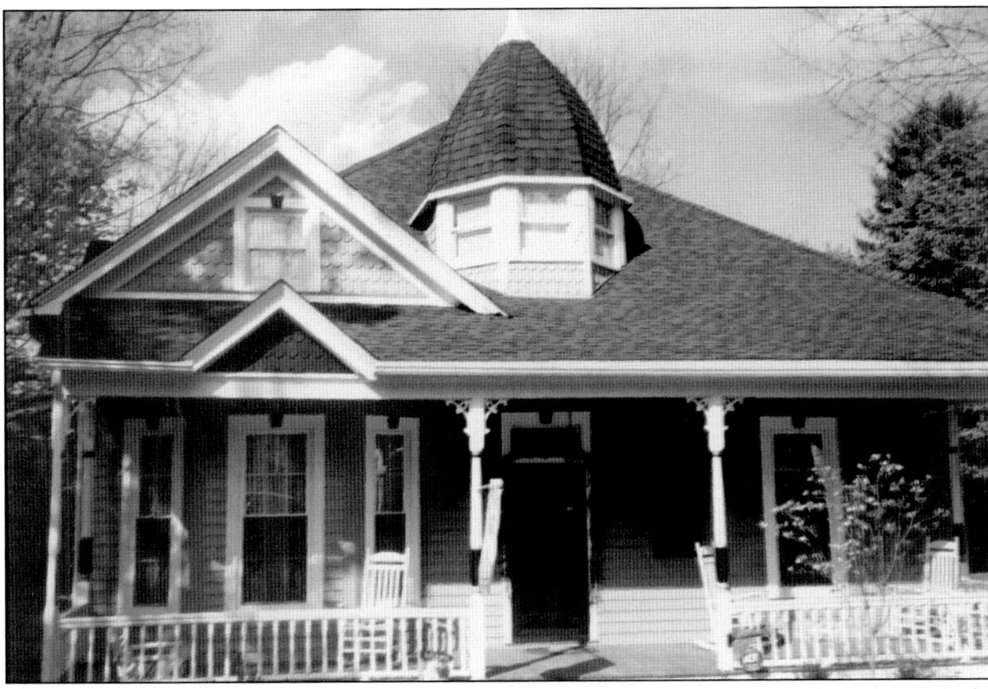
This was the Lyons Avenue home of A. M. Black, Tazewell's early photographer who took the excellent family pictures that have helped preserve much of the county's history. Black was paralyzed for the last 40 years of his life as the result of an unfortunate accident. He worked from his bed and with the help of his wife maintained a successful newspaper and magazine subscription service. (Courtesy of Mullins files.)

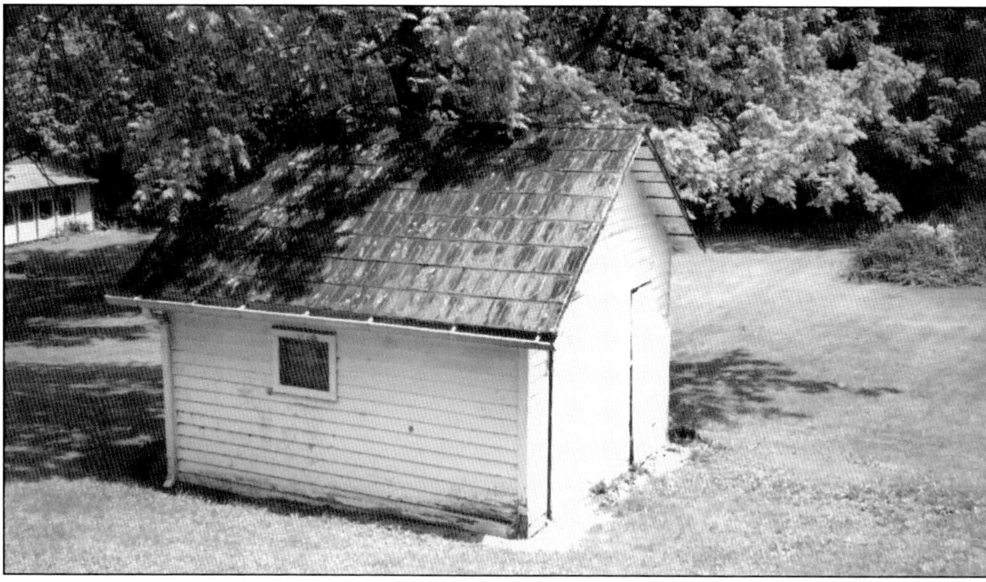

Mechanics Street connected Church Street and Tazewell Avenue in 1907. The street intersected Sun Street at the same time. A century later, Mechanics Street is known as Pine Street and Sun Street has become Lyons Avenue. In the early 1900s, a mysterious "woman in black" appeared on Pine Street and frightened the residents and the businessmen who walked down the street each night after work. She seemed to materialize from this small white building (or one just like it), which at one time housed the town hearse. It all started as a joke but became serious when the stores closed early at night so the workers could safely walk home and miss an after-dark encounter with the silent lady. Her identity was never revealed to the men she frightened. (Courtesy of Mullins files.)

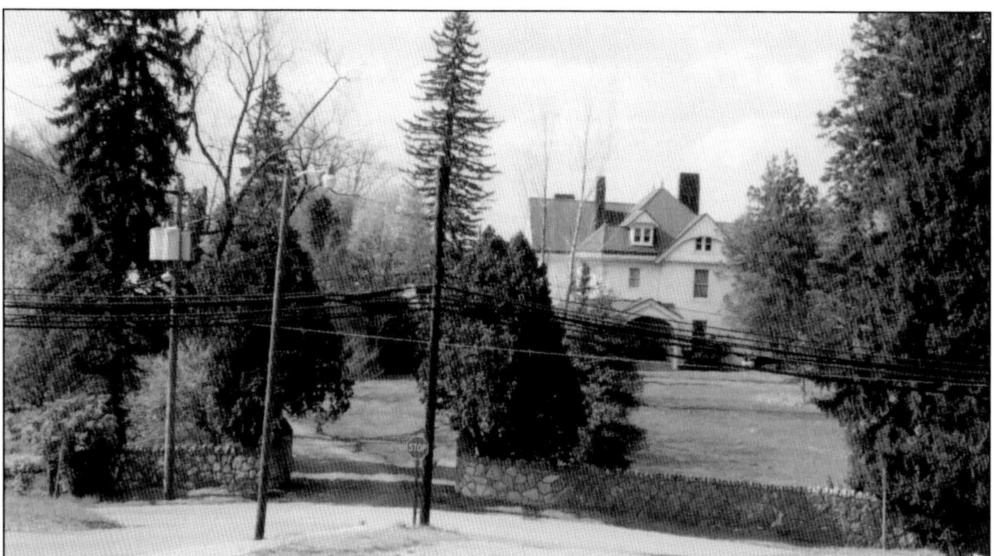

This beautiful home is now owned by the Claude VanDyke family but was originally owned by the Gillespie family. The last members of the Gillespie family to live there were Mr. and Mrs. T. Ritchie Peery. Peery, a well-known Tazewell resident in the mid-1900s, always had an interest in fine horses and often rode a favorite in the Tazewell County Fair. (Courtesy of Mullins files.)

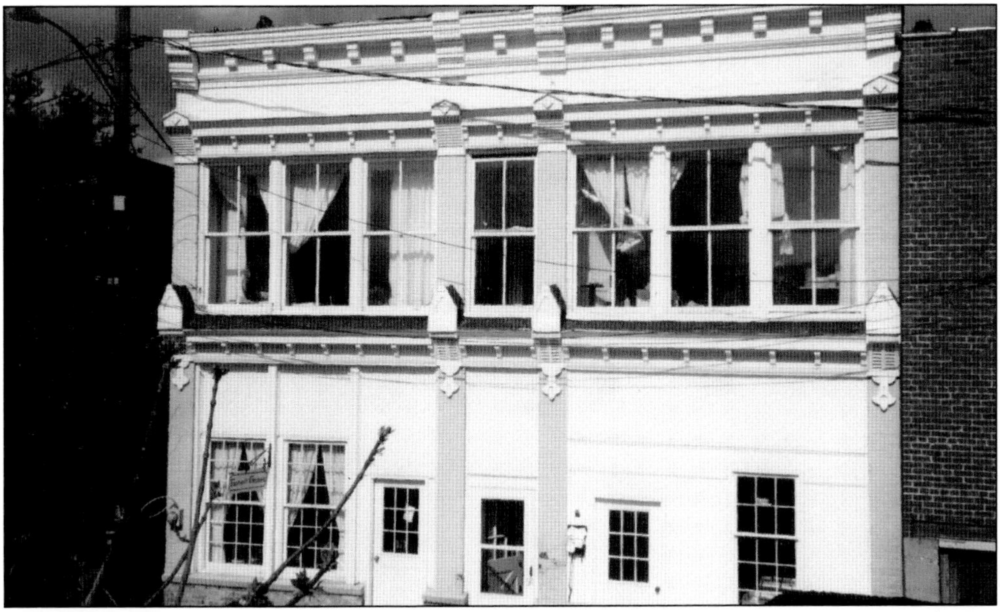

Tazewell's original telephone company was located on Elk Street. An operator named Mrs. Hiltzheimer is remembered for her memory and her advice freely given to all her customers. She even helped raise a generation of Tazewell youngsters by keeping up with them close enough to tell them it was time to go home and study. Note the ornate roof, typical of the town's early buildings. Today the building is a dry cleaning establishment. Tazewell's first telephone connection was a "home-made" device between Pobst Jewelry Store on Main Street and Kelly Groseclose Store in Burkes Garden, probably connected in the 1890s. (Courtesy of Mullins files.)

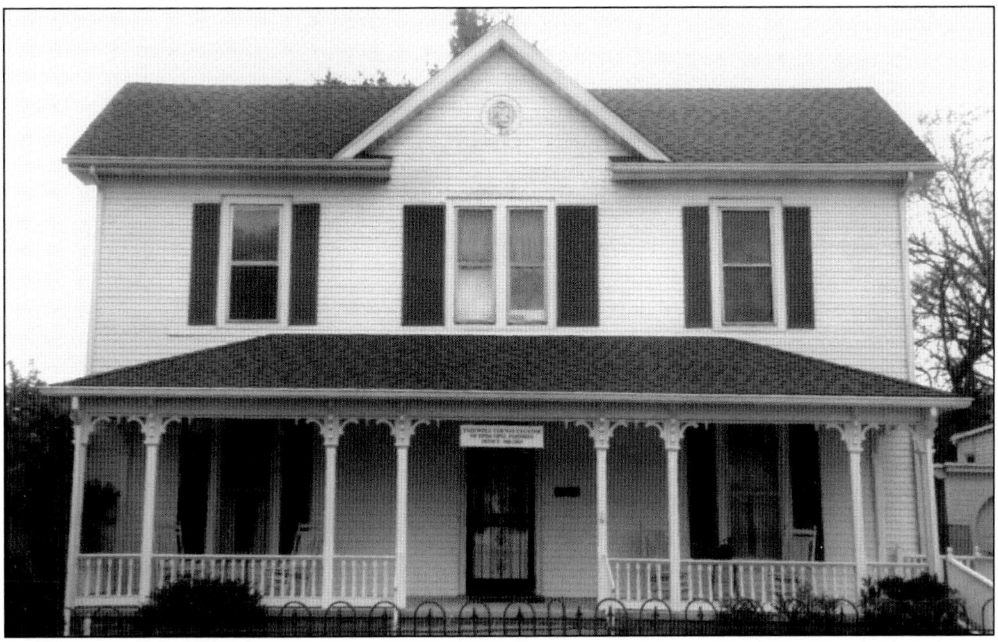

The Sexton House, built about 1897, was conveyed to the Stras Memorial Episcopal Church as a rectory in 1940. Today it serves the cluster of Episcopal congregations for various church activities. The central gable is a typical feature of houses in the late 1800s. (Courtesy of Mullins files.)

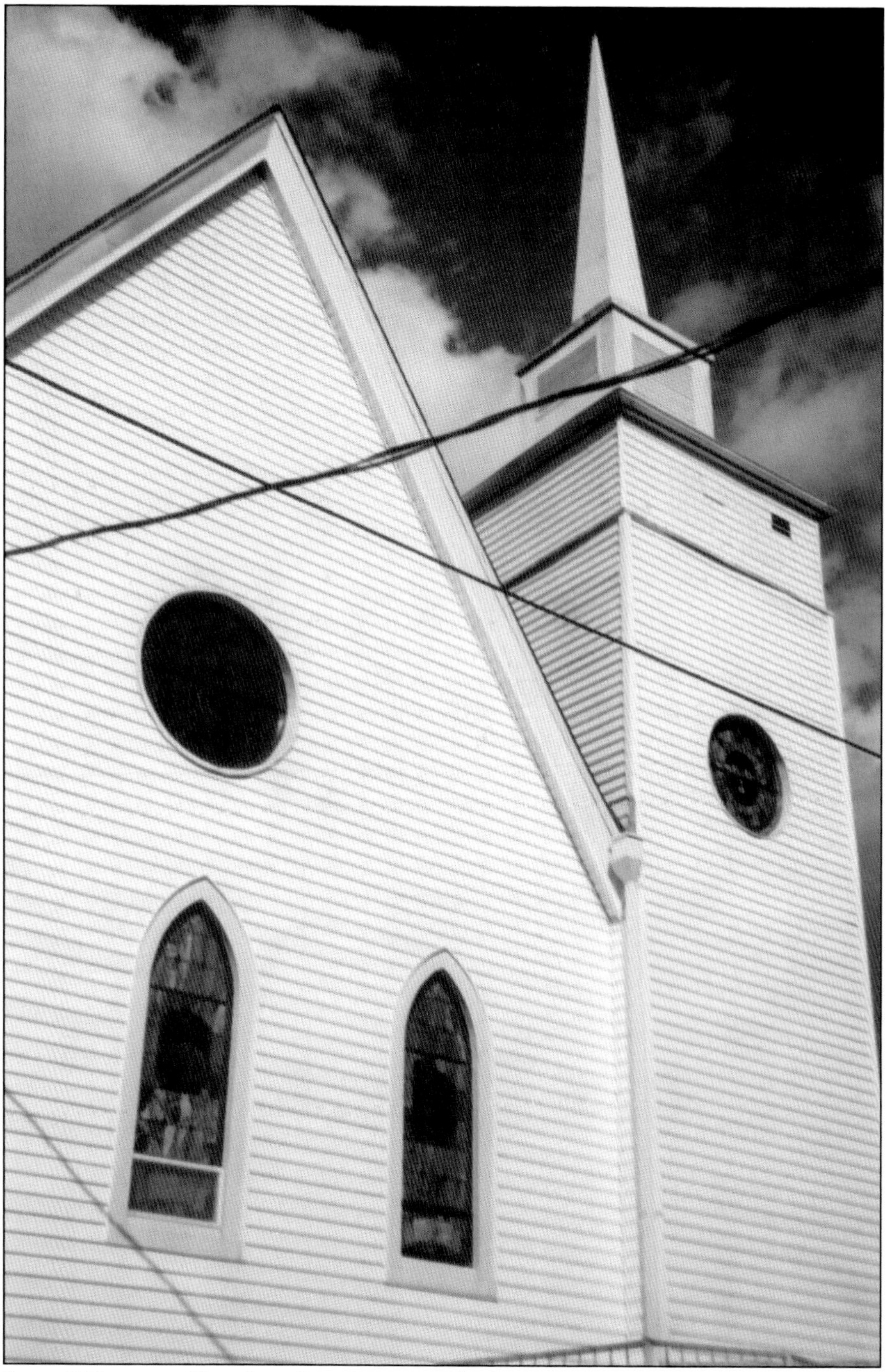

The Tazewell Christian Church on Pine Street was built in 1898. It followed an earlier congregation formed in 1883, which met in the previous Catholic church building on Marion Avenue. This old church on Marion Avenue was later used by Tazewell High School for public performances, including the annual graduation ceremony. The building has since been torn down. Leadership and support for the Tazewell Female Seminary and Tazewell College came in large part from the Christian church congregation. (Courtesy of Mullins files.)

The Tazewell Presbyterian Church was organized in 1851, and since that time, four buildings have been at the present site on Church Street. The first church was a log structure in Jeffersonville in 1853, followed by a larger frame structure in 1889. In 1924, a brick building was erected, and during renovations on this building in 1959, it was destroyed by fire. The new building, now occupied, was completed in 1960. The memorial chimes heard often from its tower were donated by Mr. and Mrs. Robert Gillespie. (Courtesy of Mullins files.)

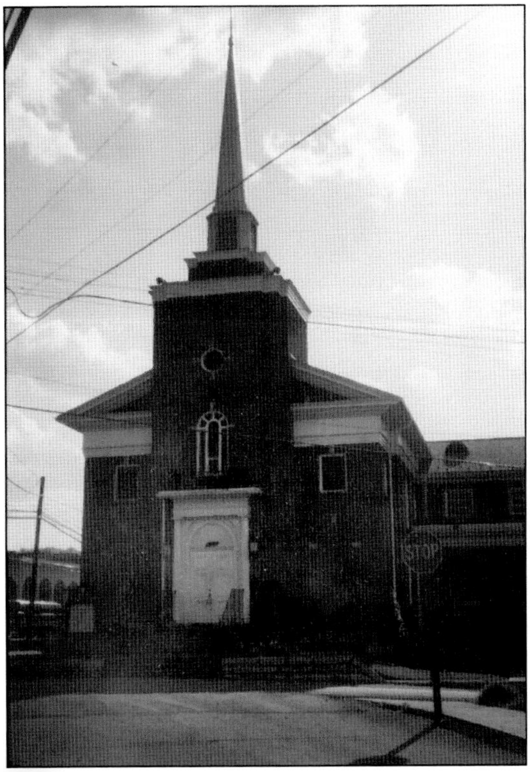

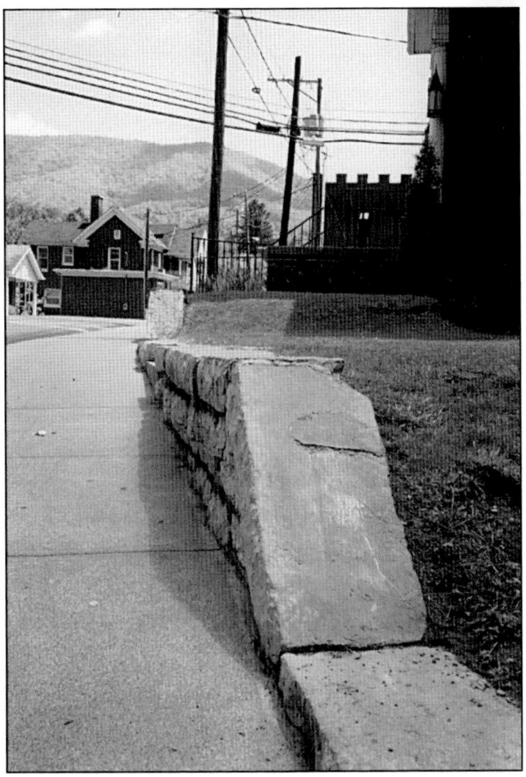

In front of the Tazewell Presbyterian Church is the "sliding place," the perfect place for children to play. In the 1940s and 1950s, when children walked to and from the Tazewell Elementary School, they always included the slide in their journey. It is still slick from use. Whoever included the slide in a building plan probably did not realize his good deed. (Courtesy of Mullins files.)

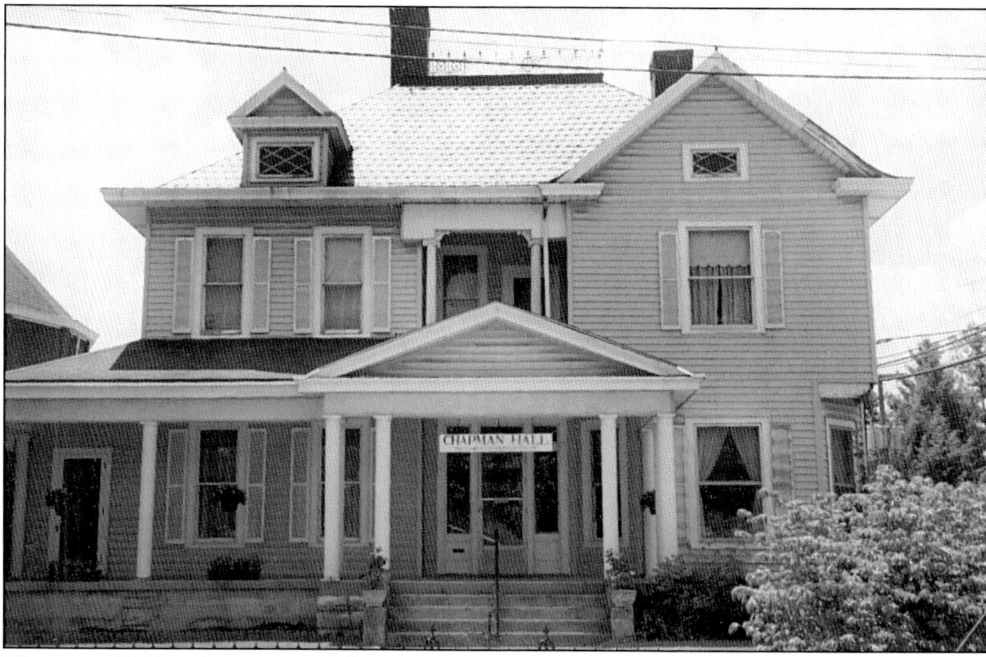

Chapman Hall is the annex of the Main Street United Methodist Church, which includes a large dining room and recreational area. Dating from 1905, it was originally the home of the Boyer and Chapman families. Pearl Johnson Crenshaw, the mother of internationally known professional golfer Ben Crenshaw, lived here before she married and moved to Texas. (Courtesy of Mullins files.)

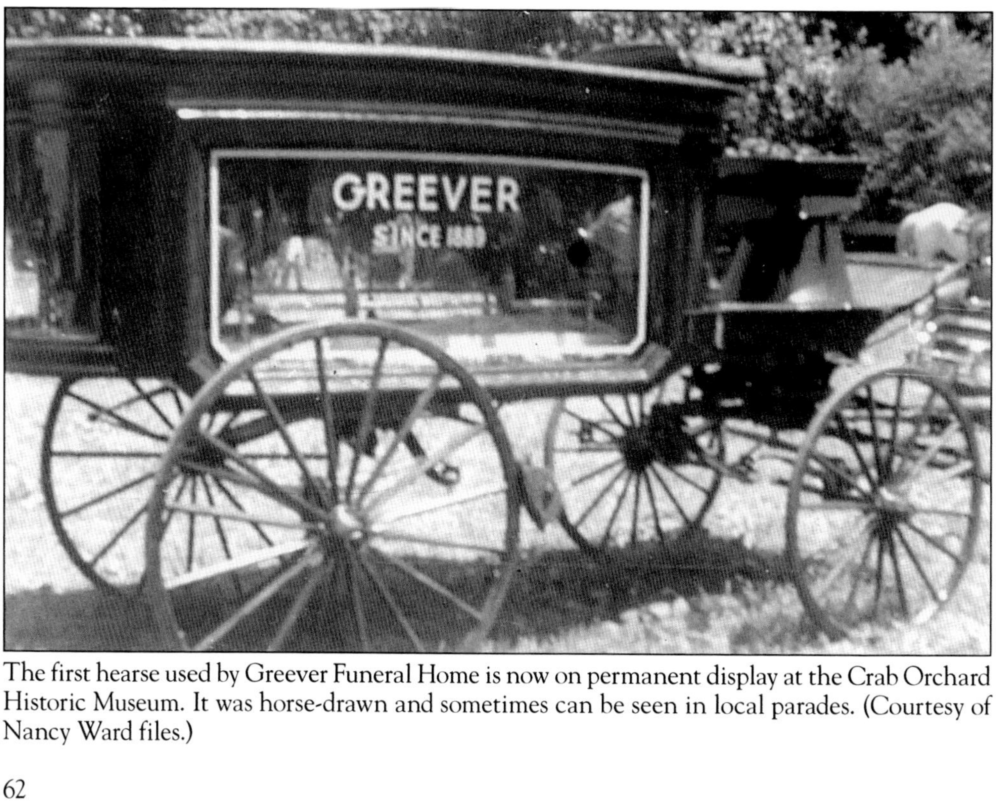

The first hearse used by Greever Funeral Home is now on permanent display at the Crab Orchard Historic Museum. It was horse-drawn and sometimes can be seen in local parades. (Courtesy of Nancy Ward files.)

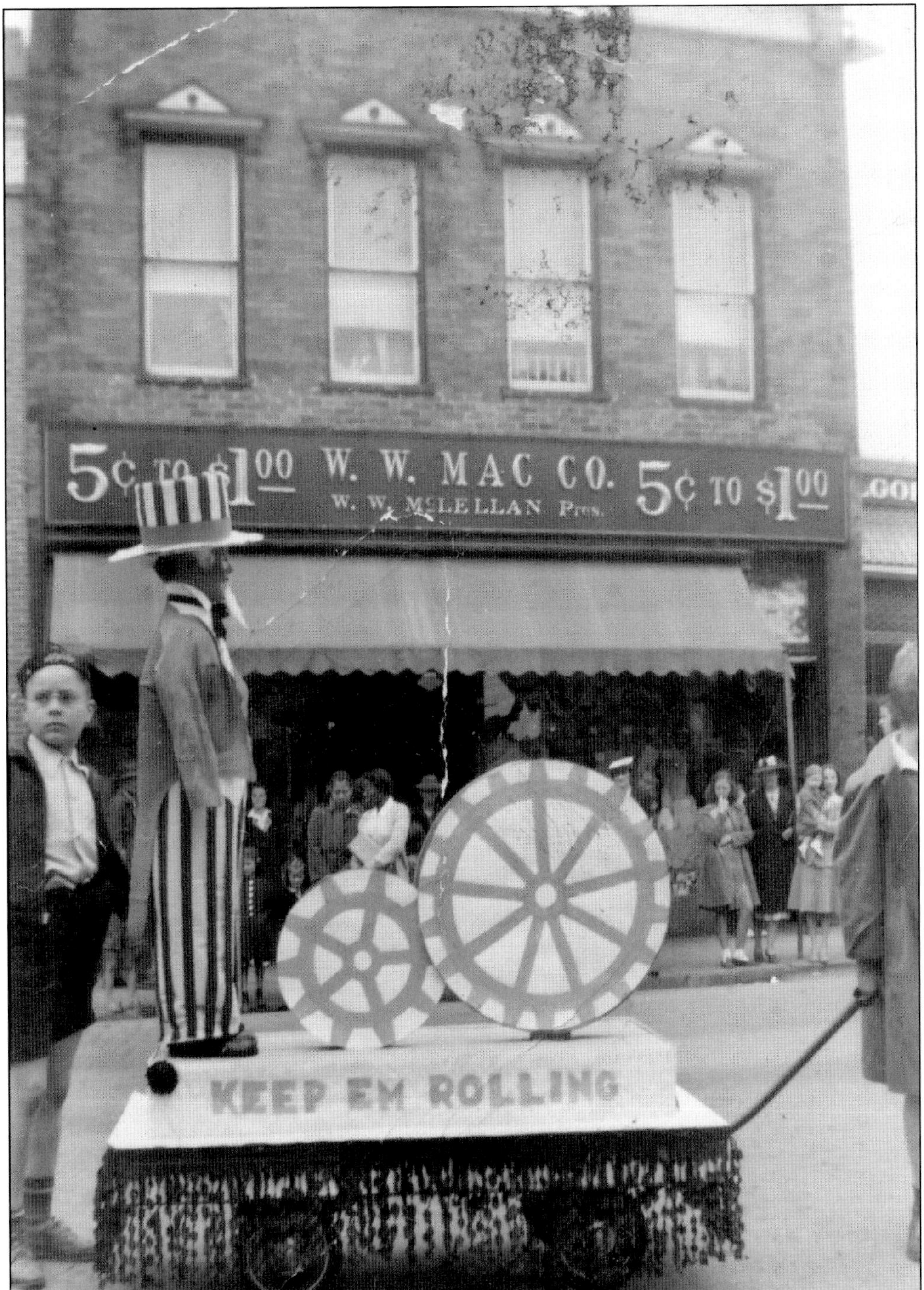

"Uncle Sam" said to "keep 'em rolling" in this 1942 war bond parade on Main Street. Note the W. W. Mac Store, which advertised merchandise from 5¢ to $1. Among others, Louise Bowen was a longtime manager of W. W. Mac. War bonds and savings stamps were a popular fund-raising effort during the World War II years. (Courtesy of June Friedl.)

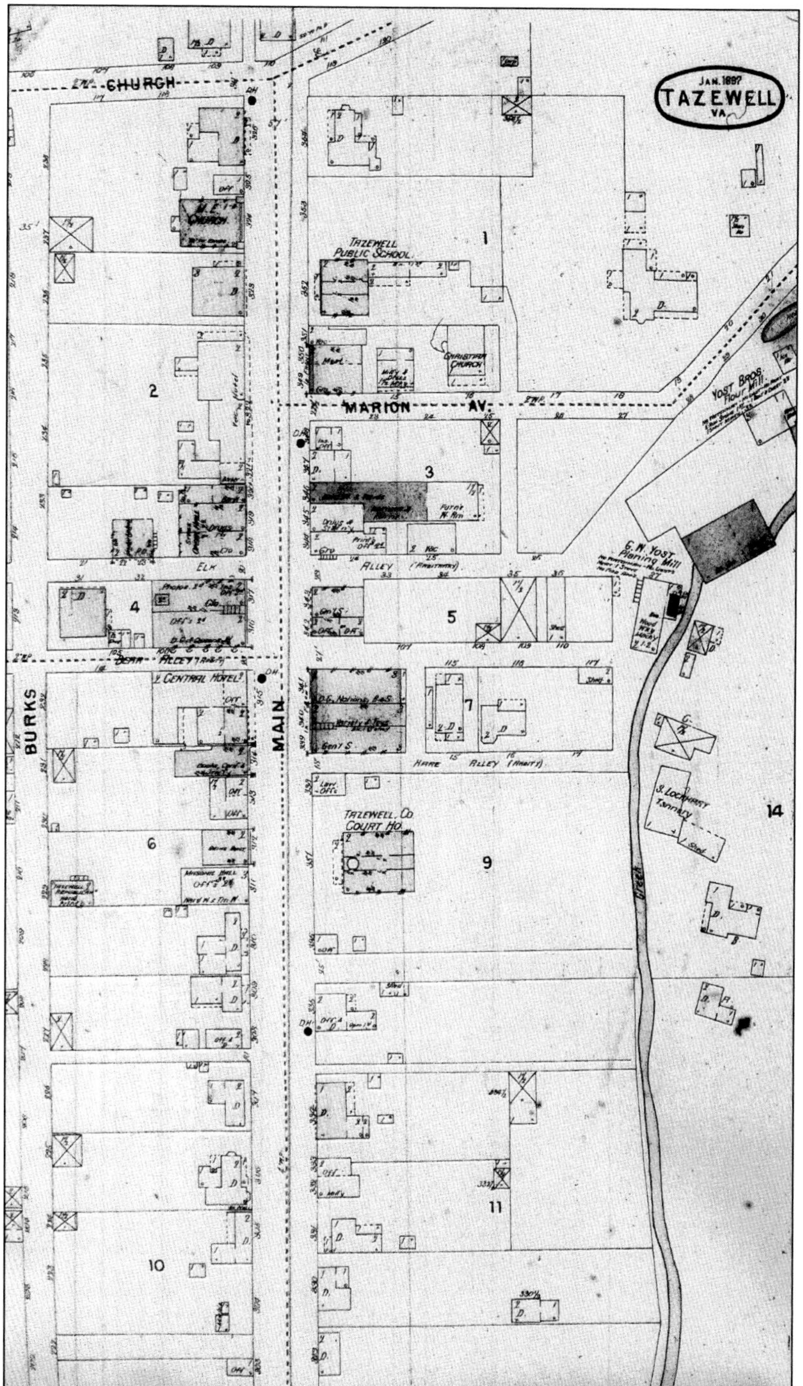

The Sanborn Insurance Map of Tazewell shows Main Street and vicinity in January 1897. Several c. 1900 businesses are labeled. The Sanborn map collection is made up of a uniform series of large-scale maps. The graphic representations of more than 12,000 cities and towns date from 1867 to the present. The maps depict commercial, industrial, and residential sections of communities in the United States, Canada, and Mexico. (Courtesy Tazewell County Public Library.)

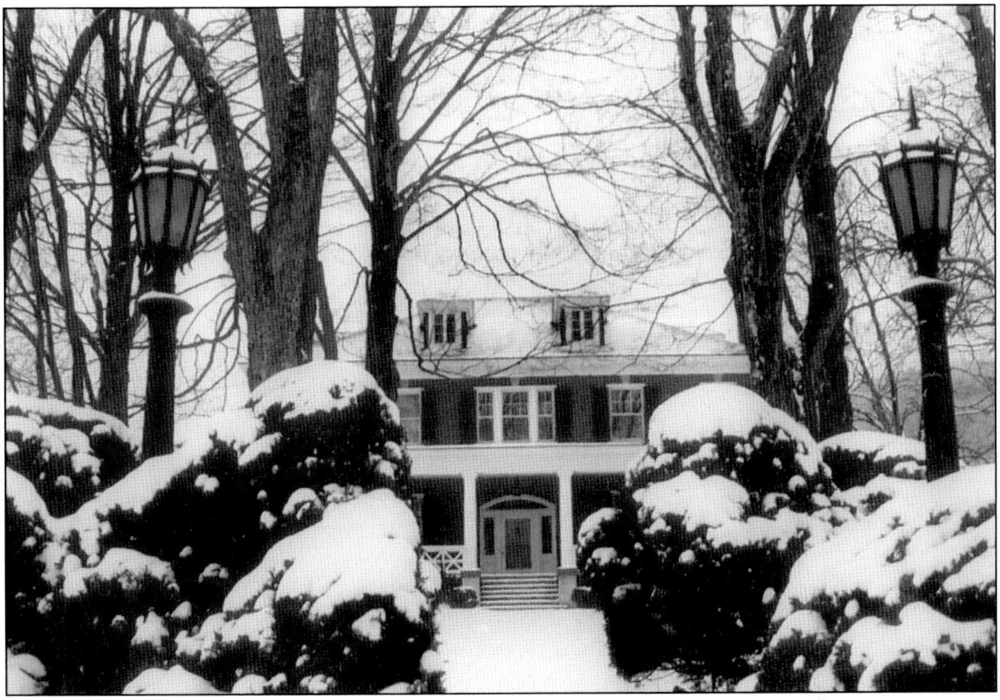

Maple Hill, the Tazewell home of Gov. and Mrs. George C. Peery, is especially beautiful on a day of snow. This peaceful day was in the winter of 1974. (Courtesy of Nancy Peery Olson.)

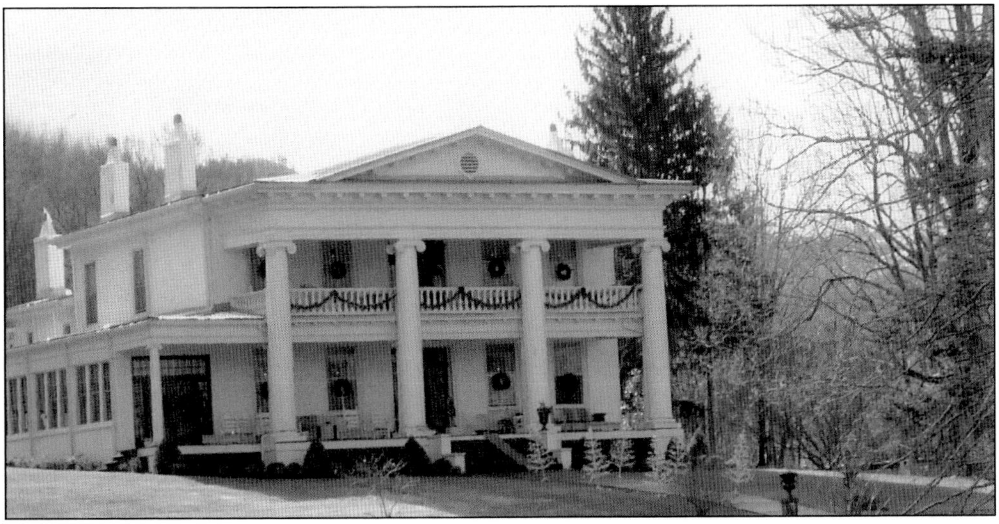

This stately home, now owned by Dr. Robert Weinacker, was built in 1859 by John W. Johnston, the father of Dr. George Ben Johnston, a famous Virginia surgeon. (Johnston Memorial Hospital in Richmond was named for him.) In later years, the Floyd family occupied the home on Marion Avenue. This political family has been compared to the Kennedys. Mrs. J. W. Johnston was a Floyd, and her father and brother were both governors of Virginia. Other occupants of the house included the Col. A. J. May family. His widow once had a school there. Some of the A. Z. Litz family lived in the beautiful home for over 60 years. (Courtesy Mullins files.)

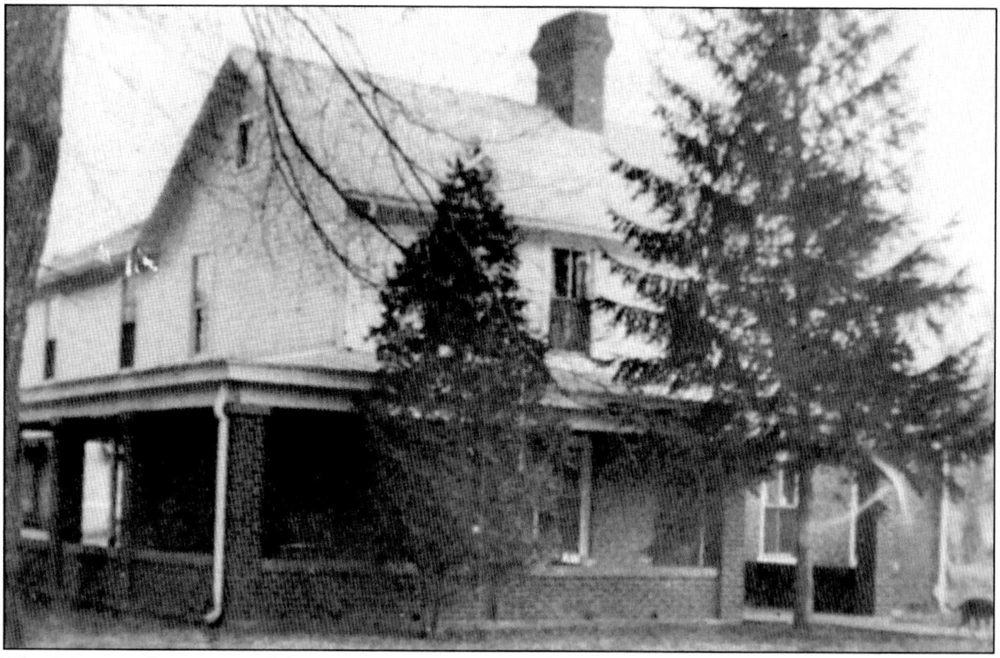

The Martingale was a well-known restaurant owned by Mr. and Mrs. Ralph P. Hawkins in the beautiful old family home of the Peerys and Martins. The home burned some years after the restaurant was closed. The Martingale name came from a former resident, George A. Martin, Tazewell County's first surveyor. (Courtesy of the *Peak*, Tazewell High School.)

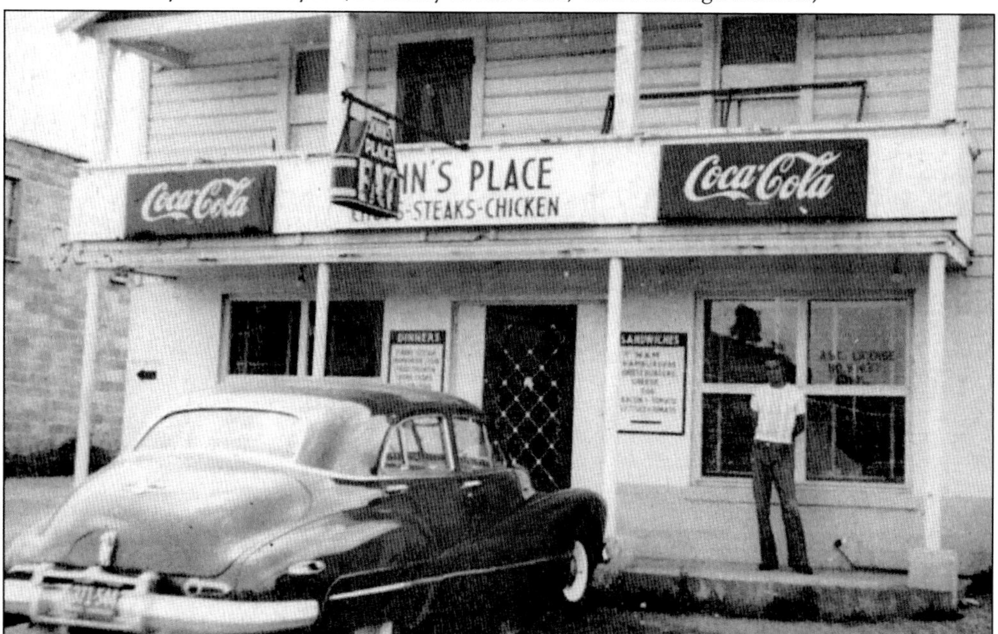

John's Restaurant, owned and operated by John Westmoreland and his family, was a popular gathering place for many years. Their special feature, along with other good food, was the Big John's Hamburger. John's was open from 1946 until 1987. A motel was also a part of the business during the second half of the establishment's existence. (Courtesy of Rae Farley.)

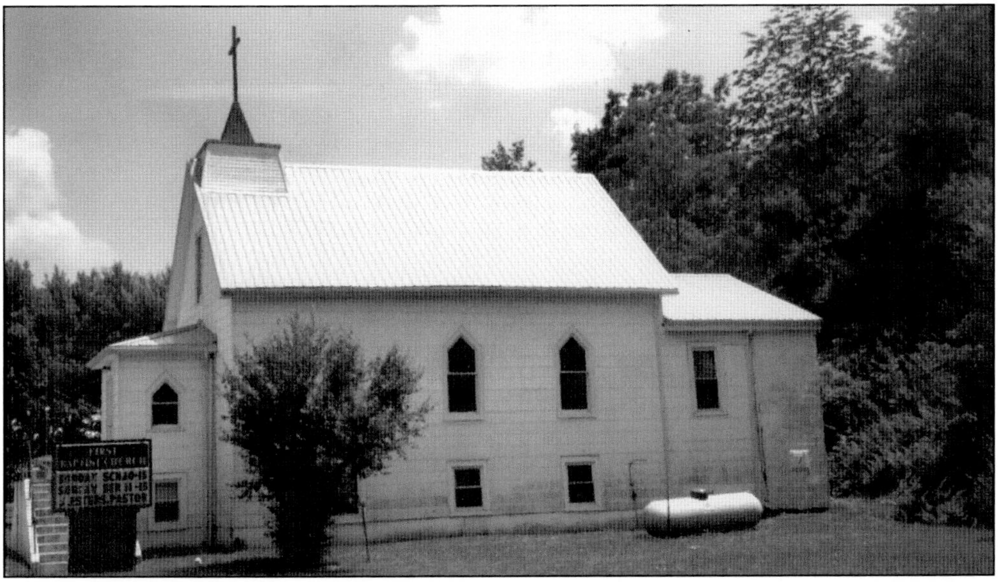

The First Baptist Church is one of the oldest churches in the African American community of Tazewell. The building was once a blacksmith shop and is believed to be more than 119 years old. A century ago, there was also a blacksmith shop operated by the Hagy family close to the present Municipal Building. Faye Viney, a lifelong member of the First Baptist Church, furnished this information. Nearby the first building of the Midway Christian Church is also more than 100 years old. This congregation has relocated to a new modern facility at a beautiful site overlooking the community. (Courtesy of Mullins files.)

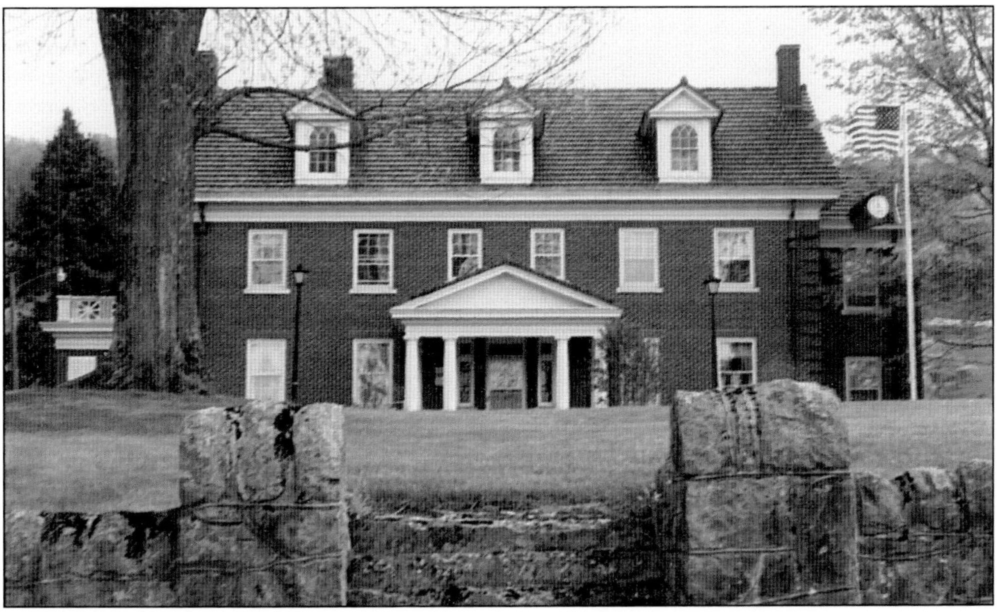

The Tazewell County School Board offices are in this Fincastle Turnpike home built in 1926 by C. Henry Harman. The Harman family sold it in 1946 to L. F. Monk, who sold it in 1969 to the county. Since that time, it has been used by the Tazewell County Health Department, the Tazewell County Development Corporation, and the Farm and Home Extension services. (Courtesy Mullins files.)

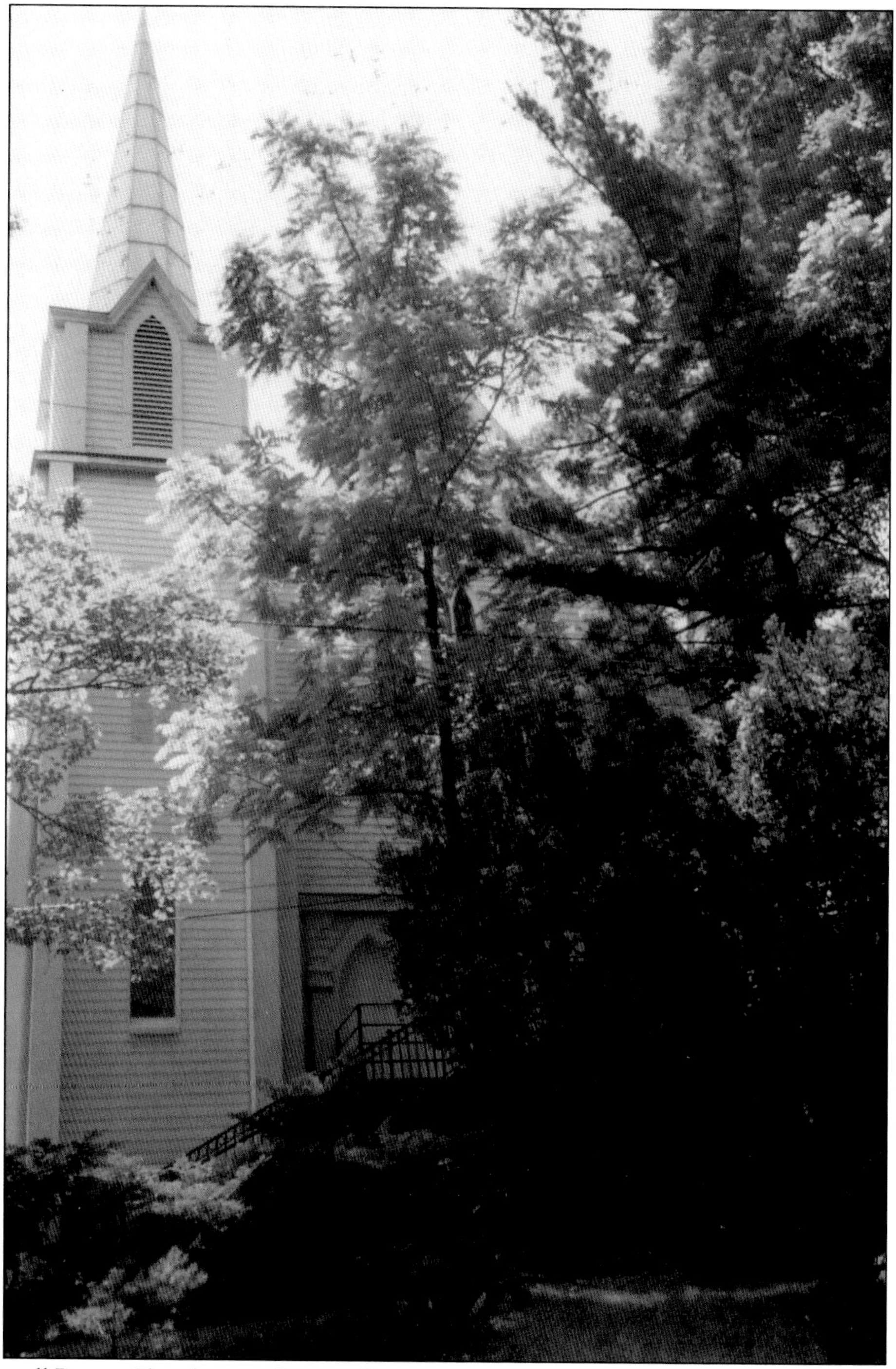

Tazewell Baptist Church, one of Tazewell's oldest places of worship, was built in 1890 by Thomas Masten Hawkins, Tazewell County's master builder and a member of the church. He weighed 300 pounds, and he tested the strength of his works of wood (such as windowsills) by sitting on them. The church bell, enclosed in the tower, was donated by John D. Rockefeller. (Courtesy of Mullins files.)

Four

Kelly Becomes North Tazewell

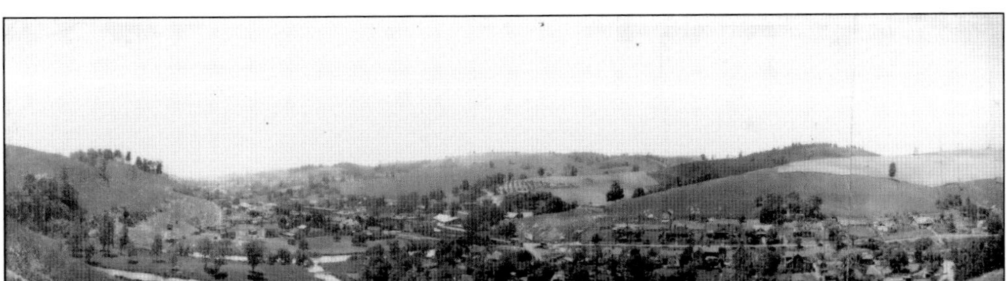

This panoramic view of North Tazewell shows a bustling riverside community that served as the commercial center of the Tazewell area. North Tazewell began as Kelly on the Clinch in the early 1800s. Residences were constructed in both directions up and down the Clinch. Later many businesses located here as well. (Courtesy of Jesse Peery.)

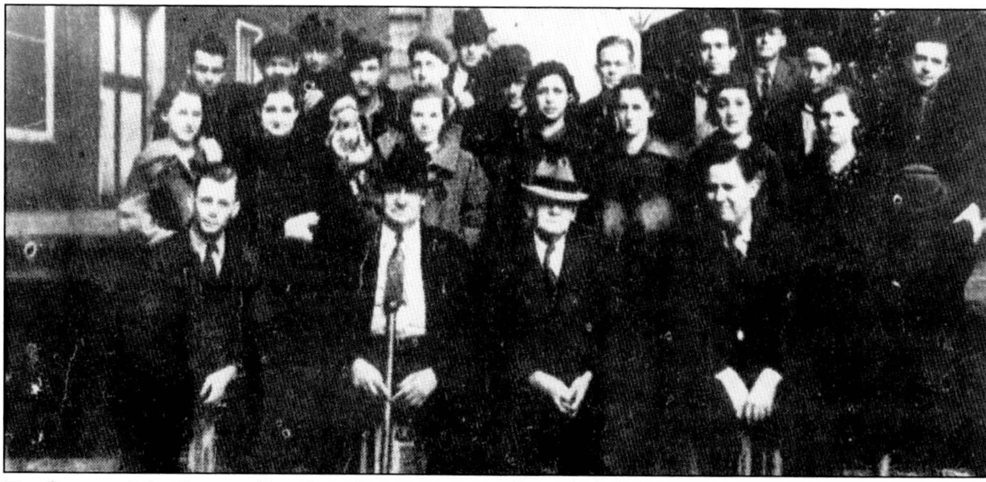

Employees of the Sunrise Bottling Company in 1937 included, from left to right, (first row) George Buston, Harry Buston, J. G. Buston, W. E. Spencer, and Francis Wilson; (second row) Margaret Spencer, Annie Johnson, Elsie Holbrooks, Ethel Beavers, Dainese Crawford, Georgie Boothe; (third row) Robert Ireson, Paul Groseclose, Hal Lawrence, Walt Lawrence, Jack Buston, Elmer Atwood, Joe Hubbard, Joe Patrick, Raymond Groseclose, Charlie Boothe, Frank Lawrence, and Tom Newman. The Sunrise Bottling Company was the home of the popular Was-cott Ginger Ale, named after its creator. William A. Scott began the manufacture of the ginger ale in 1921, and it was shipped to New York, San Francisco, and New Orleans, as well as locally. Before starting the business, Scott was a partner with Davis Diuguid, a wholesale grocer at North Tazewell. (Courtesy of Jack Repass.)

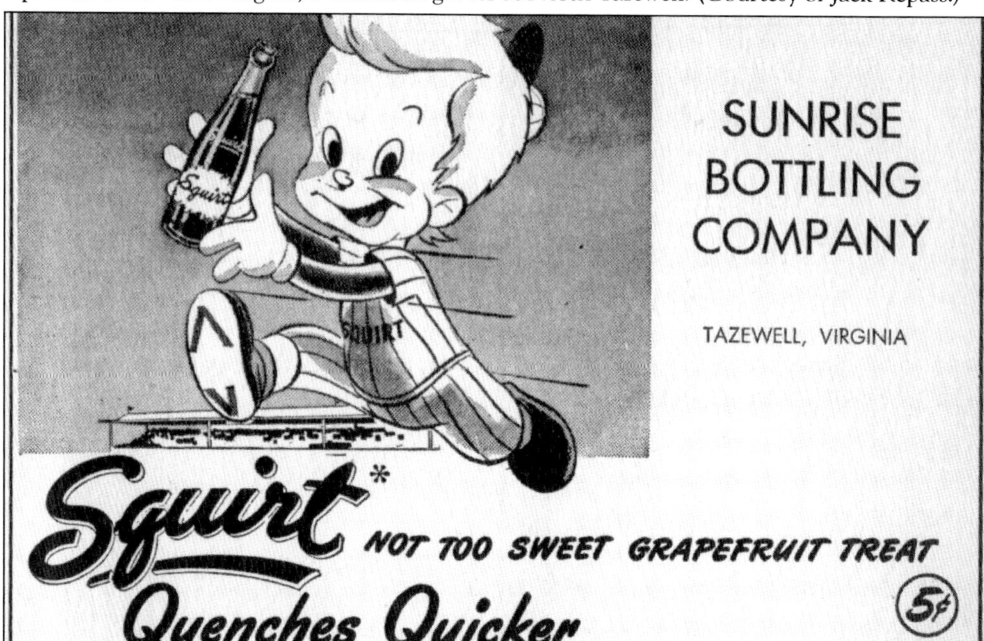

The Sunrise Bottling Company at North Tazewell made the soft drink called Squirt. This was an early advertisement that promised a "thirst quencher" that was a "not too sweet grapefruit treat" at 5¢ per bottle. In addition to Squirt and Was-cott Ginger Ale, Sunrise bottled Red Rock Cola, Rhythm Punch, Hires Root Beer, Tazewell Orange, and other Sunrise beverages. (Courtesy of Mullins files.)

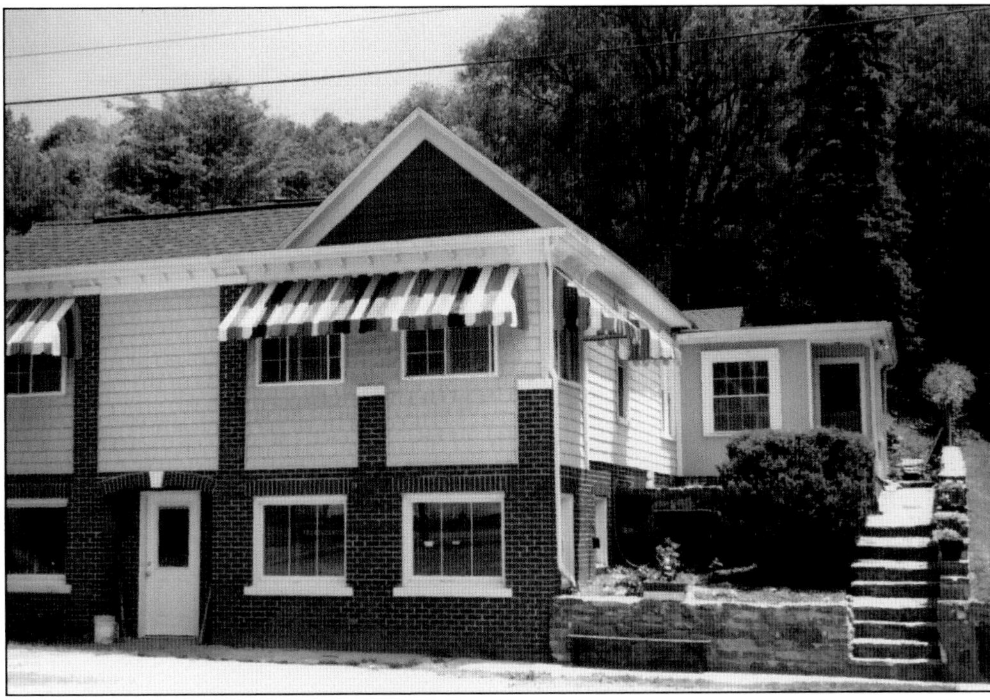

The North Tazewell home of Dr. Jack Walter Witten has been renovated by Bettye VanDyke. It reminds passersby of the days of "Doc" Witten and his household of foster sons. He is well remembered as a doctor, legislator, and humanitarian. The Witten cabin, at the Crab Orchard Historic Museum, is a popular stop for tourists and local residents who enjoy the memorabilia on display there. (Courtesy of Mullins files.)

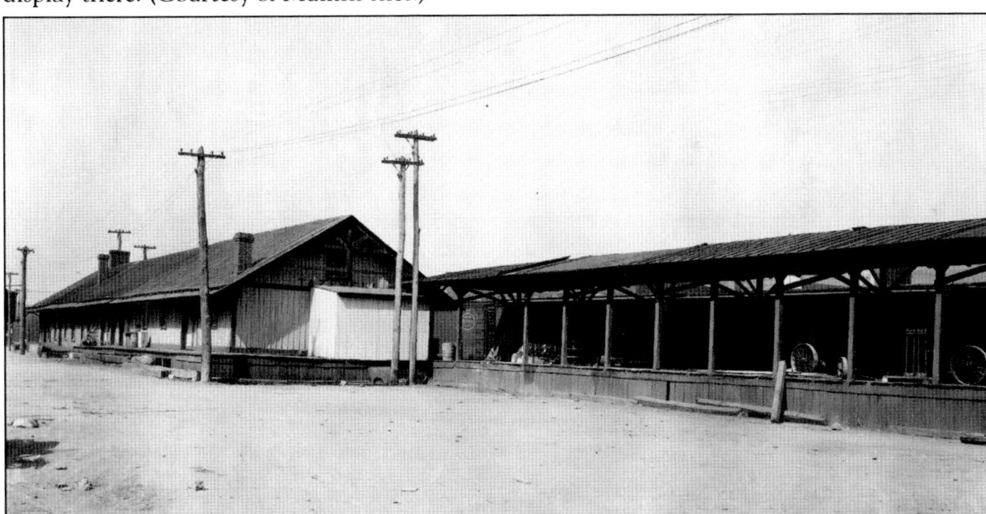

North Tazewell was a bustling business center around 1900. Many businesses and residences sprang up along the Clinch River a mile and a half north of the courthouse. With the arrival of the Clinch Valley Line of the Norfolk and Western Railroad, Kelly identified itself as North Tazewell when it secured a charter of incorporation in 1894. The town obtained its second charter in 1942. The train station, shown here, was the center of much of that business activity. (Courtesy of Norfolk and Western Historical Photograph Collection at Virginia Tech.)

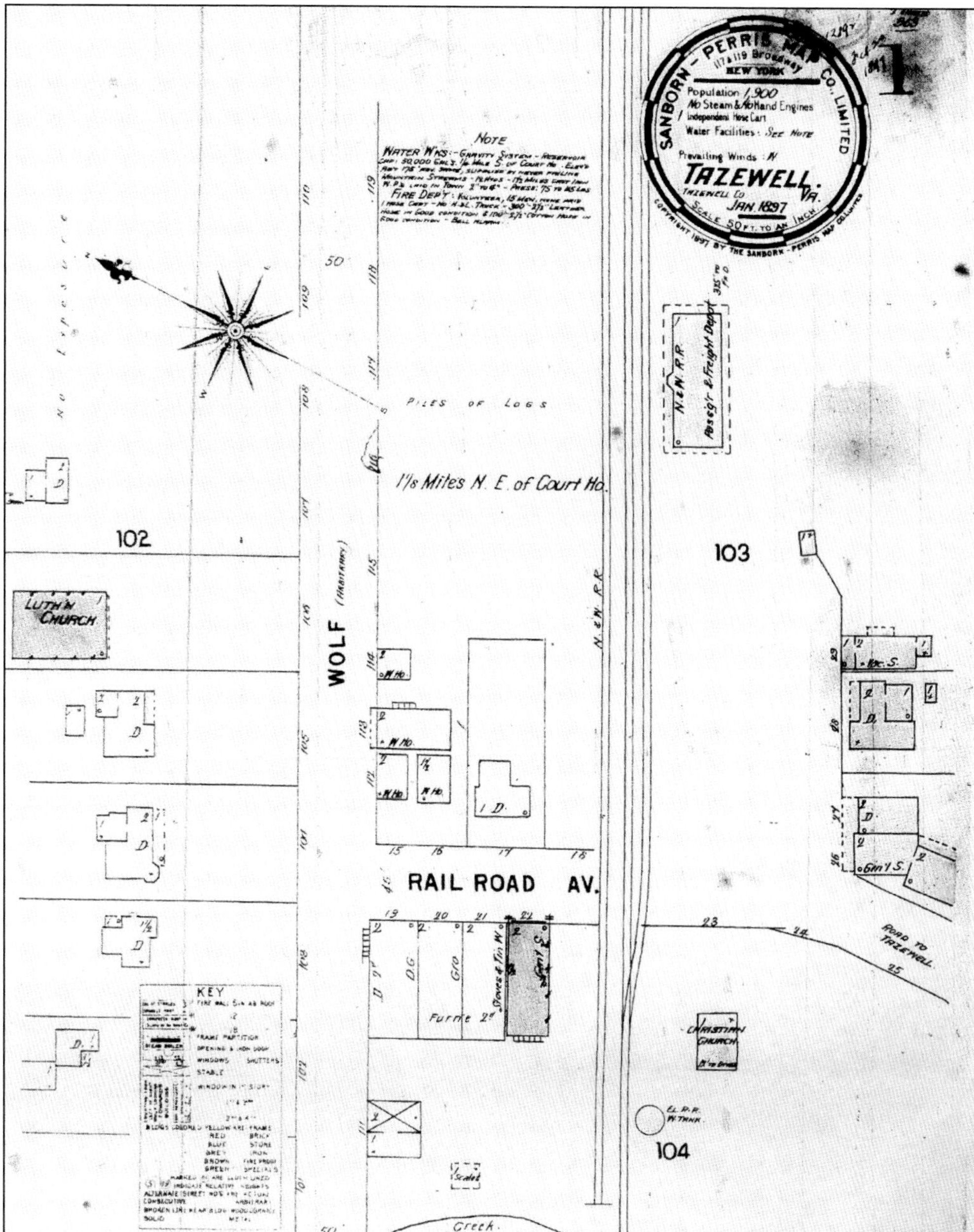

This 1897 Sanborn Insurance map shows North Tazewell. The Sanborn map collection represents more than 12,000 cities and towns in North America. The maps date from 1867 to the present. The maps indicate street names, property boundaries, building use, and house and block numbers. (Courtesy of Tazewell County Public Library.)

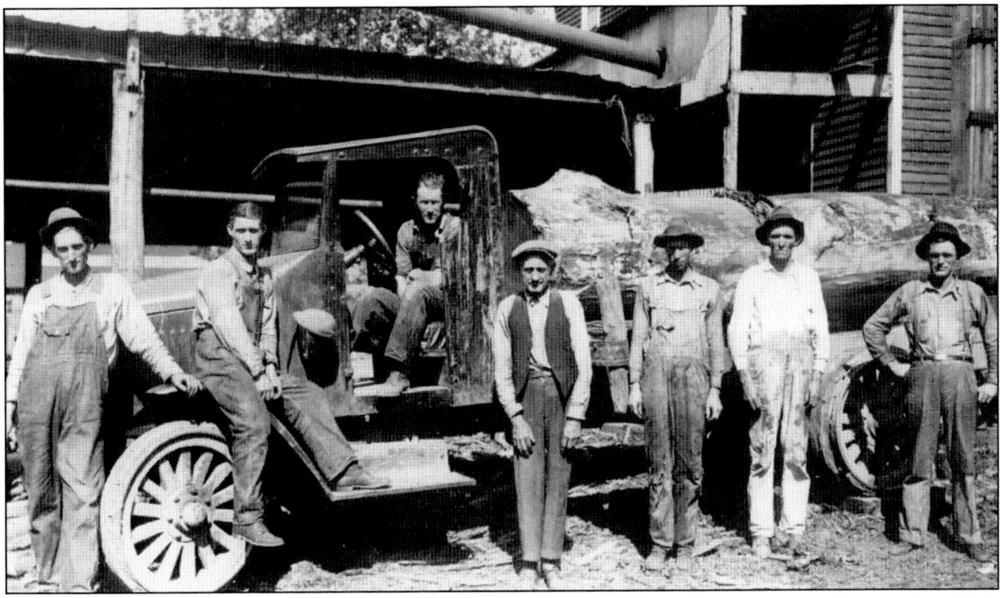

The Federal Supply Company was an important North Tazewell business well into the 20th century. Employees pictured here include, from left to right, George Davidson, Frank Neel, George Crawford, Dan Newman, Jim Crawford, George W. Burress, and W. S. Beavers. Federal Supply succeeded the 19th-century enterprise known as the T. K. Hall and Sons Planing Company. (Courtesy of Jack Repass.)

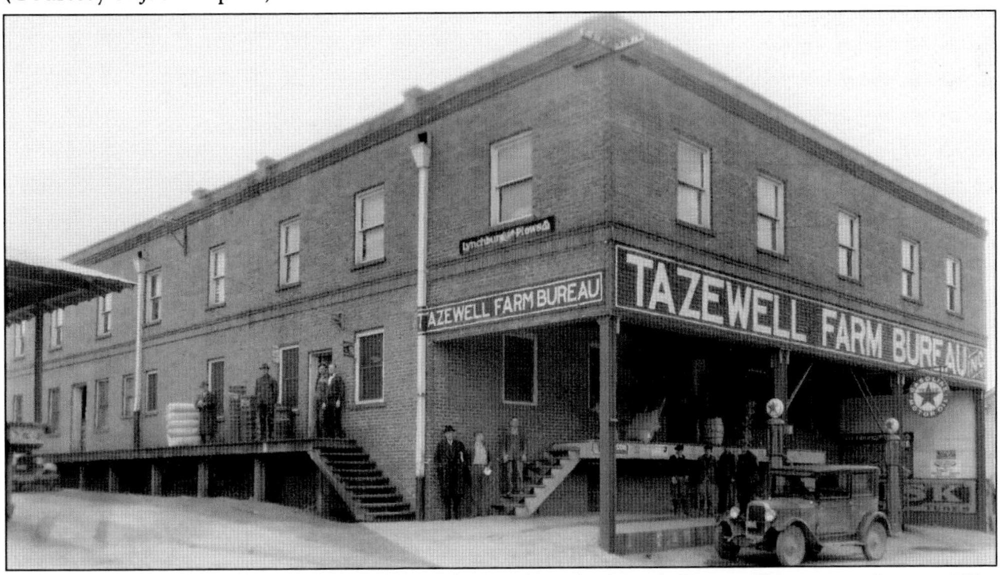

The Tazewell Farm Bureau Main Office is located in the North Tazewell business district. The business was established in 1917; the building pictured here was erected in 1921 and enlarged two years later. R. R. Wall, the Tazewell County farm agent from 1916 until 1921, became the manager of the Farm Bureau in 1922. The photograph shown here was made in 1936. When it was framed in 1957, R. D. Angles was the store manager and R. R. Wall continued as general manager. Annual sales that year totaled $370,000. Rhea Moore Sr., A. D. Torrence, Don Baker, and David Farris were other well-remembered managers of the Farm Bureau organization. (Courtesy of Tazewell Farm Bureau.)

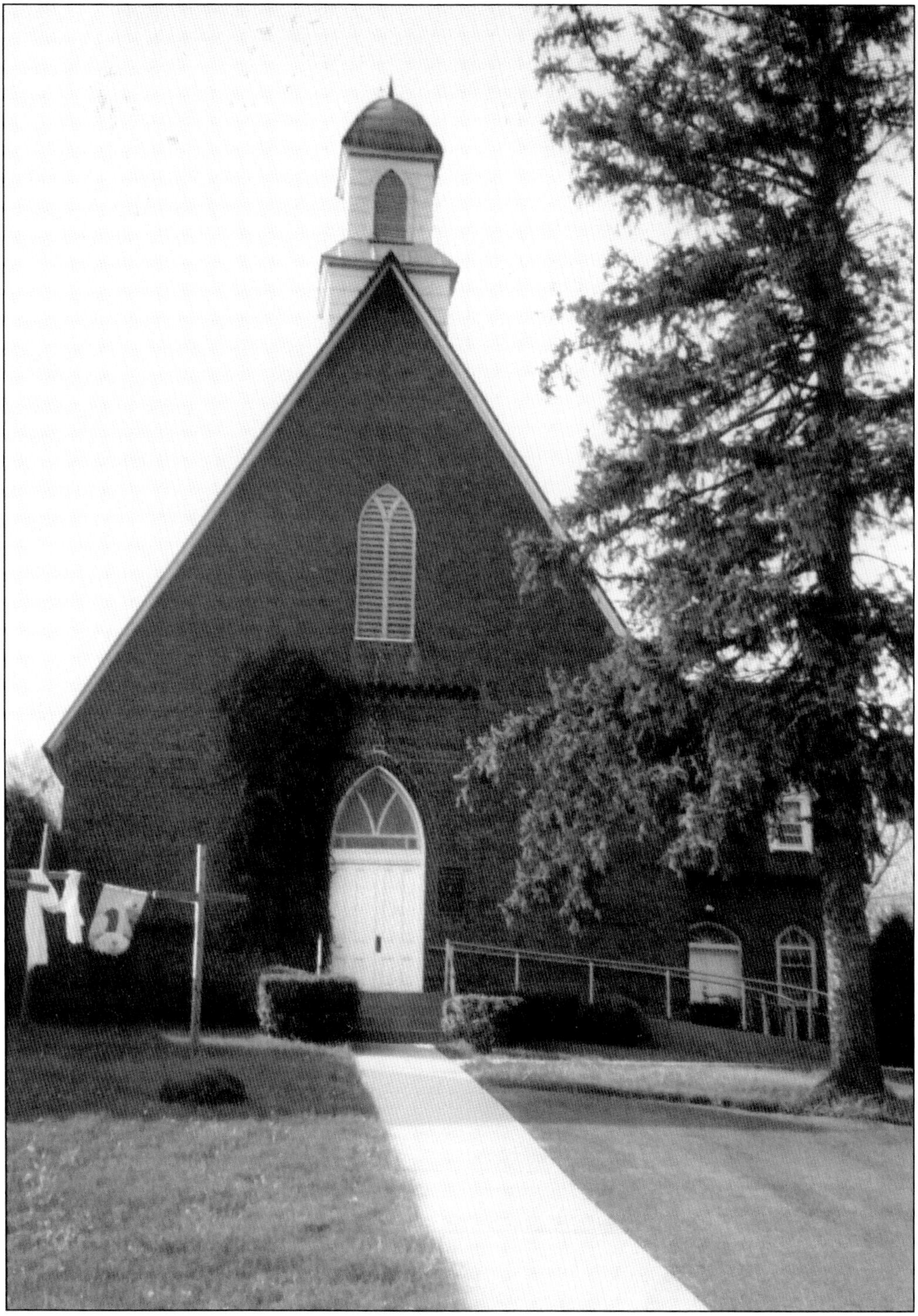

The North Tazewell United Methodist Church purchased their present building in 1899 from the Lutheran congregation, which moved to a location at the corner of Church and Pine Streets in Tazewell. The attractive brick structure was built in 1889 and continues today as an active Methodist congregation. (Courtesy of Mullins files.)

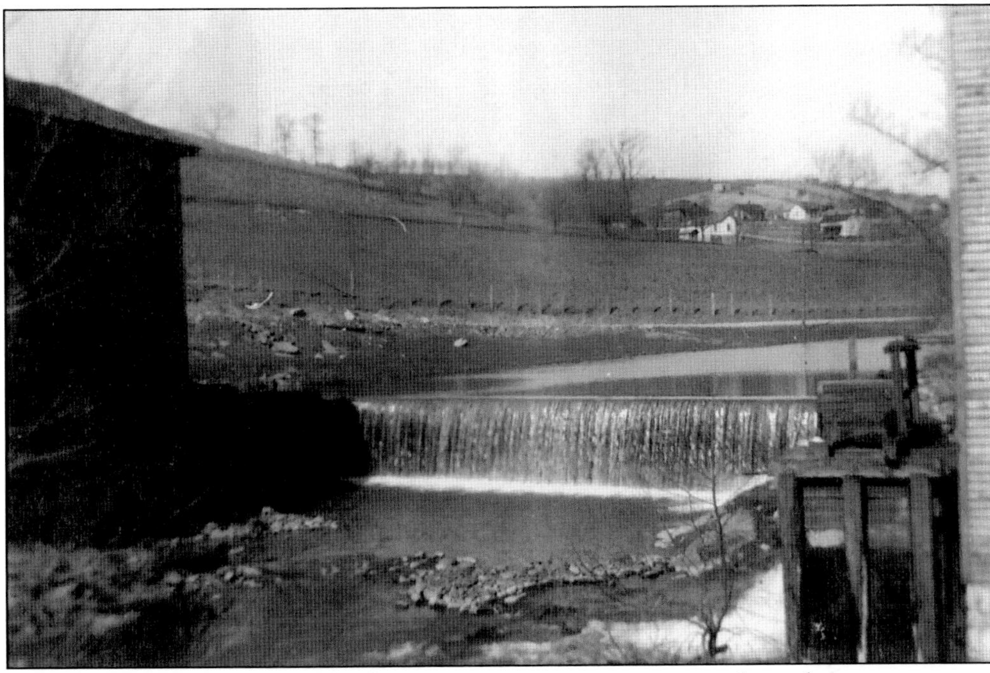

The North Tazewell dam on Clinch River, a picturesque scene, was a busy place a century ago. A woolen mill was on one side of the river and a grain mill on the opposite bank. The dam was reconstructed in 1913, and the mills were in existence as late as the 1930s. The Clinch River above the dam is a favorite of fishermen even today. (Courtesy of Jesse Peery.)

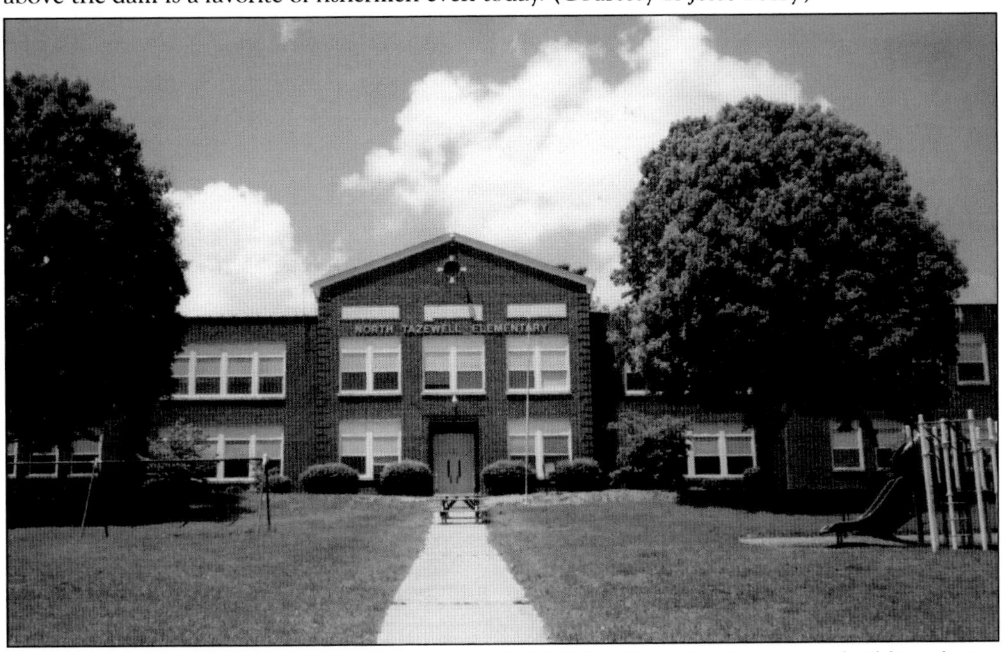

The North Tazewell Elementary School was built 1931. It followed a three-room building dating back to 1895 at the same location. There have been several additions through the years, the last one in 1994. Among many principals at the school, Jack Witten served the longest, almost 40 years at the helm. (Courtesy of Mullins files.)

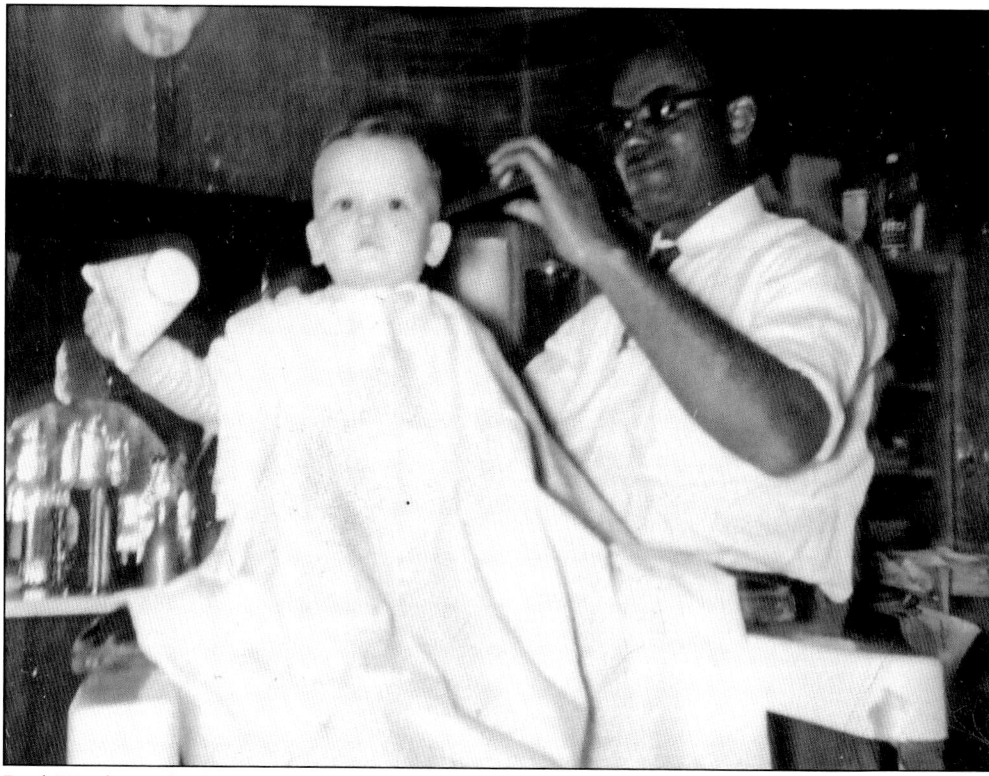

Paul Winfrey, a barber in Tazewell and North Tazewell, pleased customers of all ages. The men of the town met at Winfrey's to debate many of the great issues of the day. His young patron is Terry Mullins. (Courtesy of Terry Mullins.)

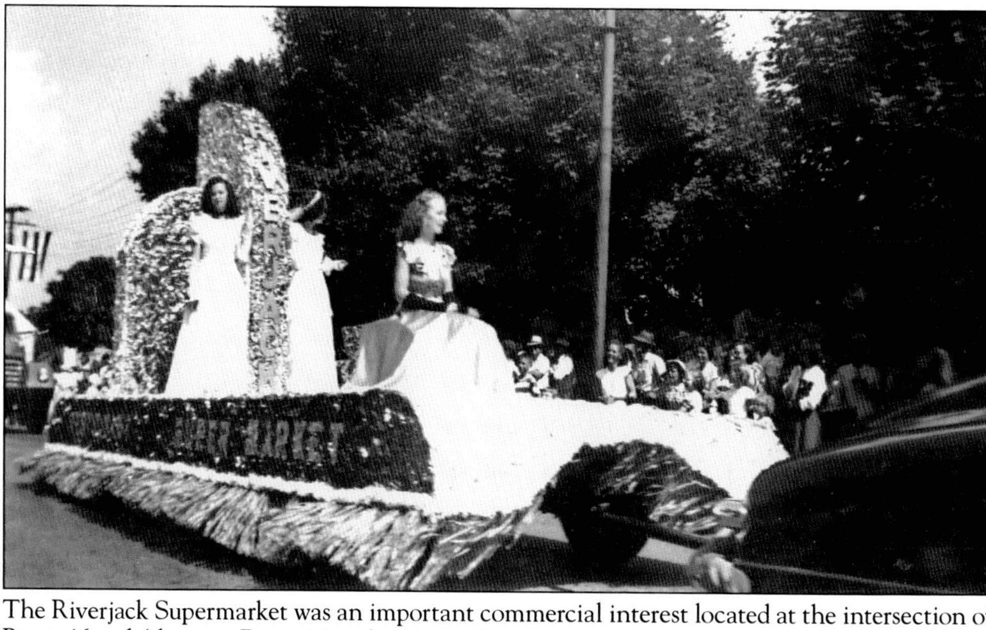

The Riverjack Supermarket was an important commercial interest located at the intersection of Route 16 and Alternate Route 16 in the Riverjack community. The business entered this impressive float in the Sesquicentennial Parade in 1950. (Courtesy of Nancy Ward files.)

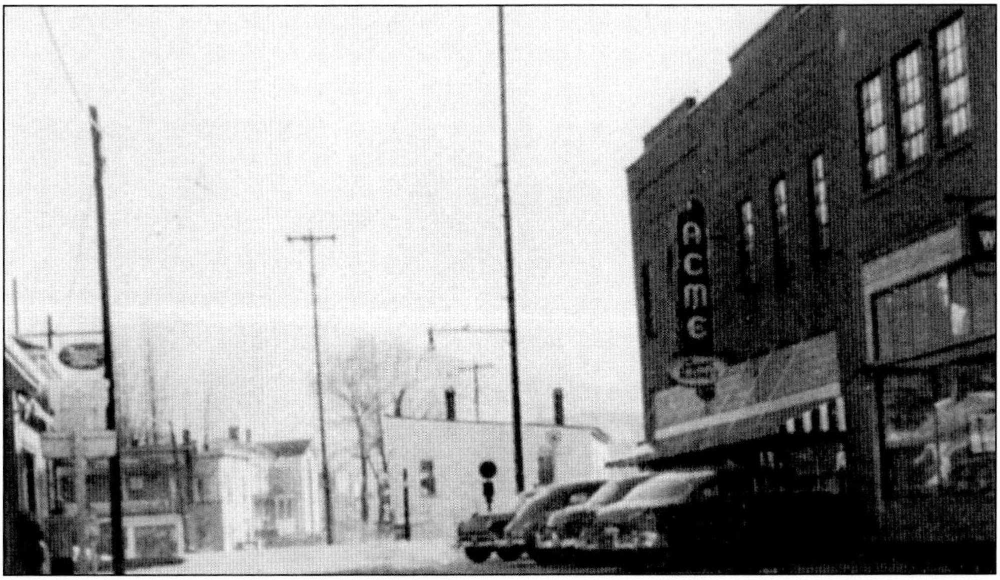

North Tazewell in 1957 was a commercial center with several businesses and many different enterprises having their offices and warehouses in the community. Many of the businesses were centered here at the intersection of Routes 16 and 61. Other enterprises were located around the railroad depot and on each side of the Norfolk and Western Railroad. (Courtesy of Terry Mullins.)

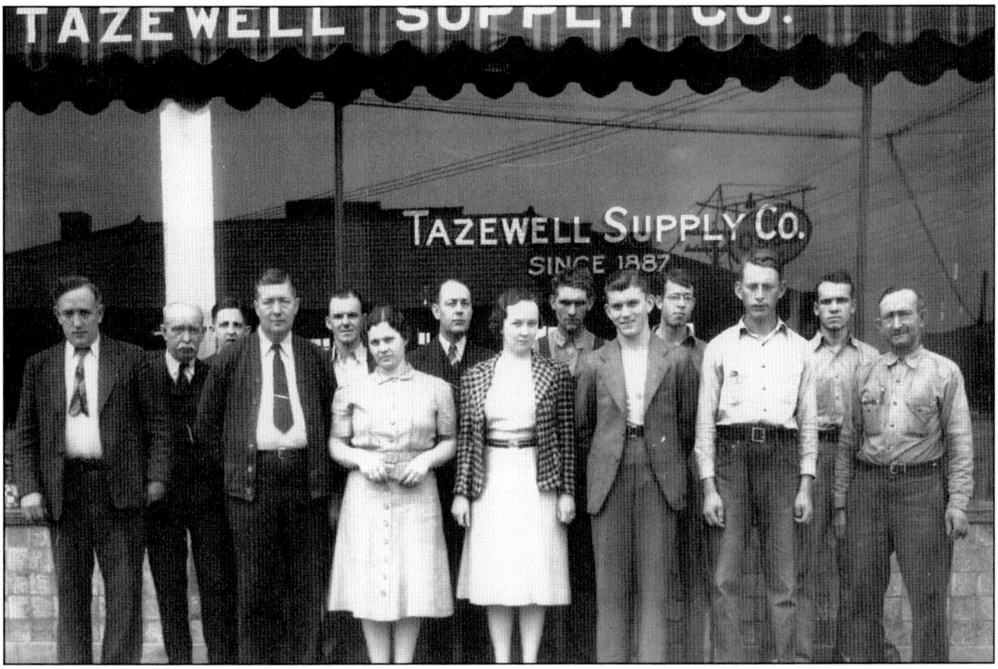

The Tazewell Supply Company was founded at North Tazewell in 1887. This employee picture from 1940 includes, from left to right, Charles E. Peery, Robert H. Ireson, J. C. Ireson, Clarence Neal, Peyton Greear, Lois Floyd, Garland Peery, Ella Greear, Jeff Asbury, Sonny Porter, two unidentified persons, Jack Ireson, and Will Moore Ireson. Tazewell Supply Company became A-Mart in 1962. (Courtesy of Ella Greear files.)

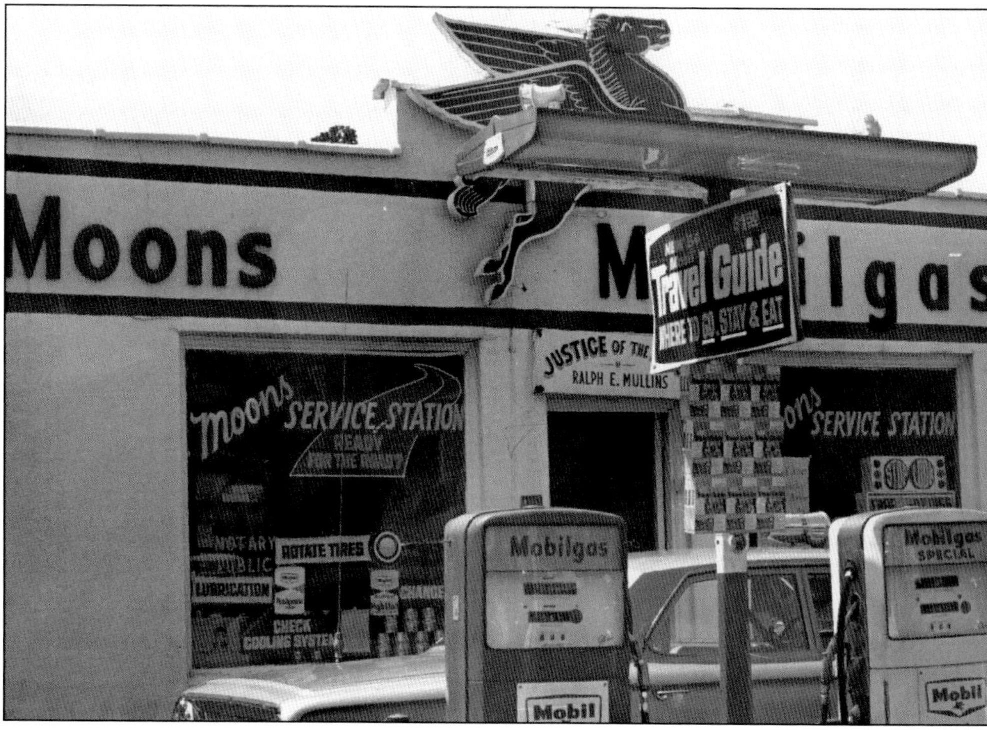

Moon's Service Station and Mullins' Body Shop were prominent businesses located on what is now West Riverside Drive in North Tazewell. The establishment served the community with Mobile gasoline products for many years beginning in 1956. Proprietors were Ralph E. Mullins and his father, James L. Mullins. (Courtesy of Ralph Mullins.)

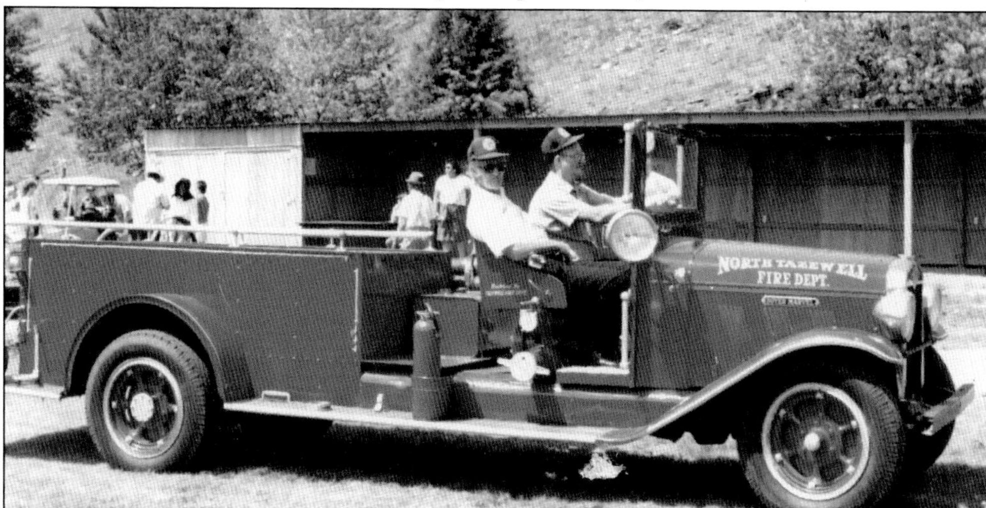

The North Tazewell Fire Department's 1929 Ford fire engine has been preserved and restored by the modern Tazewell Fire Department. The antique fire truck is a regular in community parades and celebrations. When it was put out of service, it was painted green and was used as a work vehicle when the towns consolidated. Now its original red color has been restored. Riding in the restored truck are Mac Buchanan (left) and Buck Helmandollar (right), both longtime firemen. Chief Buchanan retired in 2006 after 30 years of service. (Courtesy of Mac Buchanan.)

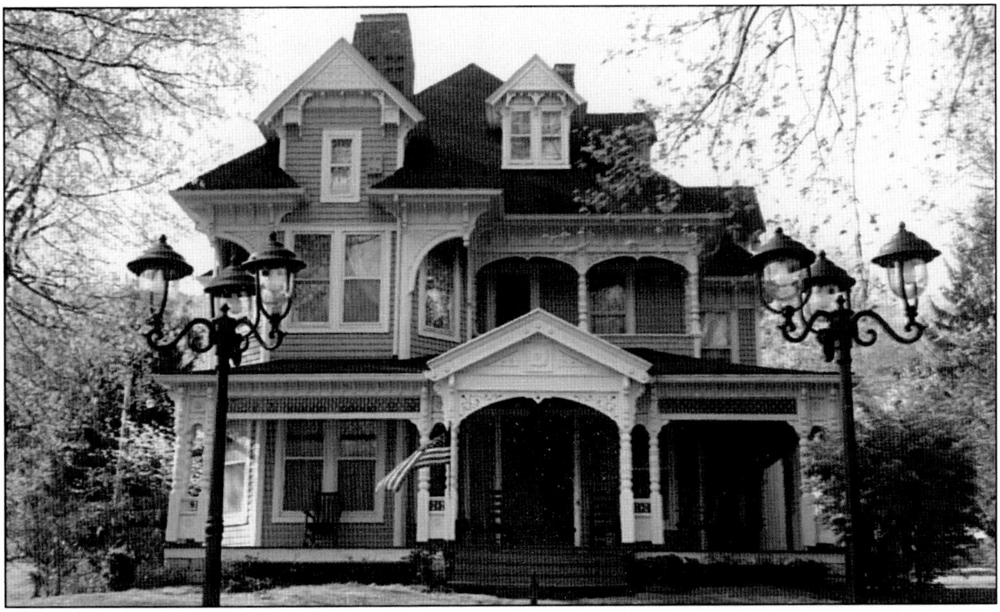

The George P. Hall house on Riverside Drive, North Tazewell, was built in 1896, and its ornate style is typical of the era. This fine home was pointed out to train passengers when they left the Tazewell Depot. T. K. Hall, father of the builder, was an early mayor of North Tazewell. The Hall house is one of the more impressive North Tazewell residences. (Courtesy of Mullins files.)

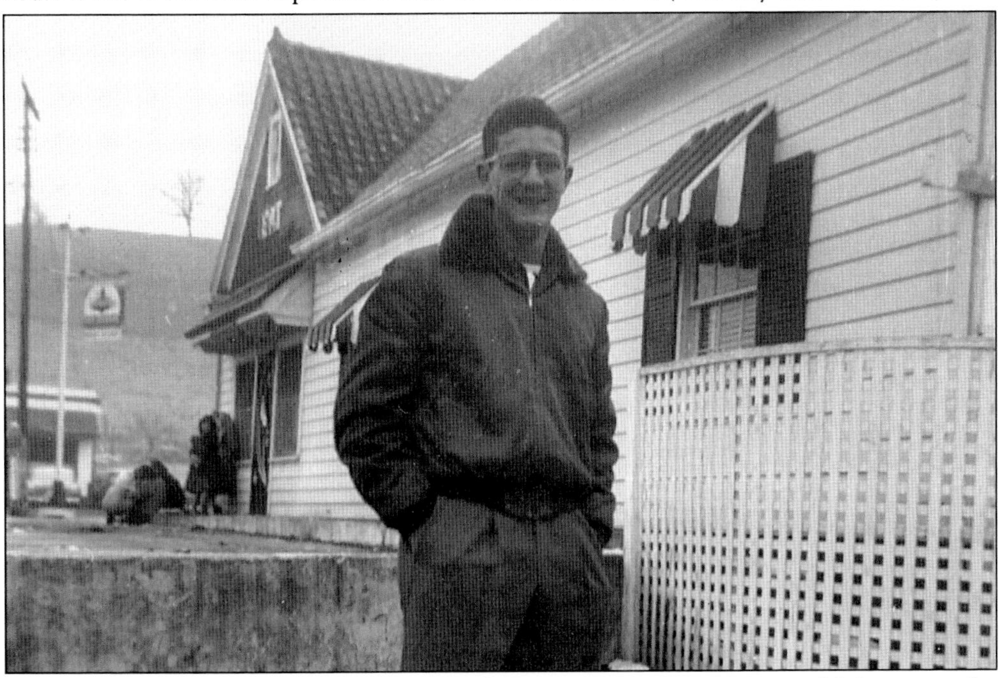

Ralph Mullins stands in front of the Riverjack Restaurant, an important establishment in the Riverjack community. The business served Virginia country ham, fried chicken, and steaks around 1950 to a varied group of patrons each day. The restaurant at Riverjack was owned by the Hayes family. An Esso service station was also part of the establishment. (Courtesy of Ralph Mullins.)

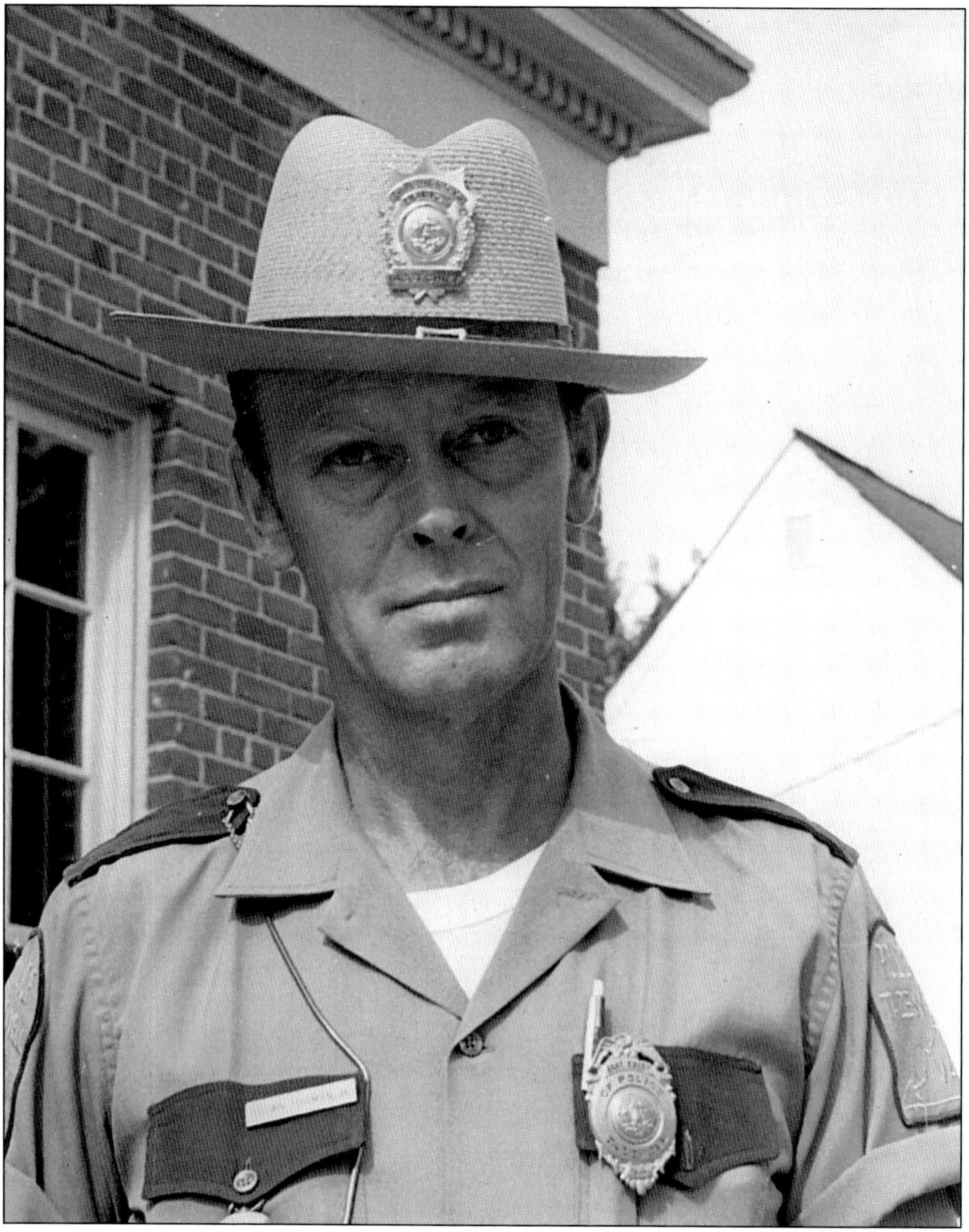

Brown Harman, a North Tazewell native whose ancestors were among the area's early settlers, was chief of police of North Tazewell before the 1963 consolidation of the two towns. After that, he served as assistant police chief in Tazewell (1963–1977) and chief from 1977 to 1986. Also serving Tazewell as chief of police was Rufus Hagy, who was a Tazewell officer and chief until his retirement in 1973. (Courtesy of Mullins files.)

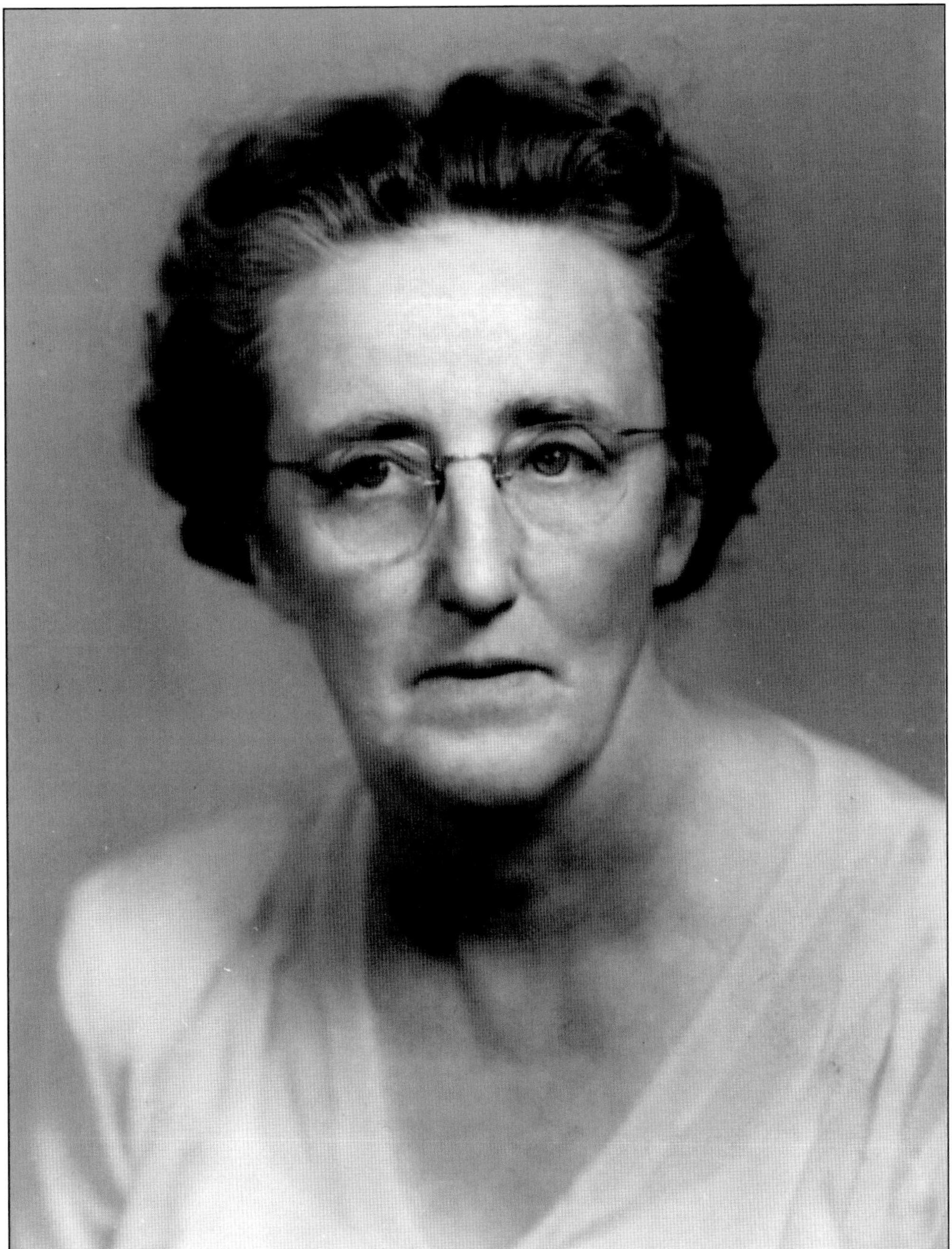

Bonnie Hall was the mayor of North Tazewell during much of the final era of the town's existence. She was the only female mayor in the Commonwealth of Virginia when she assumed that post after her husband's death. In addition to succeeding her husband, Keemer Hall, as mayor, she served several terms of her own prior to consolidation in 1963. "Miss Bonnie," as she was known throughout the county, was also the truant officer for Tazewell County schools for several years and, as such, was responsible for keeping many young students in the classroom instead of on the streets. (Courtesy of Leslie files.)

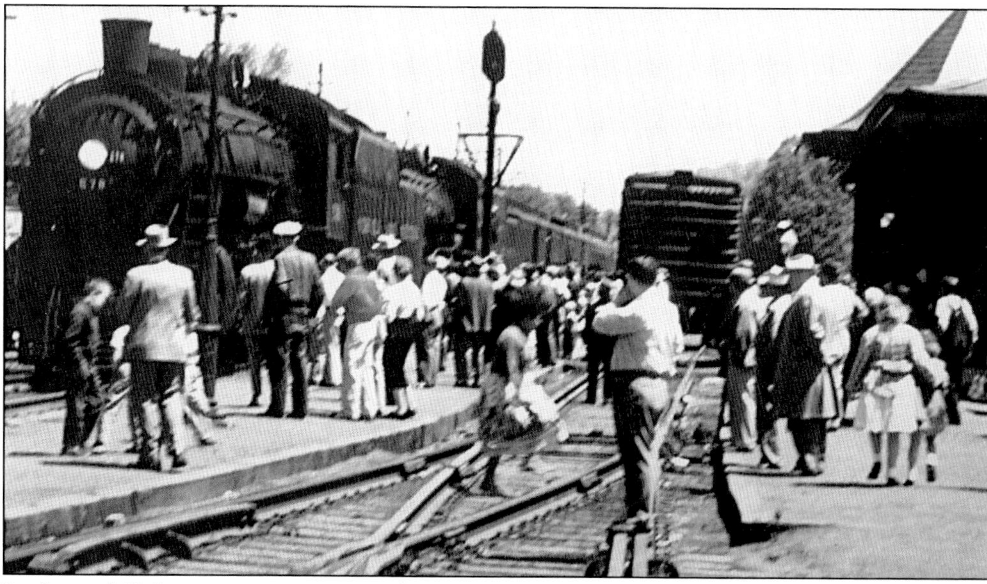

In the mid-20th century, passenger rail service continued to make North Tazewell a busy place as trains arrived, making their way up and down the Clinch Valley line. The new diesel-powered locomotives made stops at the Tazewell Station several times daily. The Norfolk and Western Railway was famous for manufacturing their steam locomotives in-house at their Roanoke Shops. Around 1960, Norfolk and Western became the last major American railroad to convert from steam to diesel motive power. Crowds were common when the locomotive made its arrival. (Courtesy of Jack Repass.)

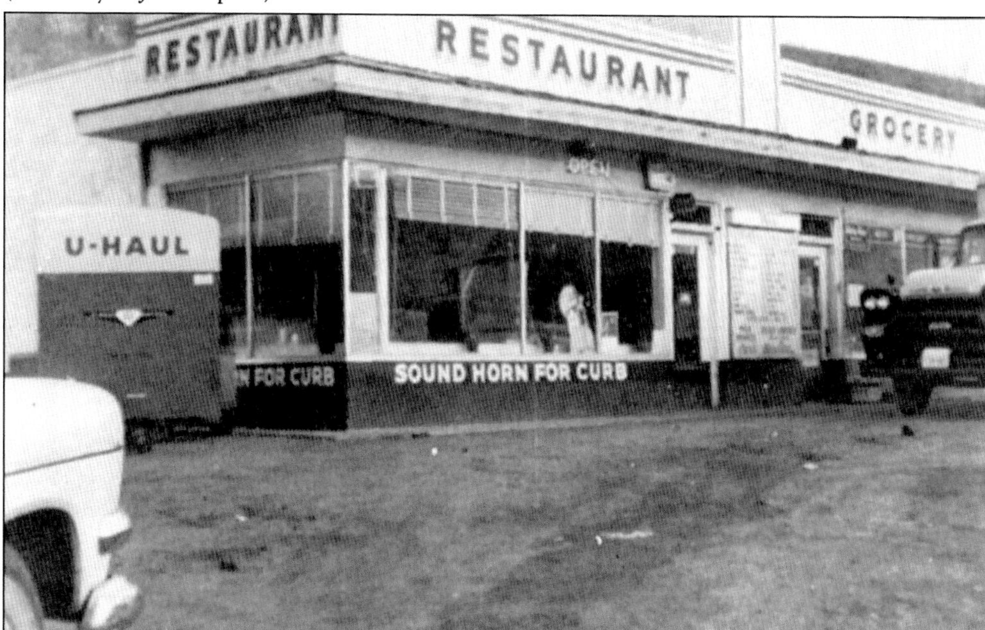

Glen's Drive-in east of the town was a popular place in the days before fast-food restaurants came to Tazewell. It was owned and operated by Glen Kinder, a prominent businessman in many fields. A favorite spot of old and young alike, Glen's was a required stopover for travelers passing through Tazewell. (Courtesy of the *Peak*, Tazewell High School.)

The Repass Barber Shop has been an institution in the North Tazewell community for over half a century. The barber shop was started in 1925 by Floyd Repass. His brother, George W. Repass, came into the business in 1928. The five sons in that family became registered barbers and worked in their shop at North Tazewell. (Courtesy of Jack Repass.)

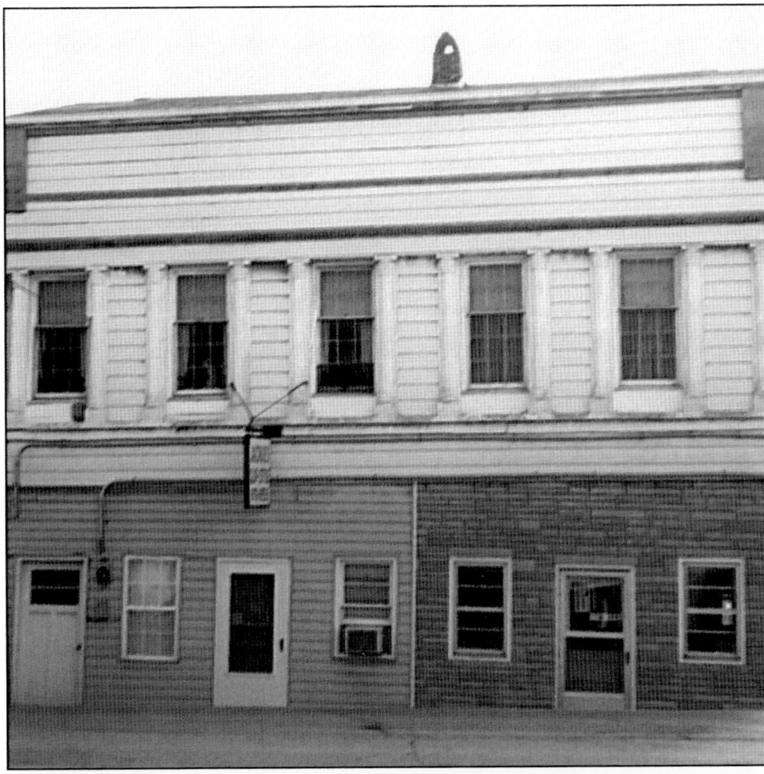

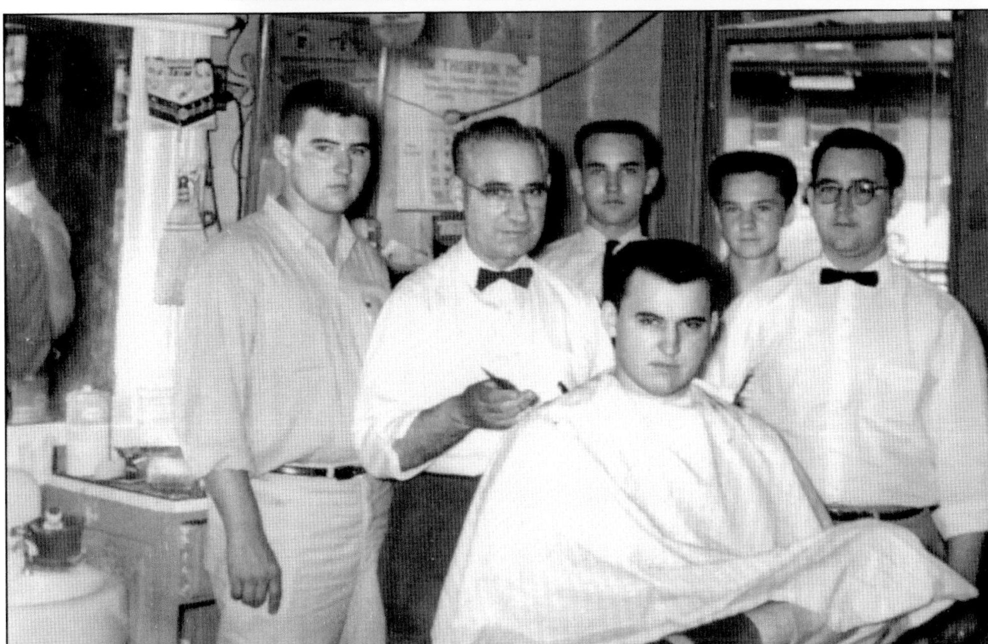

The Repass family barbers were pictured as a group in their family business and included, from left to right, Ralph, George W. (father), Douglass, Marshall, Jack, and Bob (seated). The Repass family has been prominent in Tazewell County for four generations. The art of barbering, according to the Repasses, is becoming rare in the 21st century. (Courtesy of Jack Repass.)

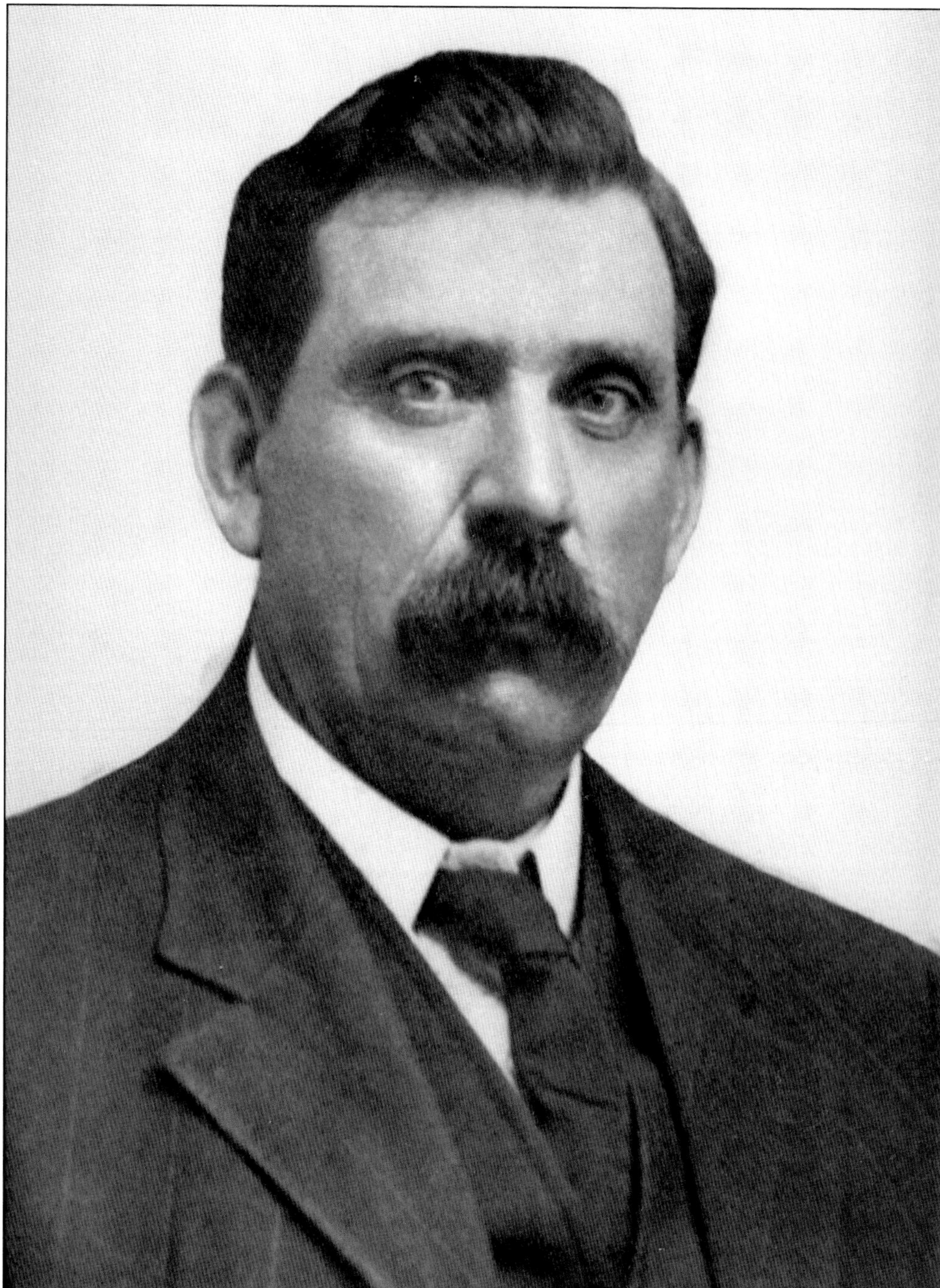

The first mayor of North Tazewell, when the town was incorporated in 1894, was William L. Britts. He was first employed by the W. P. Hall Lumber Company, predecessor of Federal Lumber Company, in North Tazewell. Later in his career, he became a co-owner of the same company. He was widely known as a master cabinet maker. Britts had three sons and a daughter. Members of this family later owned and operated the popular Britts Restaurant in North Tazewell. Later their restaurant was located on Main Street in Tazewell. (Courtesy of Town of Tazewell.)

Five

FACES AROUND TAZEWELL TOWN

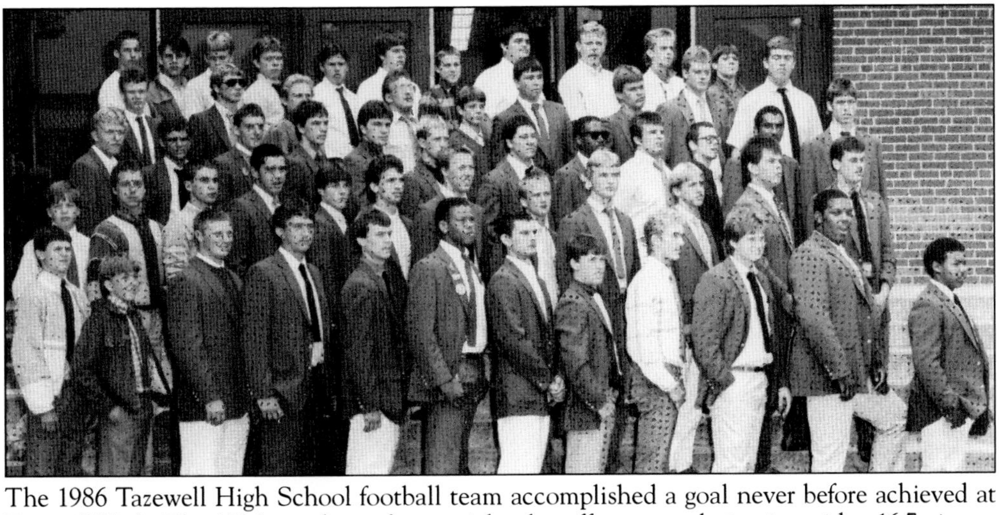

The 1986 Tazewell High School football team accomplished a goal never before achieved at Tazewell High. The 1986 squad won four straight play-off games, culminating with a 16-7 victory over Nottoway High School, to secure the first Virginia State Football Championship for Tazewell. Team members included, from left to right, (first row) David Canady, Mark Beggs, John Blankenship, Donnie Hankins, Kevin Hicks, Jesse Davis, Gary Matney, Jeff McCann, Marty Garrett, Troy Wright, Robert Viney, and Steve Rainey; (second row) Clifford Dale, Gary Dixon, Robbi Peery, Keith Stinson, Larry Murphy, Bobby Stallard, Jim Compton, Dusty Woods, Jeff Lamie, Anthony Brewster, Stephan Holloway, and Craig Clifton; (third row) Mark Ferguson, Scott Rasnake, Dennis Smith, Mark Queen, Joey Ratliff, Brad Laney, Chris McCall, Link Thompson, Tom Williams, Jeff Wilson, Quentin Reed, and Mark Burnett; (fourth row) Kevin McCall, Richie Mays, Chris Linkous, Charles Gills, Billy Wagner, Robbie Colley, Freddie Howery, Robbie Smith, and Barclay Sisk; (fifth row) Tom Moore, Wesley Comer, Jeff Brewster, Chris Toney, David Hash, Scott Kitts, Roger Brown, Jerry Smith, Marc Waddell Brent Matney, and Scott Burress. Dave Litz was the head coach of the 1986 state champion Tazewell Bulldogs. (Courtesy of the *Peak*, Tazewell High School.)

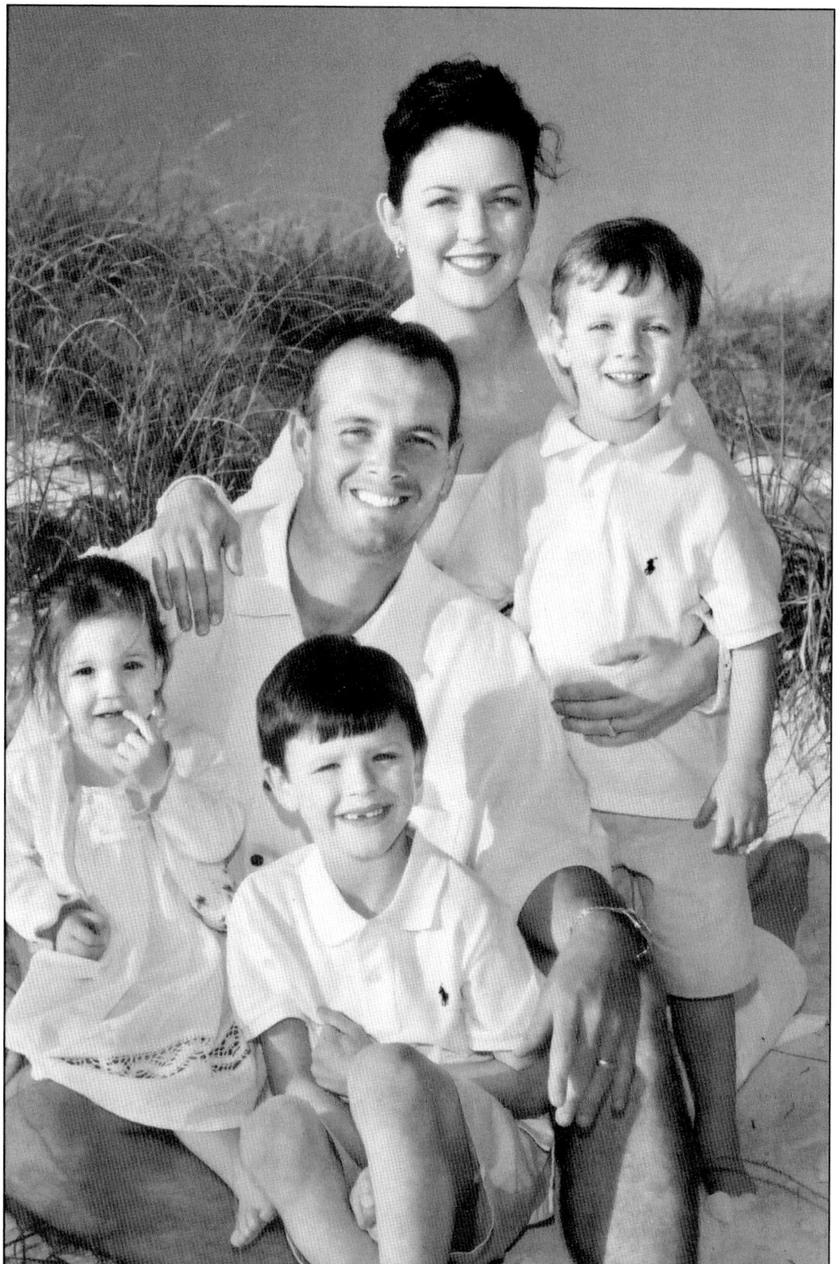

Billy Wagner is Tazewell's true "hometown hero." The Tannersville, Virginia, native was a member of the 1986 Tazewell High School state championship football team but excelled in baseball, becoming a First-Team All-State pitcher in 1990 under the guidance of Tazewell coach Lou Peery. Wagner later set an NCAA strikeout record at Ferrum College before being the number-one draft choice of the Houston Astros in 1993. Wagner, who got his 300th save on July 4, 2006, has also played for the Philadelphia Phillies and is now a member of the New York Mets. He and his family live in Albemarle County near Charlottesville. They are shown here on a 2005 family vacation. Pictured are, from left to right, (first row) Olivia and Will; (second row) Billy and Jeremy; (third row) Sarah. (Courtesy of Eric Robinson and Rick Farris.)

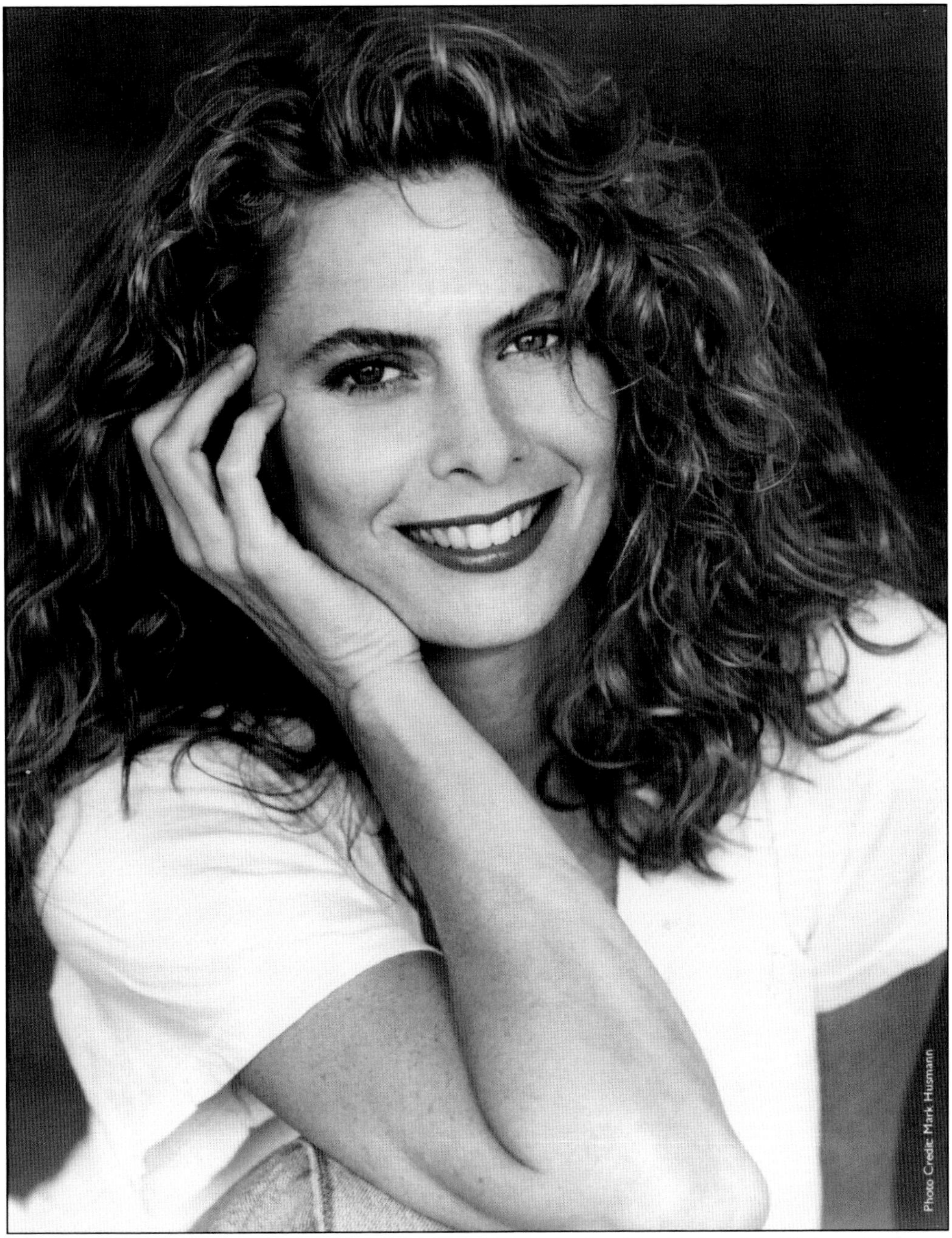

Kathryn Harrold, the daughter of Carolyn Harrold and the late D. H. Harrold of Witten Valley, is an acclaimed actress in both motion pictures and television. She has starred in 12 modern movies as the main character and in many television series, including the highly rated *Picket Fences* and the popular series *Rockford Files.* As a youngster, she attended Tazewell schools, and her artistic abilities were recognized at an early age. She is one of Tazewell's best-known personalities today. (Courtesy of Carolyn Harrold.)

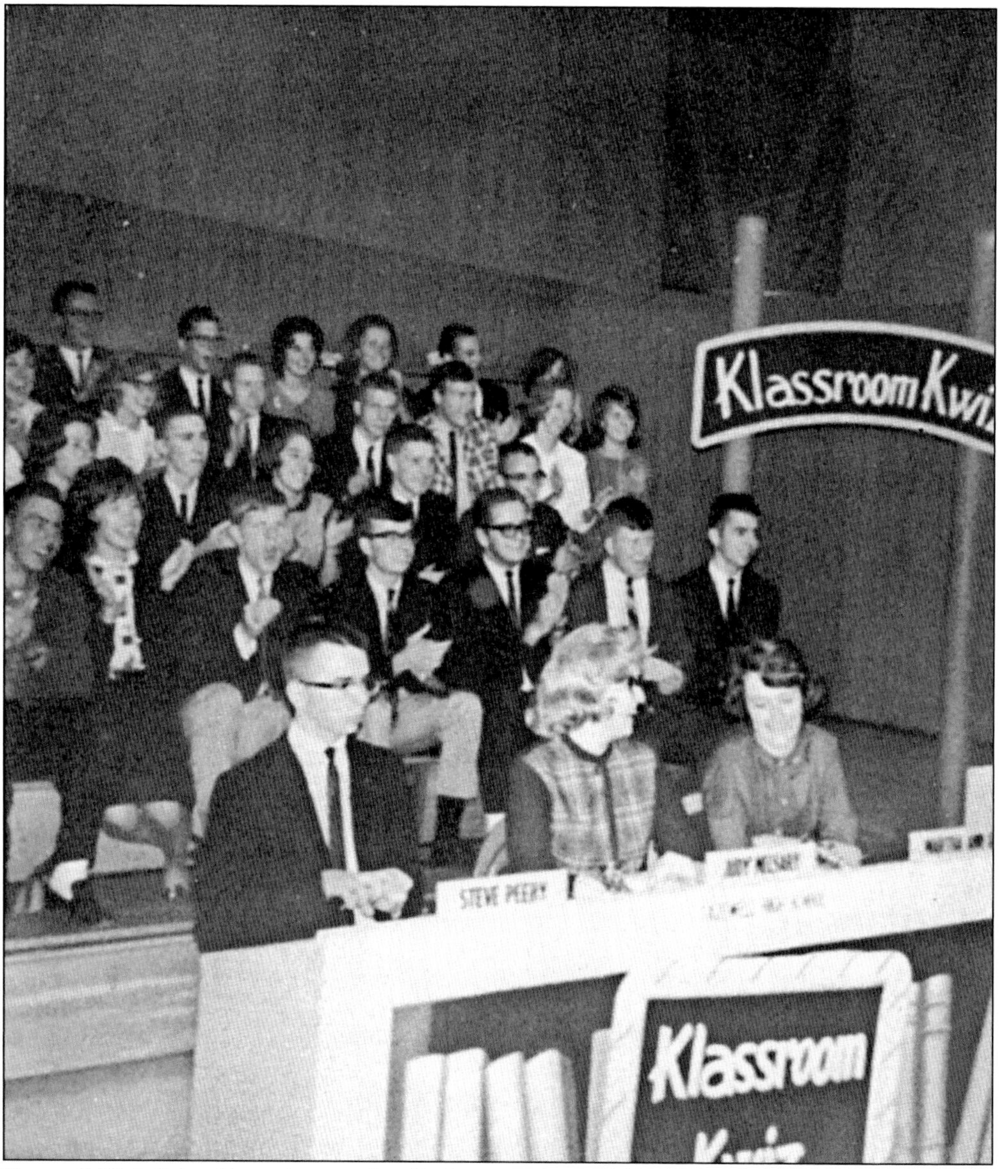

Tazewell High School has a long and stellar history in not only athletics but academics as well. In addition to winning many district, regional, and state honors in many endeavors, students have also represented the school well in other competitions, such as the long-running Klassroom Kwiz on Roanoke's WDBJ Television Channel 7. The captain of the 1965 team representing Tazewell High School was Steve Peery. Teammates seated next to Peery are Judy Necsary (center) and Martha Ann George (right). (Courtesy of the *Peak*, Tazewell High School.)

An academic contest that has become an institution at Tazewell High School is the annual Voice of Democracy competition. The Barnes-Beavers Post of the Veterans of Foreign Wars in Tazewell cosponsors the competition along with the Tazewell High School social studies department. Since its inception, more than 10,000 Tazewell High School students have written essays to be submitted in the competition. Only two Tazewell County students have placed first in the Virginia State Voice of Democracy. Both state winners were Tazewell High School students. Carroll Sluss won the state Voice of Democracy in 1976. (Courtesy of the *Peak*, Tazewell High School.)

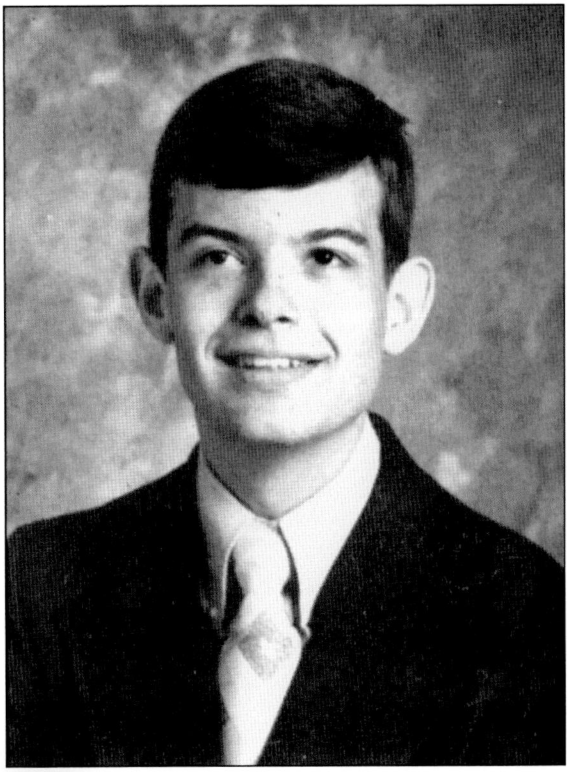

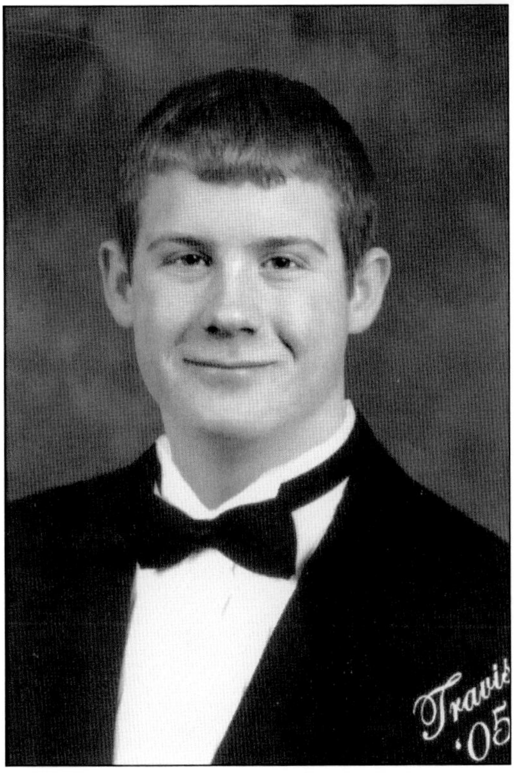

Travis Mitchell placed first in the Commonwealth Voice of Democracy competition in 2005. Mitchell is continuing his pre-med studies at the University of Virginia in Charlottesville. Mitchell presented his winning essay with a unique personal outlook of growing up in Tazewell. (Courtesy of Mullins files.)

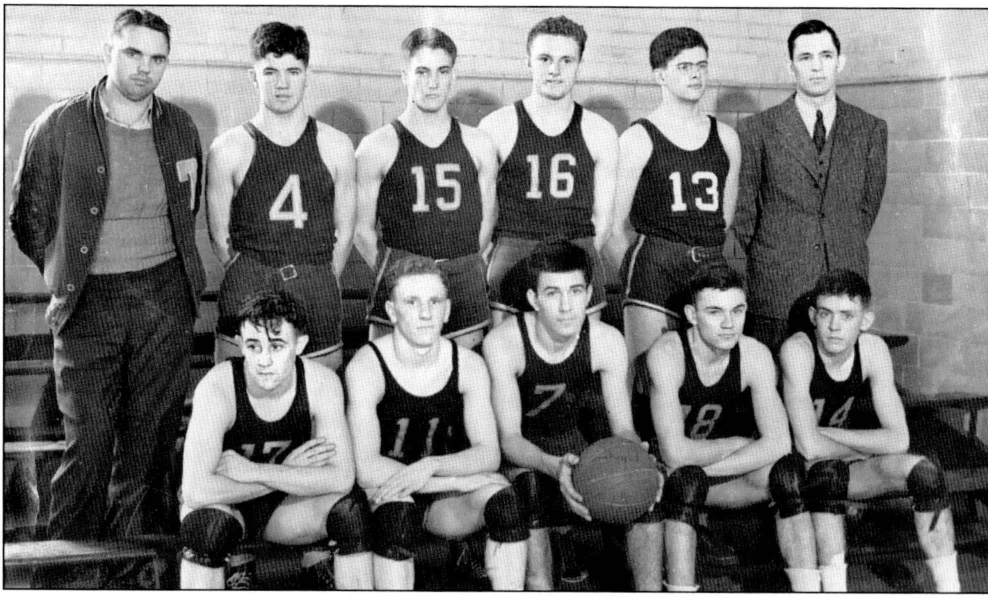

Basketball has been a major sport for the students of Tazewell High School for many generations. The 1939–1940 Tazewell High School basketball team won the Virginia AA State Basketball Championship, defeating Suffolk by a score of 46-38. Team members of the state championship basketball team pictured here are, from left to right, (first row) Bill Grimes, Lee Murray, Carl Young, Harry Smith (captain), and Junior Hall; (second row) Peg Booth (manager), Bill Kiser, Sonny Peery, John Turzi, Robert Crockett, and Conley Snidow (coach). Other members not pictured included George Grimes and Jack Britts (manager). Tazewell reigned as state champion for six years, since there was not another AA state champion until after World War II. (Courtesy of Mary Bowen Peery Colley.)

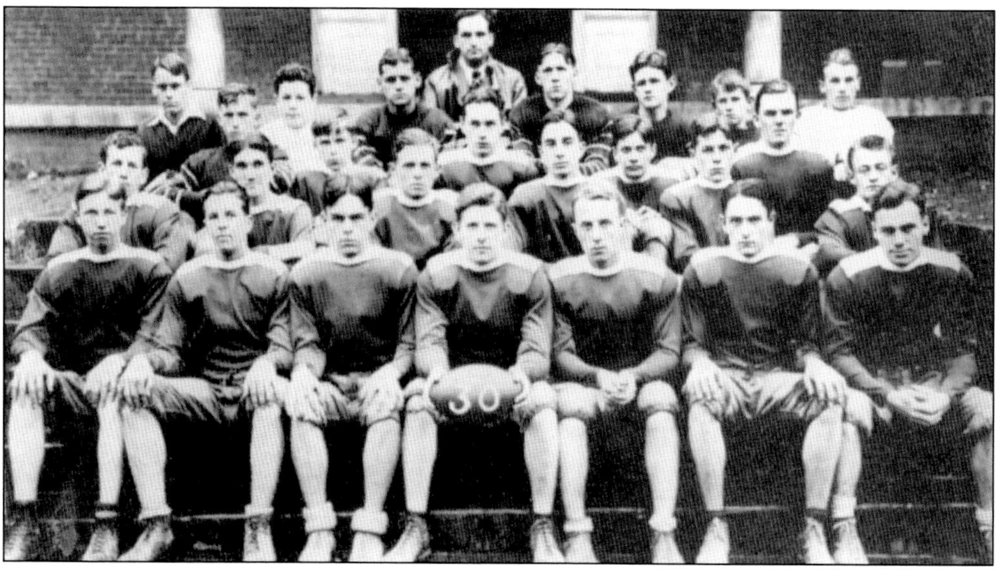

Tazewell has been a football town since the first team was fielded in 1926. Rivalries with neighboring Richlands, Big Creek, Graham, and Bluefield High Schools have been highlights of many fall football seasons in "T" town. One of the earliest football teams, the 1930 squad, is pictured here. (Courtesy of the *Peak*, Tazewell High School.)

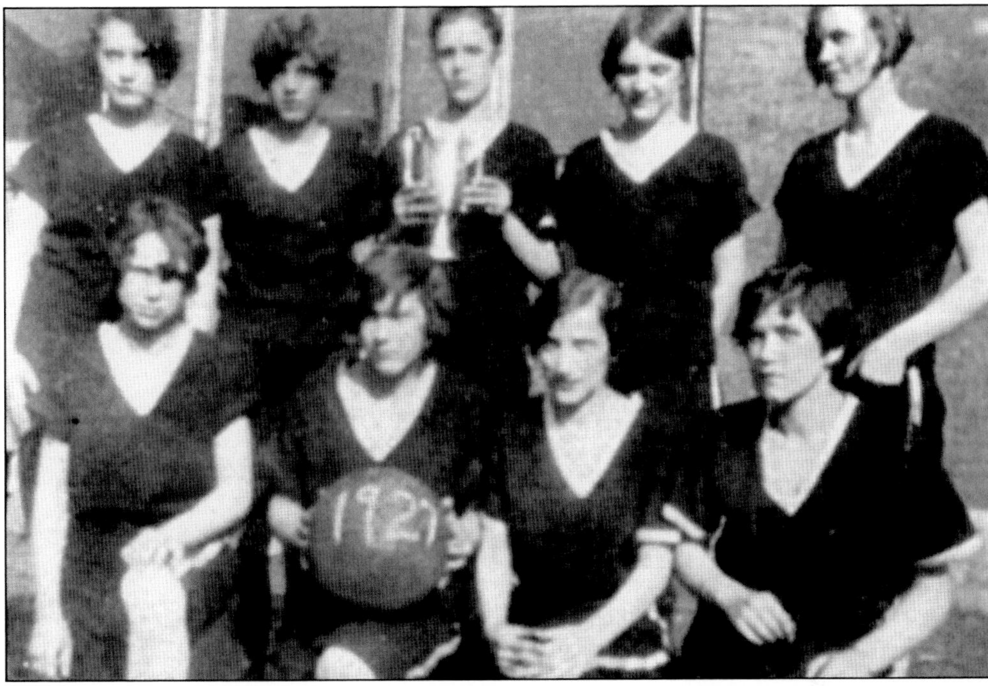

Girls' sports have also been an important part of Tazewell High School's interscholastic competition through the years. The girl's basketball team of 1936–1937 posed here for a team picture. (Courtesy of the *Peak*, Tazewell High School.)

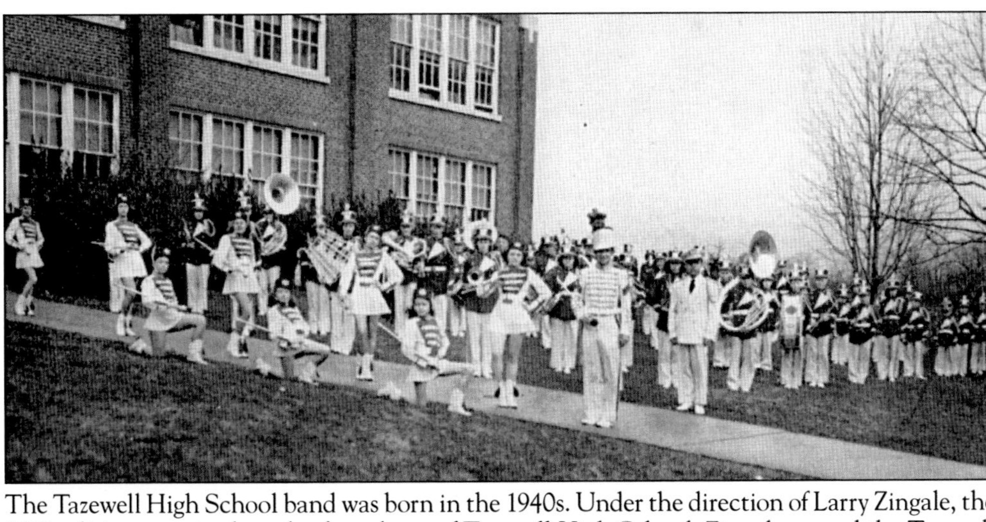

The Tazewell High School band was born in the 1940s. Under the direction of Larry Zingale, the 1949 edition practiced on the front lawn of Tazewell High School. Zingale started the Tazewell band program, which continues today. Now back in the area, he directs a modern band that is often heard at community events. (Courtesy of June Friedl.)

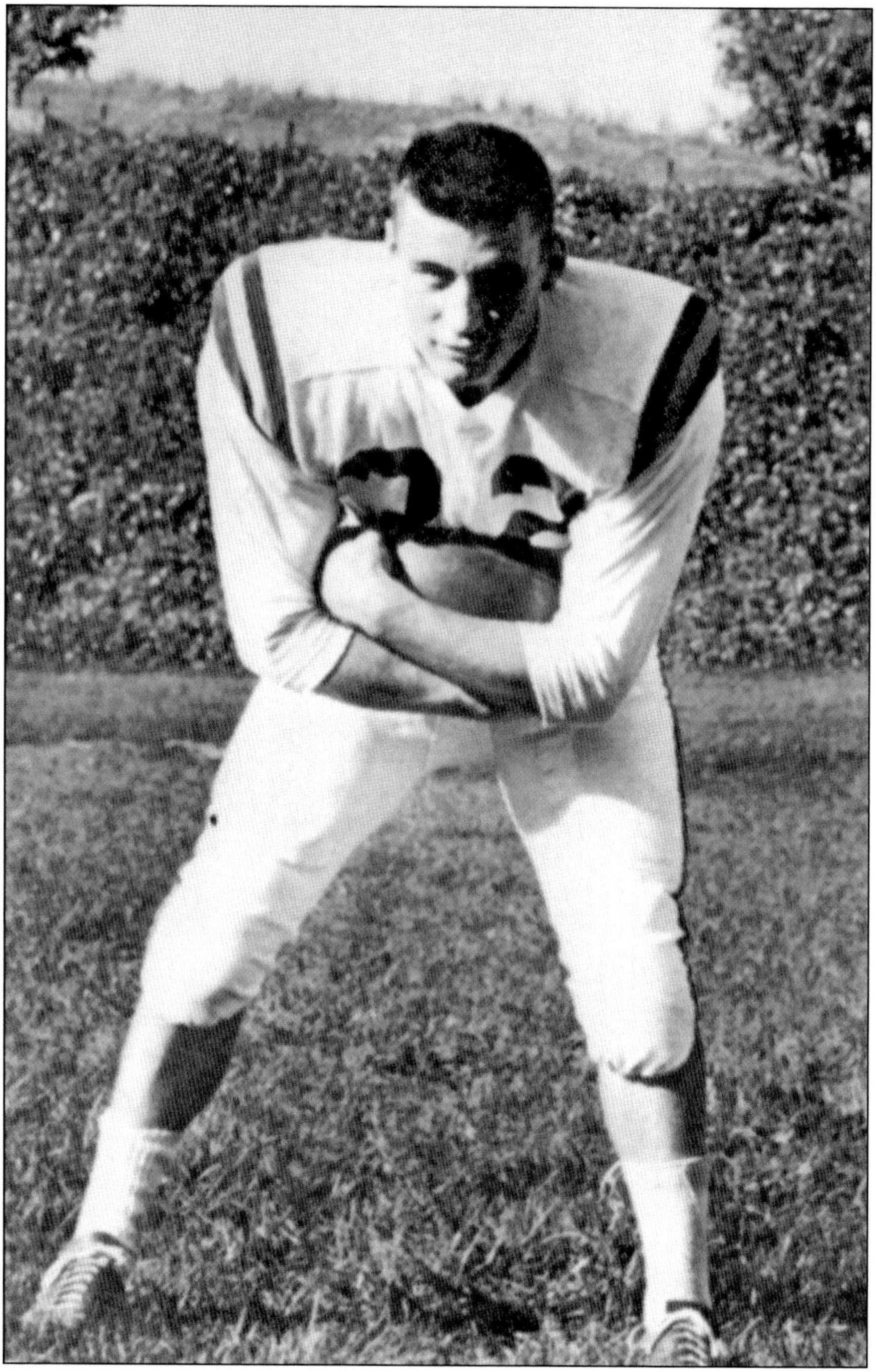

Don Barnes and John Rainey are the only two Tazewell Bulldogs in the history of the football program to be named to the All-American Team. Barnes helped lead the 1962 Bulldogs to a record of nine wins and one loss. The squad's only loss was a 7-6 setback to rival Graham, who went on to become the 1962 Virginia State Champions. Barnes also scored 132 points during his senior year and 201 career points for Tazewell High School. (Courtesy of the *Peak*, Tazewell High School.)

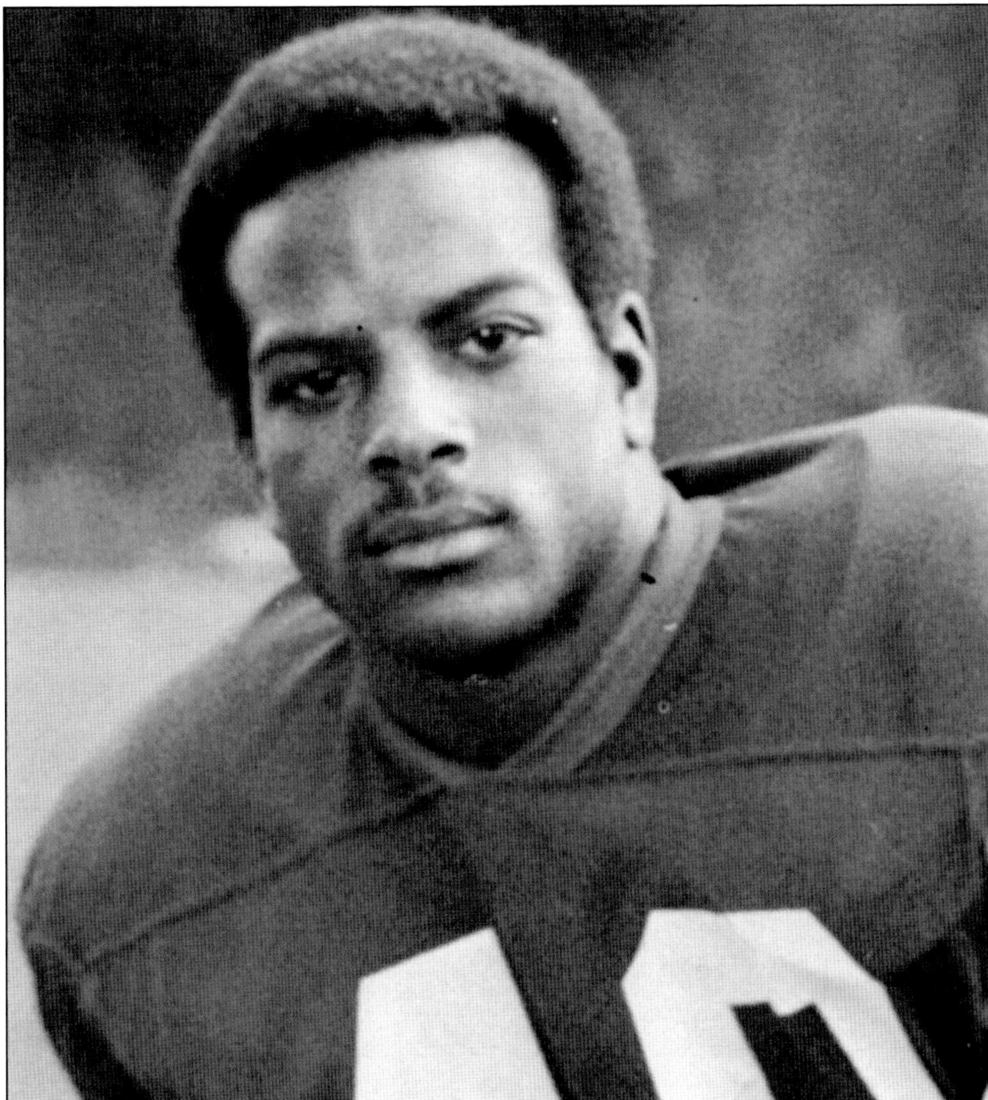

Tazewell's second All-American, John Rainey, helped guide the 1969 Bulldogs to an undefeated regular season with a record of nine wins and one tie. Tazewell and Big Creek battled to a 6-6 tie that year in an otherwise unblemished regular season. Rainey scored 160 points during his senior year and had a career total of 349 points during his tenure at Tazewell High. (Courtesy of the *Peak*, Tazewell High School.)

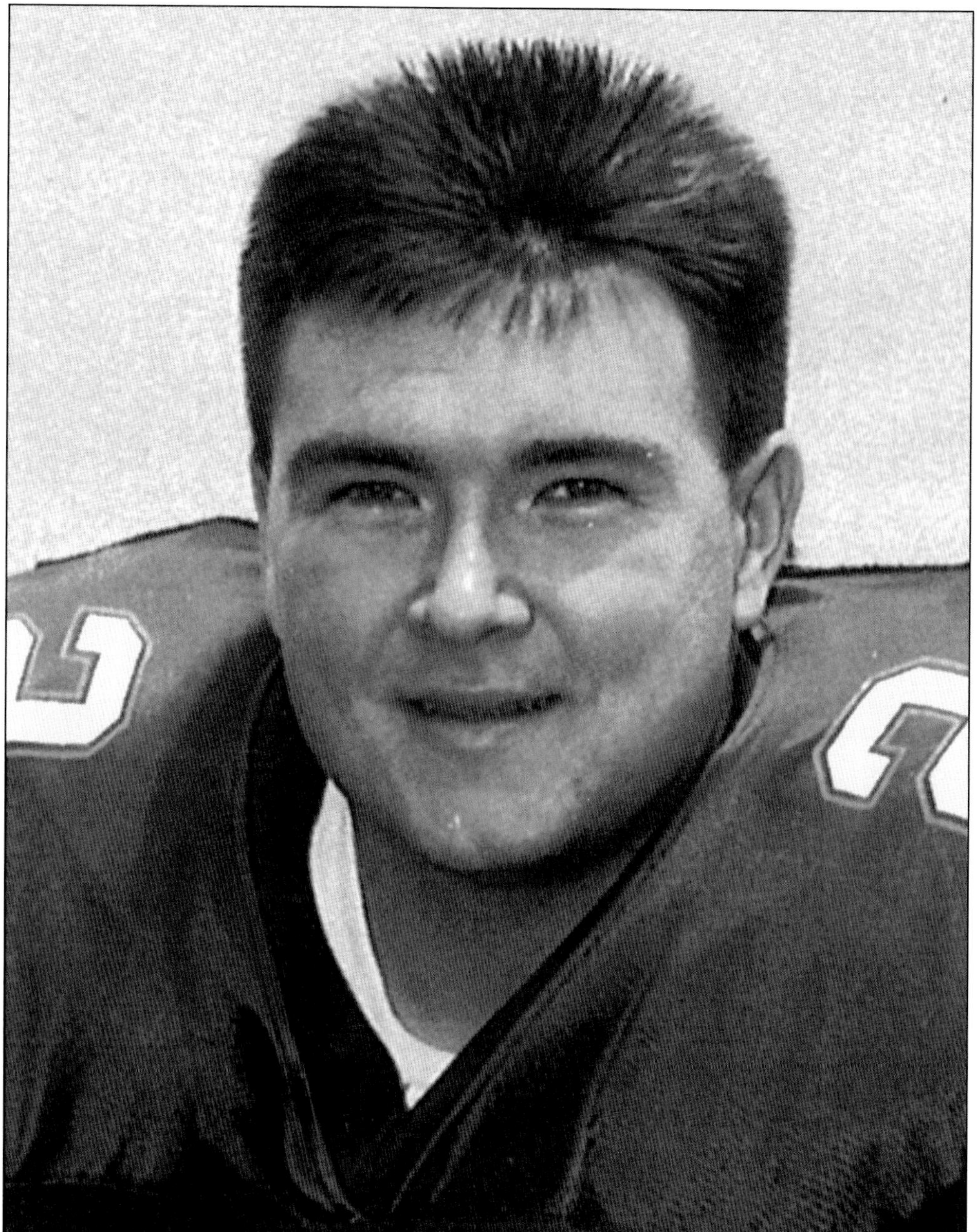

Robbie Colley was also a member of the 1986 Tazewell High School state championship football team, excelling as a punter and place kicker under the guidance of former Green Bay Packer Bill Renner. From 1991 to 1995, Colley played for the Virginia Tech Hokies under Coach Frank Beamer. Following graduation from Virginia Tech, Colley signed with the San Francisco 49ers, where he remained until placed on waiver after a three-month stint. At that point, he signed with the Tampa Bay Buccaneers. In addition to the 49ers and Buccaneers, Colley also garnered playing experience with the London Monarchs of the World League. He returned to Virginia Tech to earn his master's degree and taught history at Rustburg High School. Now living in Lynchburg, he is employed in the corporate world of pharmaceuticals. (Courtesy of Wilma Colley.)

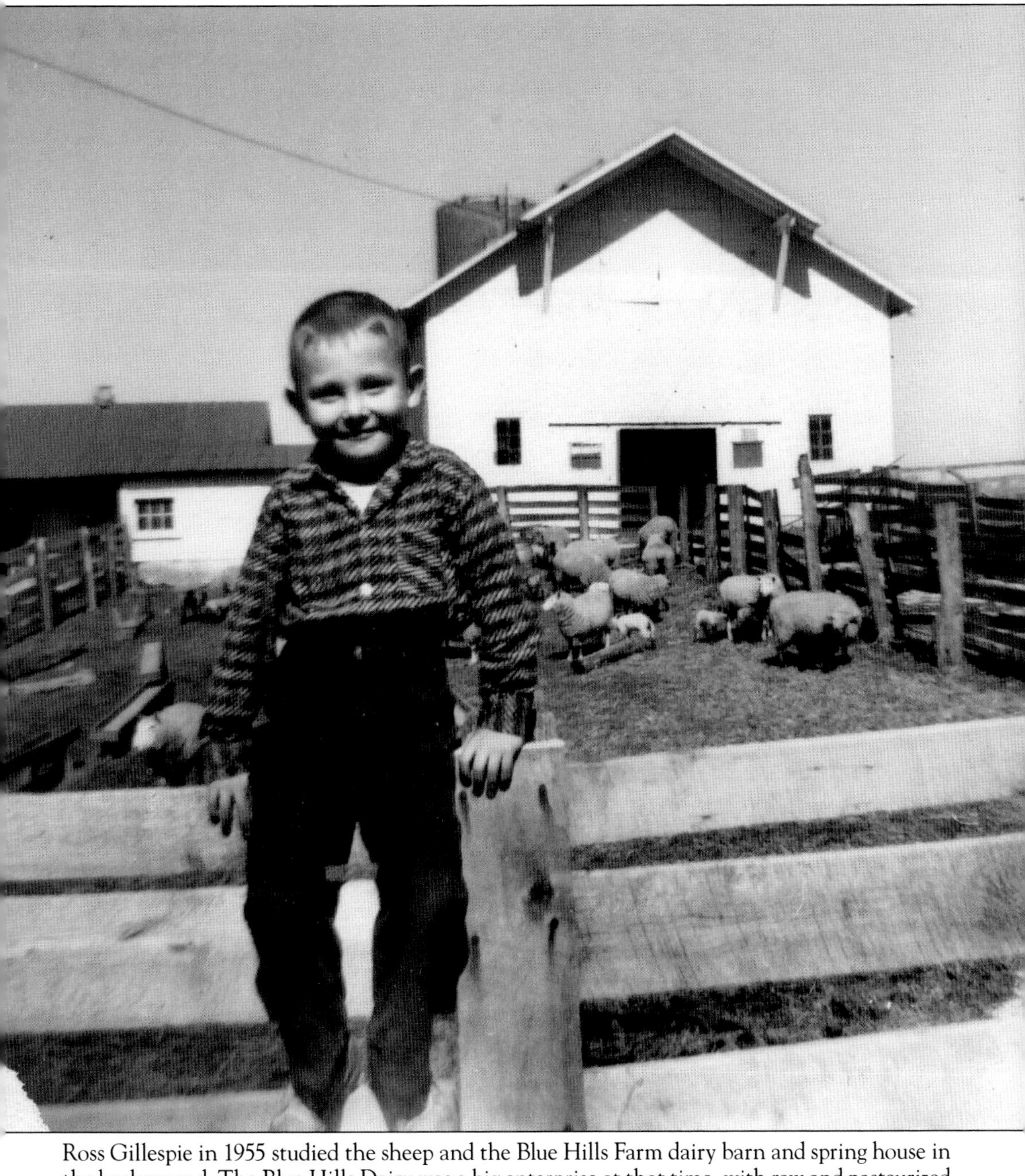

Ross Gillespie in 1955 studied the sheep and the Blue Hills Farm dairy barn and spring house in the background. The Blue Hills Dairy was a big enterprise at that time, with raw and pasteurized Guernsey milk bottled and sold from the dairy. It was owned by the Hart family. (Courtesy of Elsie Jackson.)

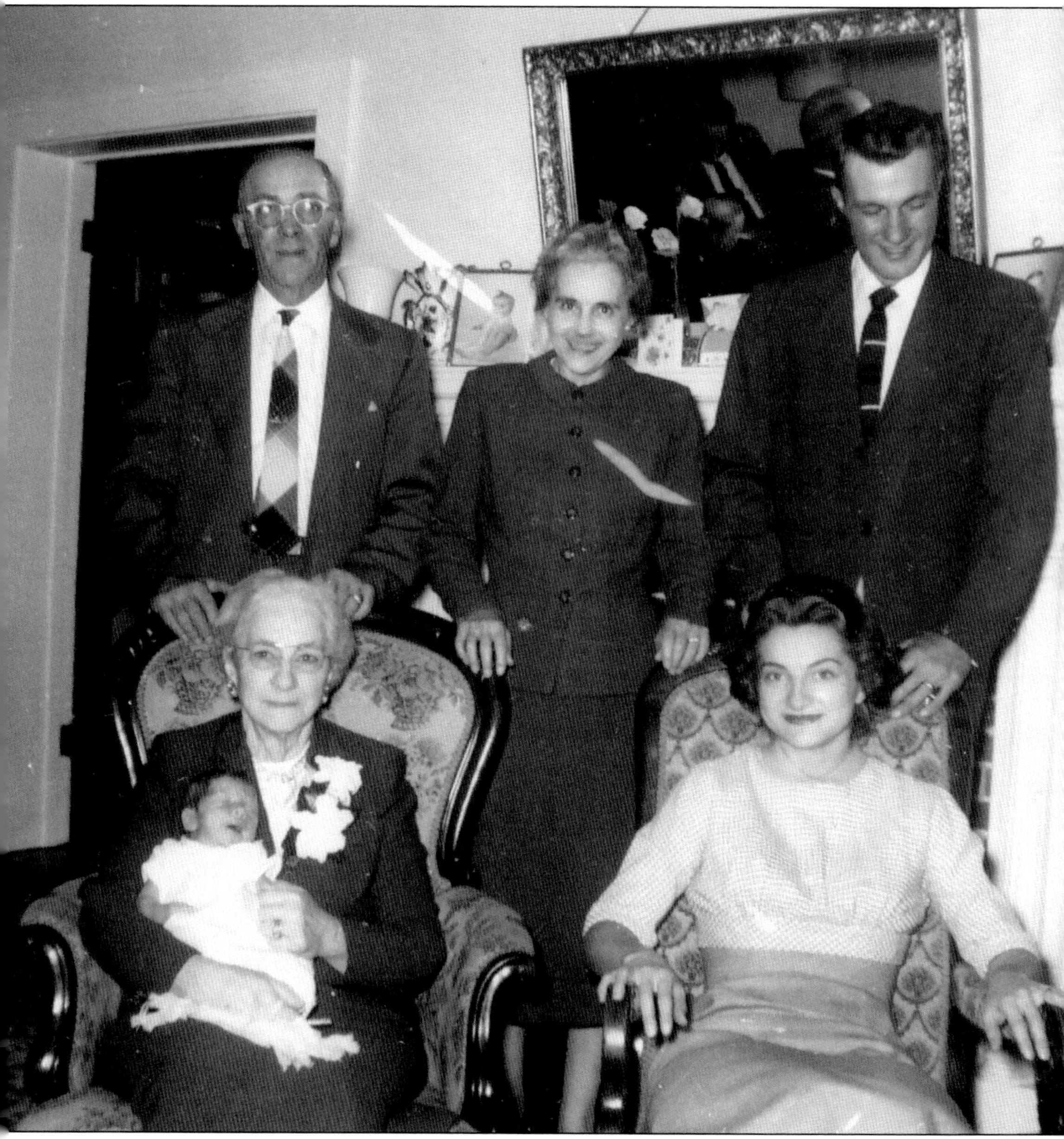

A family portrait of the Gillespies of Bowen's Cove, known locally as the "Cove," was taken in 1958 when Bob Moss was a baby. He is now a member of the Tazewell High School faculty. Moss is being held by his great-grandmother, Grace Gillespie. To their right is his mother, Katherine Gillespie Moss (Huffman), and behind her is his father, Robert Moss, of Burkes Garden. The grandparents are John C. Gillespie and Katherine Kiser Gillespie. Bowen's Cover is where the movie *Lassie: Best Friends Are Forever,* was filmed in 1994; the film grossed Paramount Pictures more than $8 million. (Courtesy of Bob Moss.)

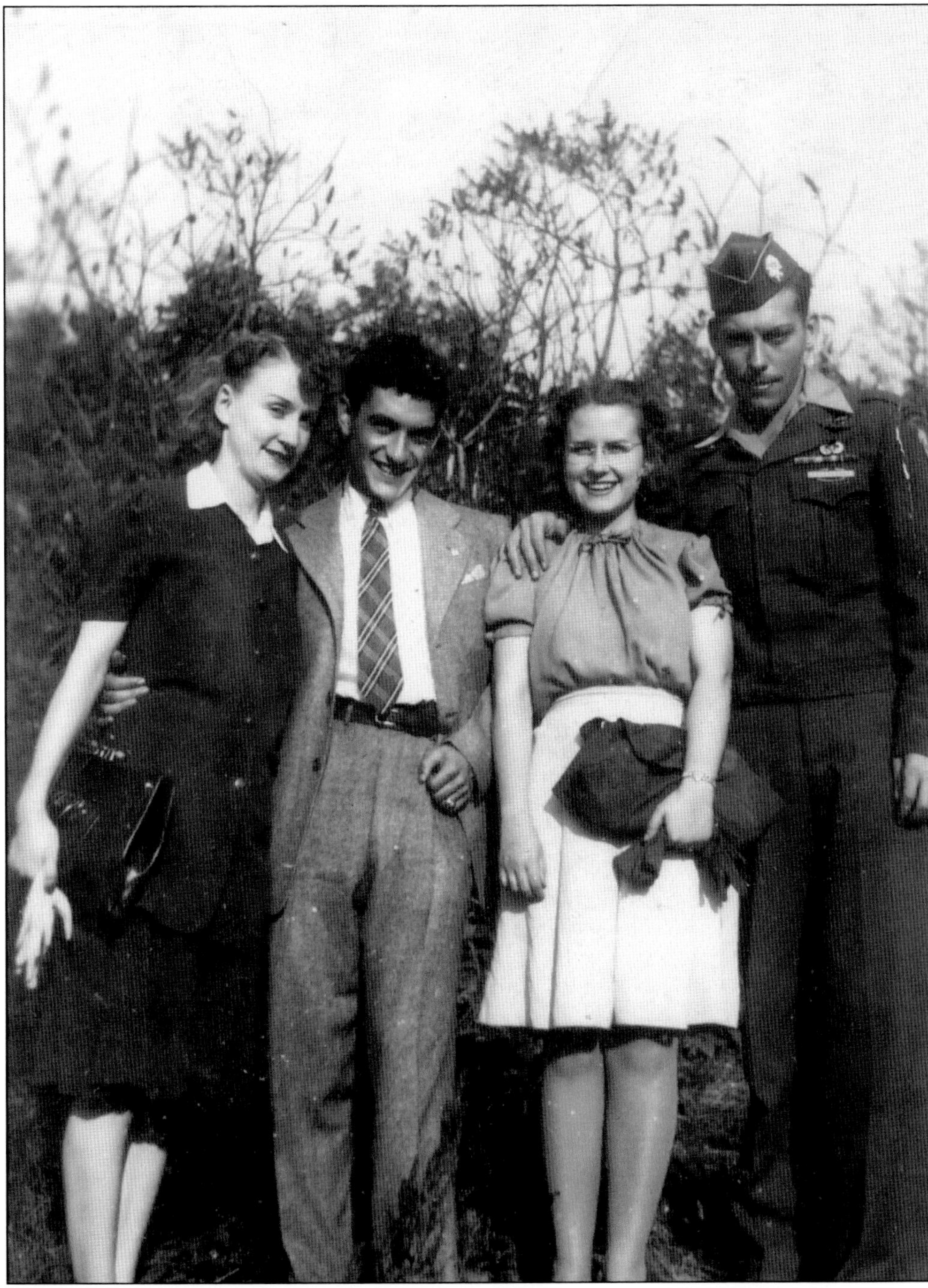

World War II gave these four young people few opportunities to get together as young people would normally do. Pictured in Cliffield in 1943 are, from left to right, Edythe Allen, Johnny Mullins, Evelyn Allen, and Pierce White. Edythe later was the proprietor of the Four Way Beauty Bar; John managed Peery and St. Clair Furniture Store and Funeral Home, while Evelyn and Pierce lived in many Virginia, West Virginia, and Ohio communities during his tenure with the Norfolk and Western Railroad. (Courtesy of Mullins files.)

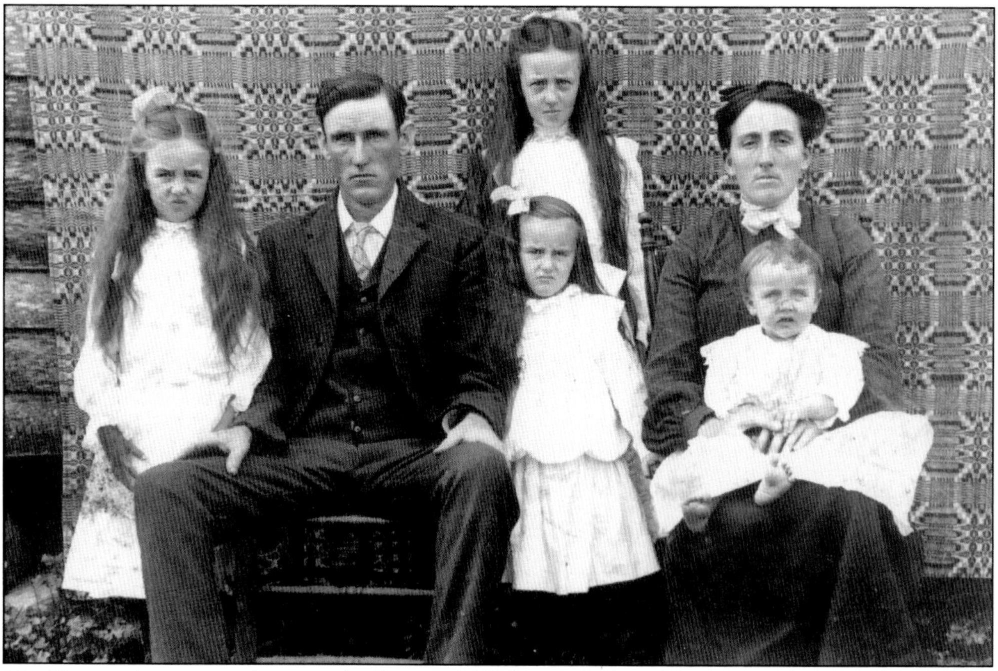

The Barrett family was photographed around 1905 outside their home near Plum Creek. Pictured from left to right are Grace Barrett, John Patton Barrett (father), Bonnie Barrett (later mayor of North Tazewell), Elizabeth Barrett (who died at the age of five), "Maggie" Elizabeth Fox Barrett (mother), and baby Marjorie or Bowen. (Courtesy of Mary Barrett.)

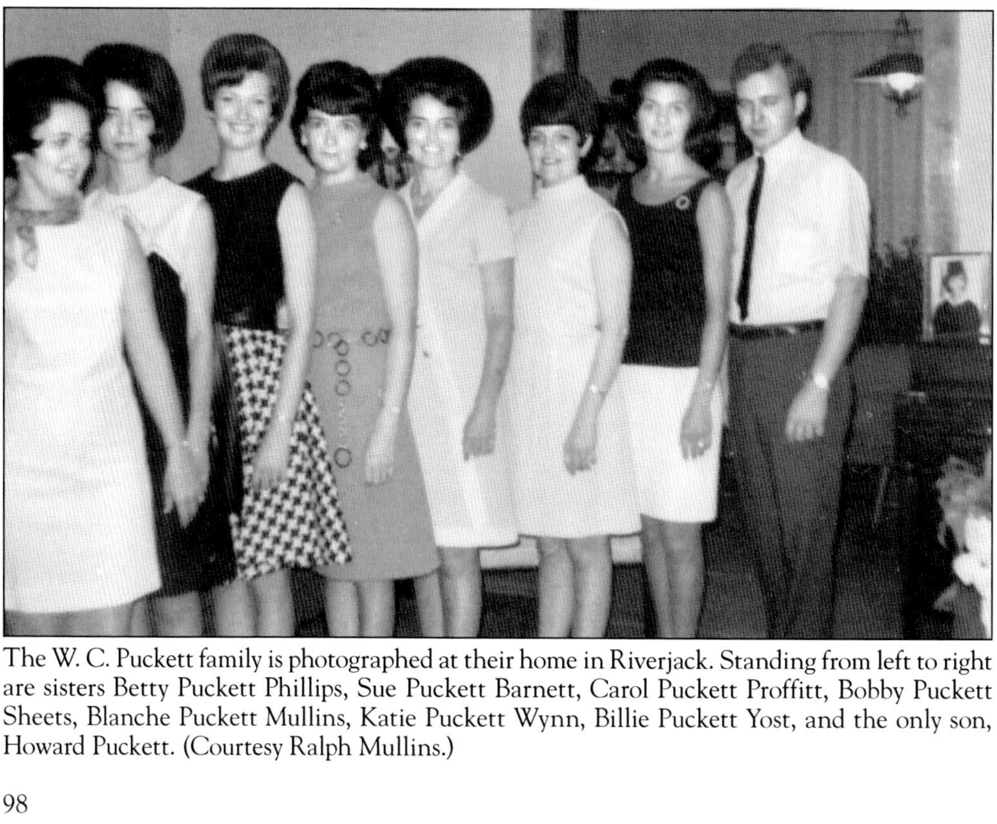

The W. C. Puckett family is photographed at their home in Riverjack. Standing from left to right are sisters Betty Puckett Phillips, Sue Puckett Barnett, Carol Puckett Proffitt, Bobby Puckett Sheets, Blanche Puckett Mullins, Katie Puckett Wynn, Billie Puckett Yost, and the only son, Howard Puckett. (Courtesy Ralph Mullins.)

Dick Kelly was one of the bridesmaids at the "womanless wedding" given for the public's entertainment in 1951. In Shakespeare's time, only men could take to the stage, so all parts were played by men. Progress had been made to accept female entertainers in this country, but in military camp settings, the men had no choice but to play all the parts. Apparently Tazewell's womanless wedding was a continuation of that tradition. (Courtesy of June Friedl.)

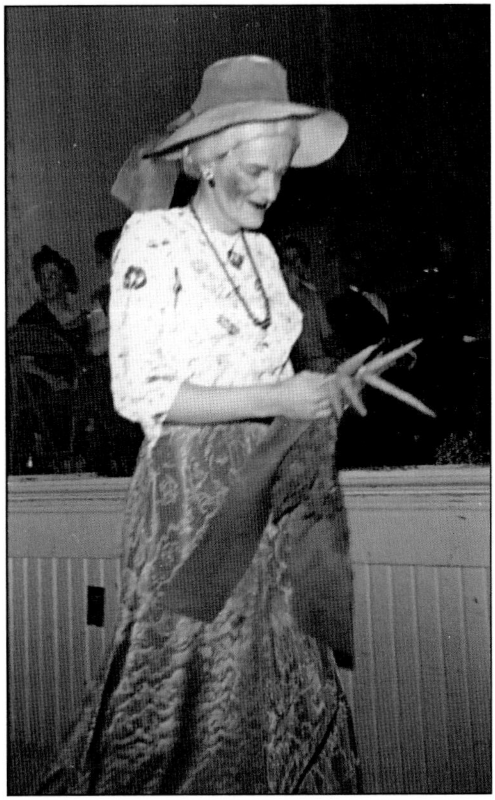

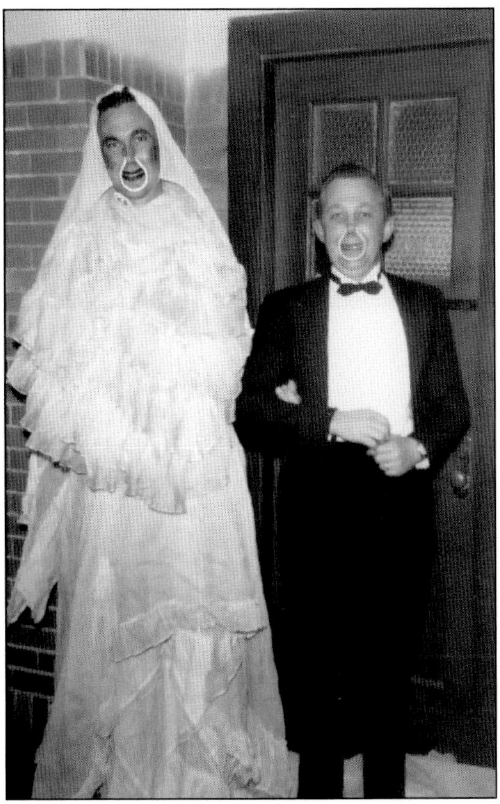

In 1951, a womanless wedding was staged for the public by a group of Tazewell businessmen. The bride was T. C. Bowen Jr., and the groom was Noland Dennison. Note the rings in their noses, not on their hands. Those who saw it as well as those who were in it will always remember the womanless wedding as one of the most hilarious exhibitions ever staged in Tazewell. In fact, at the conclusion of the show, it was not clear who enjoyed themselves more—the audience or the cast. (Courtesy of June Friedl.)

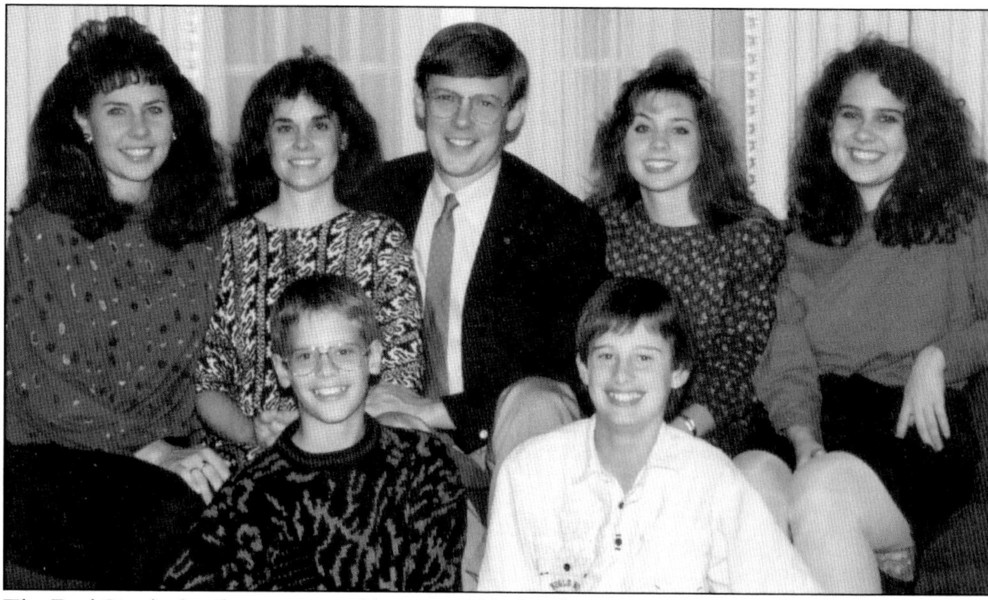

The Fred Combs family was pictured here in 1990. Combs was a Tazewell attorney and later general district court judge in Tazewell County. He was known for his interest in and support for young people in the community. As a member of the Tazewell Rotary Club, Combs was instrumental in promoting the international relationships that the local club enjoys. This program included numerous foreign exchange students who visited here and the sponsorship of scores of Tazewell students who visited countries around the world. The Combs family included, from left to right, (first row) Mark Goodwin Combs and Eric Reynolds Combs; (second row) Kelly Noel Combs (Necessary), Elene Monk Combs, Frederick Harman Combs II, Amy Carter Combs, and Emily Reeves Combs. (Courtesy of Elene Combs.)

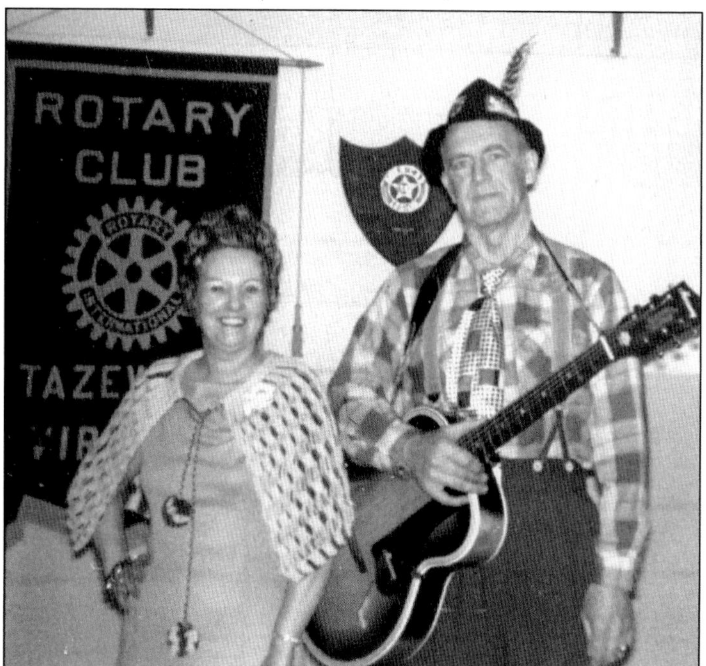

Major and Mildred Hatfield played important roles in the Tazewell/North Tazewell Lions Club's variety shows presented in the 1950s–1970s. He played the guitar and sang while she helped the actors with their makeup. Major Hatfield was the station agent for the Norfolk and Western Railway at the Tazewell Depot. He followed Mr. and Mrs. L. L. Dickenson, who were agents for many years and wrote many historical articles for local newspapers. (Courtesy of Rusty Hatfield.)

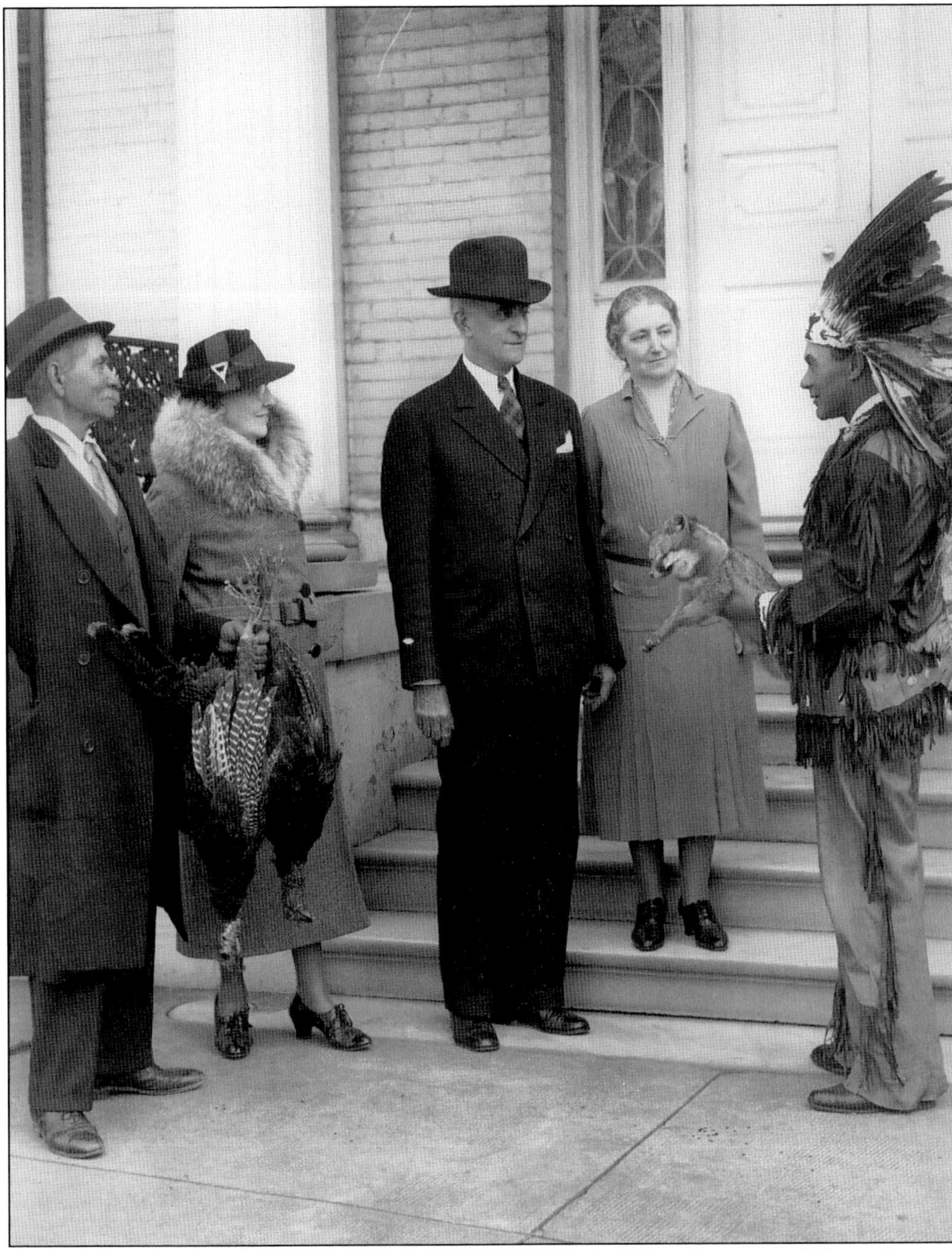

In 1935, when George C. Peery of Tazewell was governor of Virginia, he received the traditional payment from the Virginia Indian tribes. This Thanksgiving custom goes back to the first governing body in the commonwealth. Governor and Mrs. Peery received a fox and a turkey from the Pamunkey, Chickahominy, and Mattapon tribes. Webster Custalow wore the headdress of the Pamunkeys. (Courtesy of Nancy Peery Olson.)

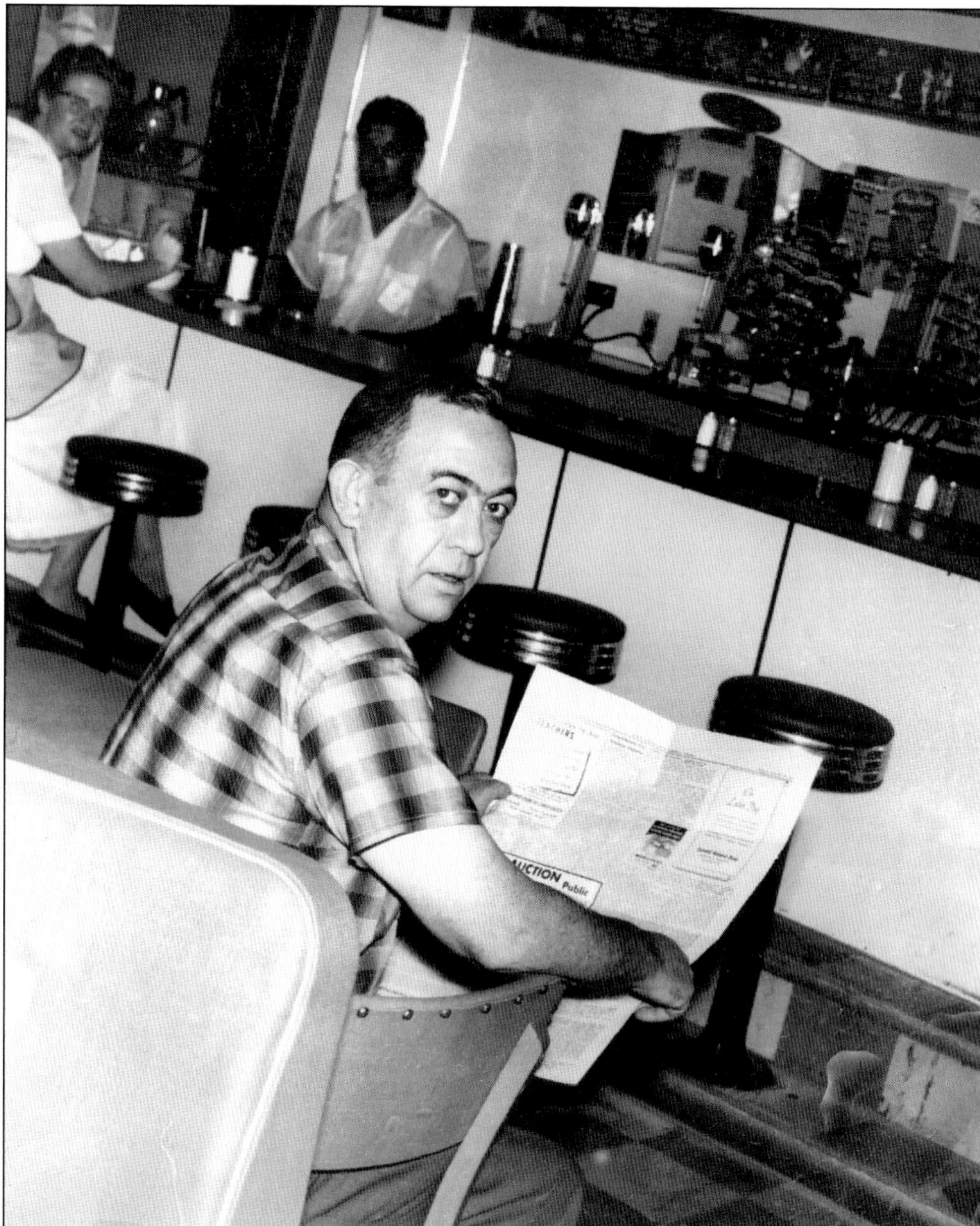

John Westmoreland seems ready for his busy day at John's Restaurant in the 1950s, a well-known place of business that will always be remembered by those many customers who appreciated the good food and the friendly atmosphere. In the background are his daughter, Rae Farley, and her husband, Jack Farley, who joined the other family members in operating the popular restaurant and motel. (Courtesy of Rae Farley.)

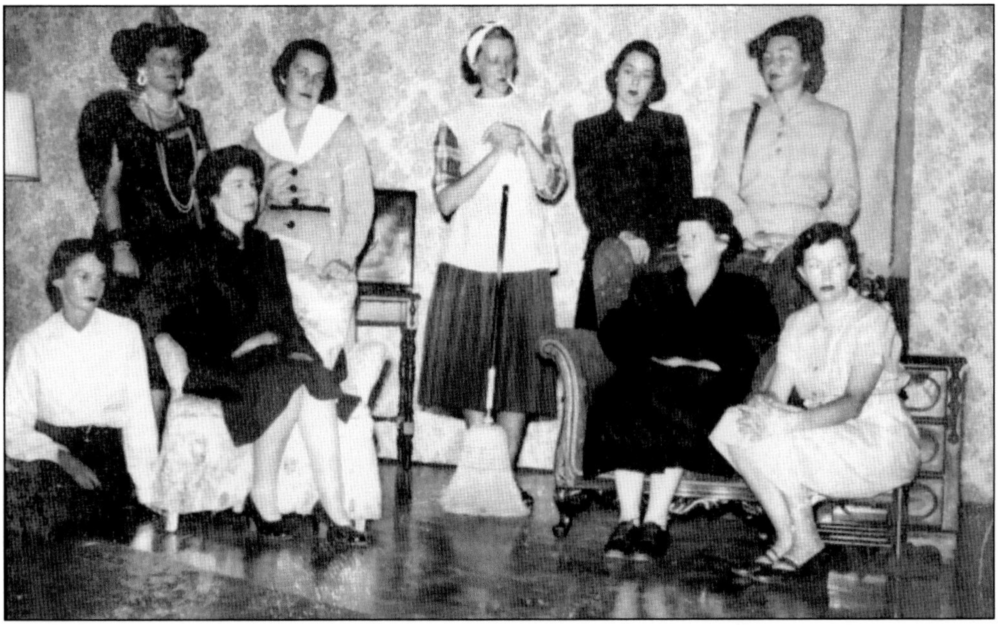

The Jeffersonville Woman's Club has been a very active part of Tazewell's civic organizations. In October 1954, they presented the play *Sister Craven* with this cast; from left to right are Phyllis Proffitt, Sydney Peery, Ann Montgomery, Jane Peery, Nancy Harman, Emmy Dennison, Pauline Wilson, Dottie Mock, and Virginia Coates. (Courtesy of Emmy Dennison.)

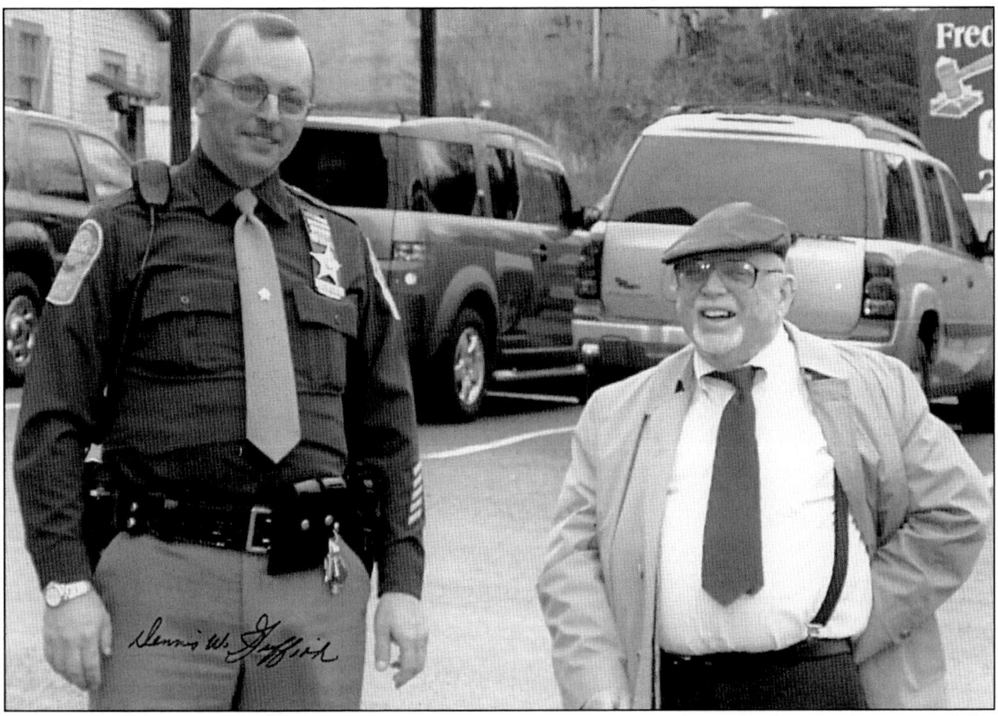

Judge Wade S. Coates (right) and Deputy Dennis Griffith seemed satisfied with the state of the world on this summer day on Main Street. The art of conversation continues to be alive and flavorful when friends meet on Tazewell streets. (Courtesy of June Friedl.)

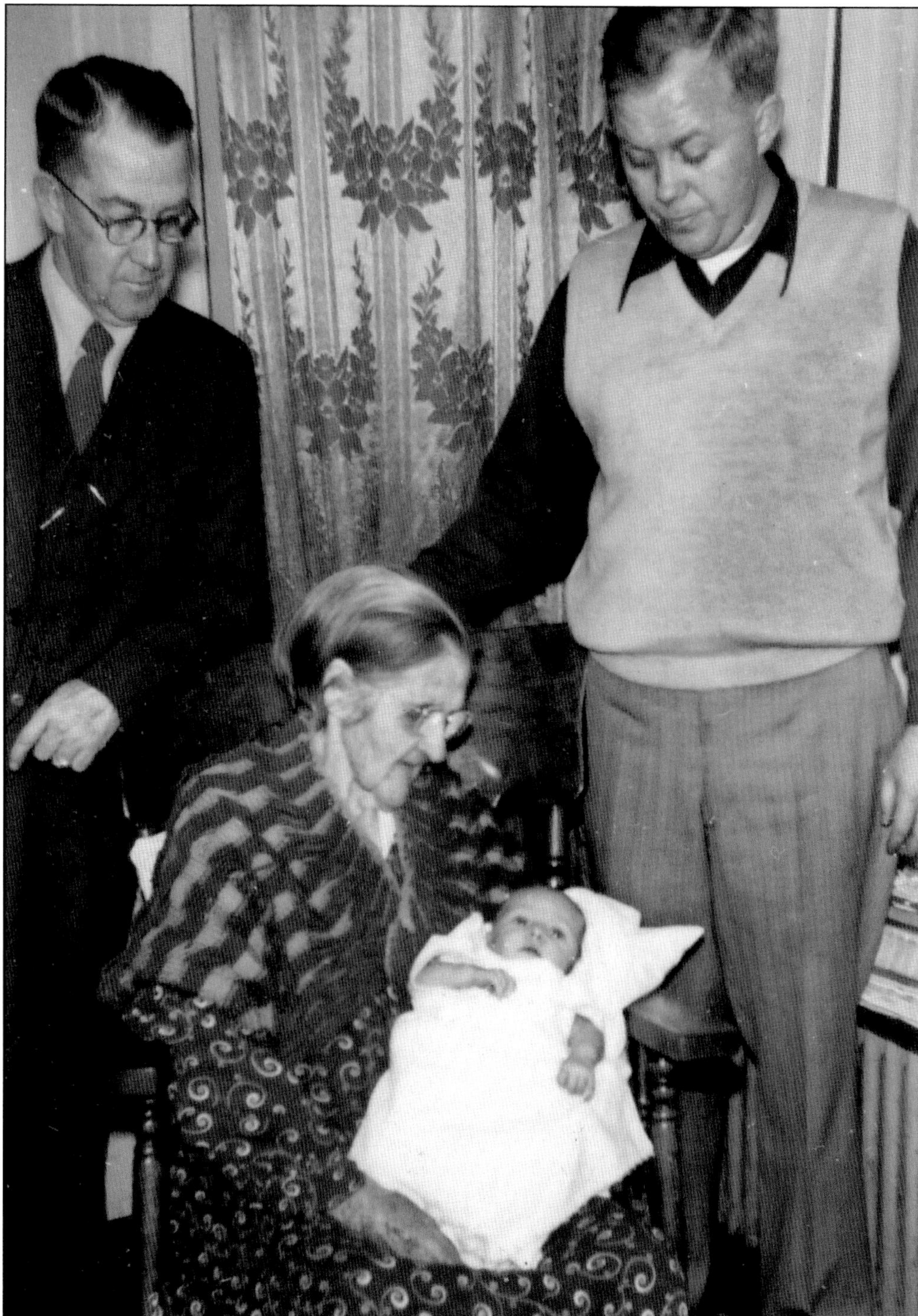

When Ned Dennison was a baby in Tazewell, he was the focus of this four-generation photograph. Holding Ned is his great-grandmother, Corinthea A. Dennison. Standing at left is Ned's grandfather, A. Ward Dennison, and to the right is his father, Noland Dennison. The family-owned Dennison Dry Cleaners was a well-known local business for many years. (Courtesy of Emmy Dennison.)

This was a bad day for young Billy Friedl even if his father, Chester, was close by and the barber, Rudolph Valentine, was kind. Valentine worked in the barbershop of Barnes Moore. This barber shop followed the long tradition of the Warren family, who had a business for several generations in Tazewell. In the early 1800s, the barbers also had bathing facilities for the men of the community. (Courtesy of June Friedl.)

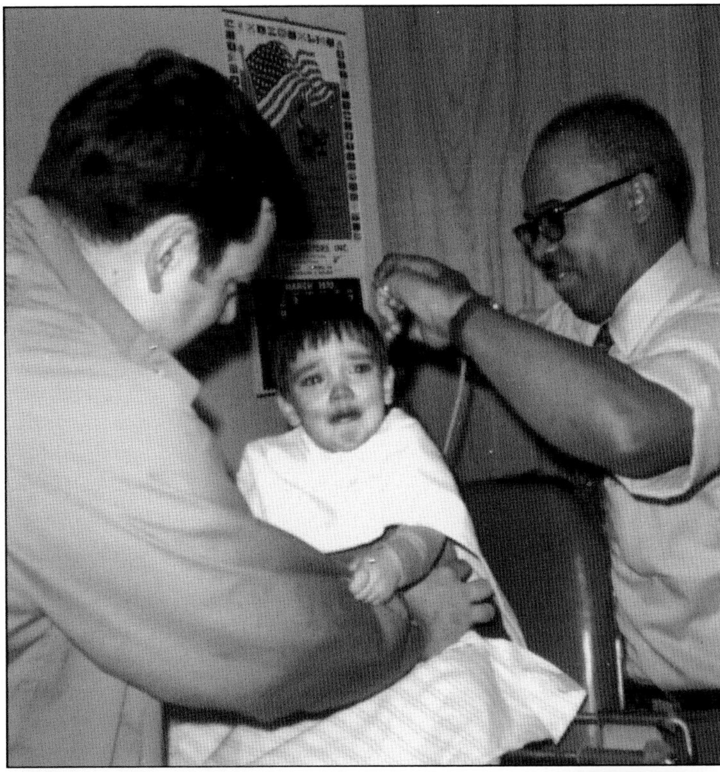

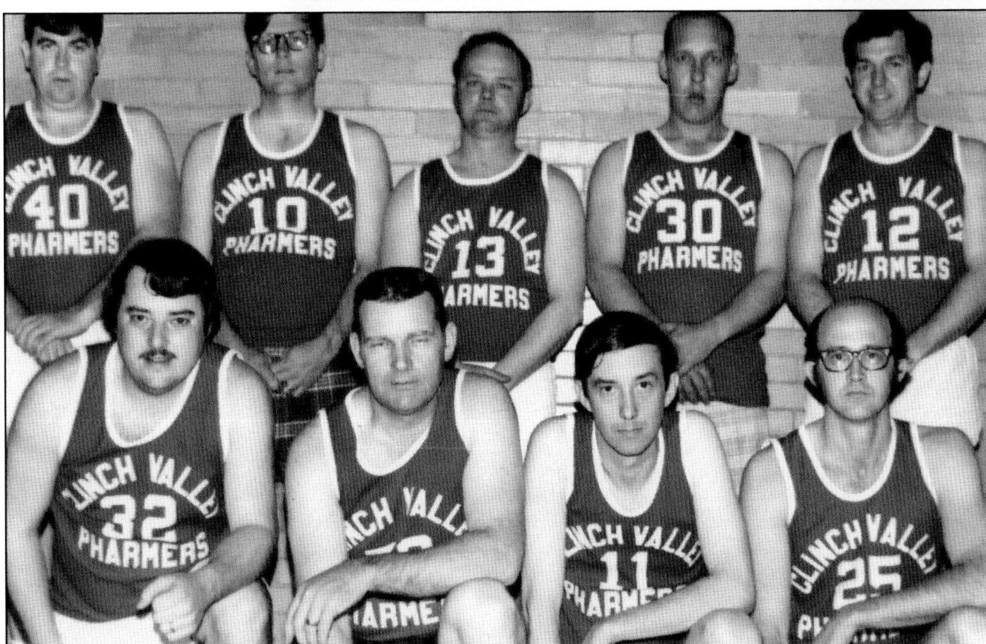

The Clinch Valley Pharmacy sponsored this basketball team in the late 1960s. Members of the "Pharmers" were, from left to right, (first row) Chester Friedl, Glen Nash, Bill Allison, and John Mundy; (second row) Charlie Frye, J. E. King, unidentified, Bill Benson, and Dennis Witt. (Courtesy of June Friedl.)

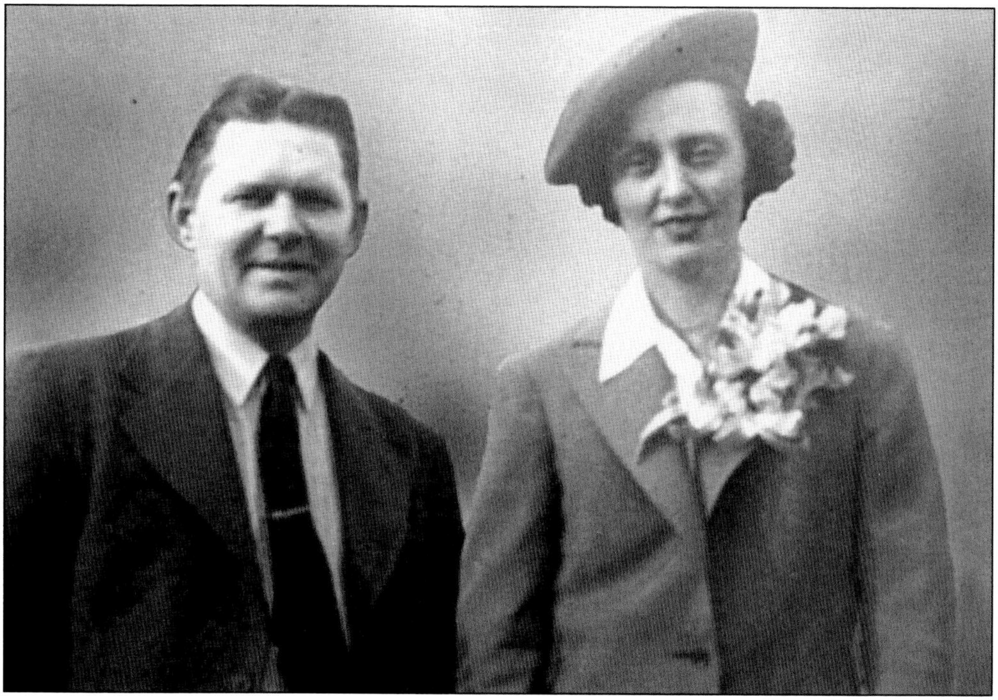

W. E. Hughes (Bill) and Katherine Kincer Hughes were pictured on Easter Sunday, April 25, 1943. At the time, they were both employed by the Sayer Brothers Department Store, which stood at the corner of Main Street and Marion Avenue. Later they were owners of Hughes Shoe Store. Their three children are Jimmy, Janita, and June. (Courtesy of June Friedl.)

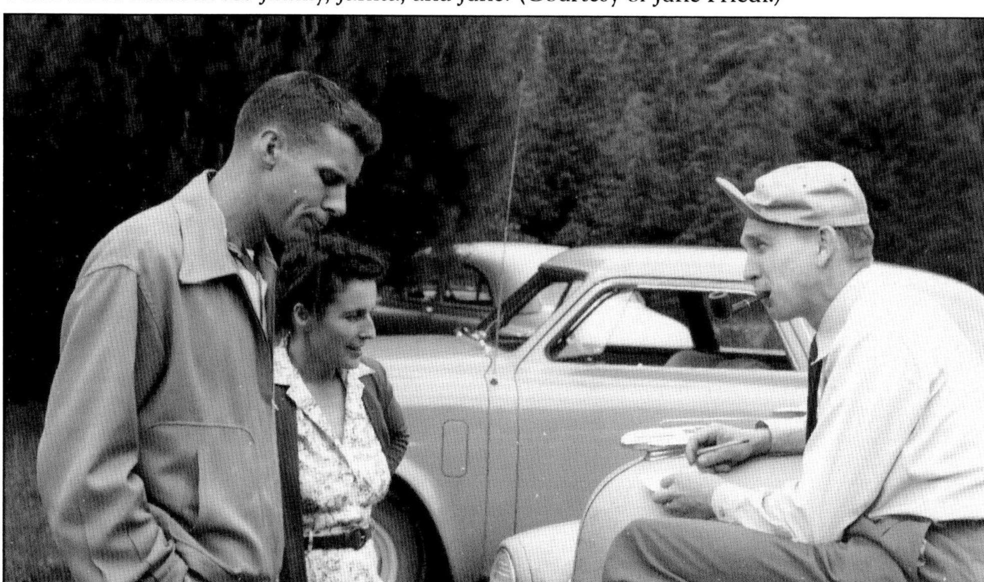

From left to right, Roie Godsey, assistant county agent, Vivian Grubb, home agent, and Luke Russell, Tazewell County farm agent, in 1952 discuss the advances in farming techniques in the Clinch Valley since the first county agent, R. R. Wall, started the local extension program. (Courtesy of Emmy Dennison.)

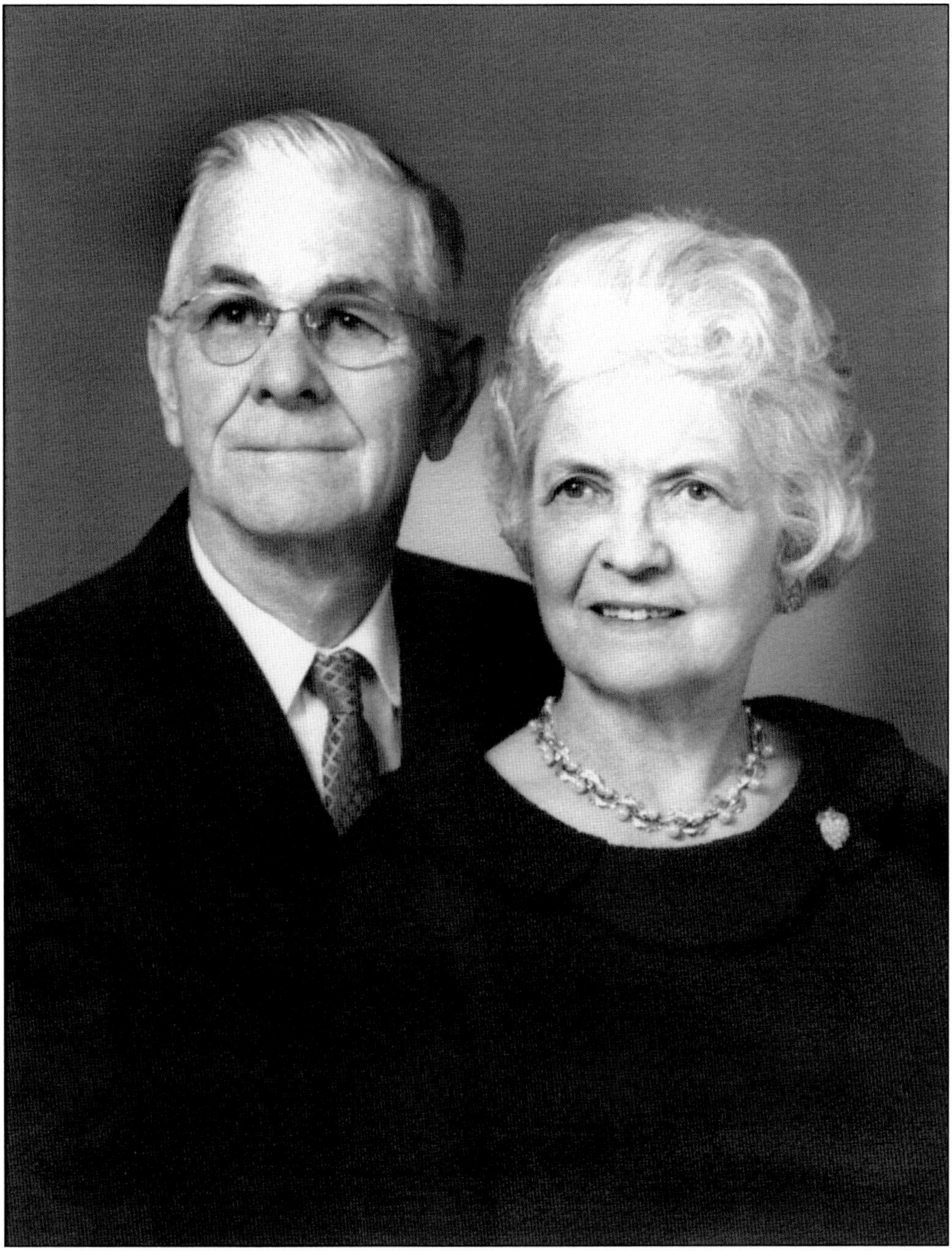

Dr. and Mrs. Peyton L. Rowlett and their family were community leaders when they lived on Tower Street in Tazewell. Dr. Rowlett was a Tazewell dentist for 47 years, beginning his local practice in 1923. His work today is remembered for its excellence. The Rowlett family was active in the Methodist church. Their three children are Peyton, Marianna, and Martha. At about the same time, Dr. Rufus Copenhaver was a Tazewell dentist, and he and his family were also widely known in the area. Dr. Hirlye Lutz also practiced dentistry in Tazewell for many years, as has his son, Steven, who has a modern practice. (Courtesy of Marianna Rowlett Harris and Peyton L. Rowlett Jr.)

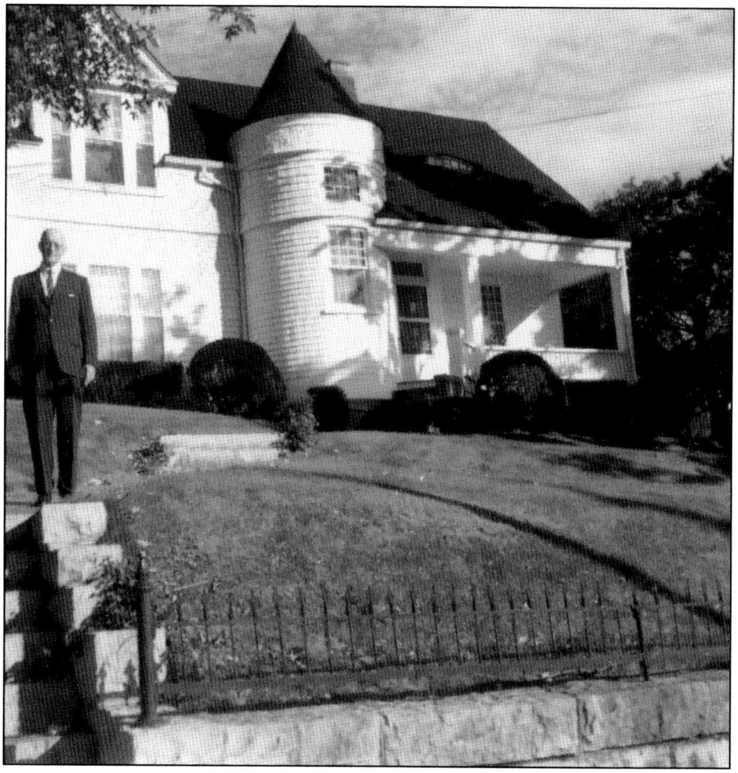

Justice and Mrs. A. C. Buchanan lived in this house on Tower Street while he served as Tazewell circuit court judge and later as justice of the Virginia Supreme Court. The house was torn down in the 1970s to make room for the expansion of the Tazewell Baptist Church. Also at this time, the house occupied by the Coulling family, adjacent to the Buchanans', was incorporated into the new church addition. Justice Buchanan is seen on the walkway in front of his home. (Courtesy of Louise McKinney.)

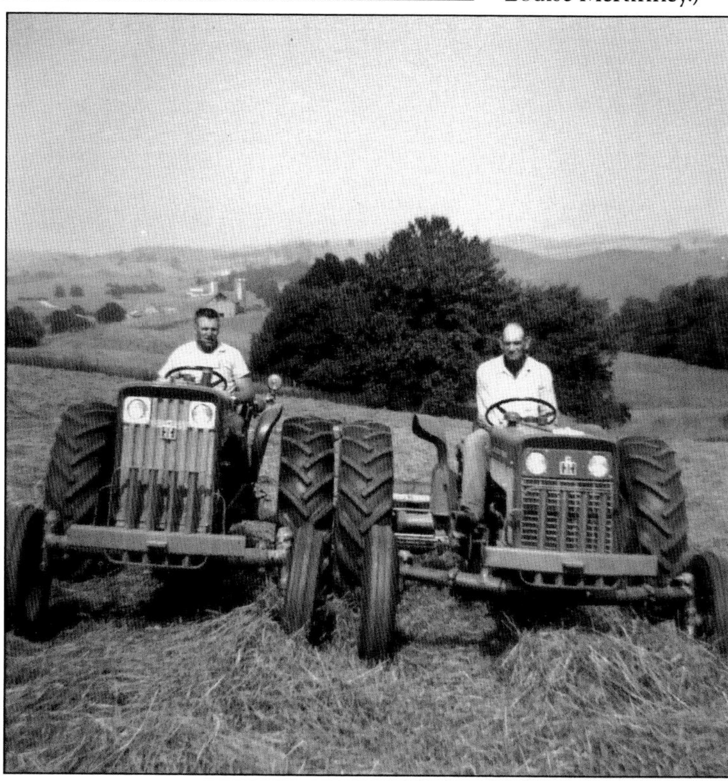

Henry P. Gillespie (right) and his father, Buford Gillespie, had finished mowing this field in 1969 on the Blue Hills Farm at Dial Rock and rested while looking west toward the Four Way section of Tazewell. (Courtesy of Ross and Barbara Gillespie.)

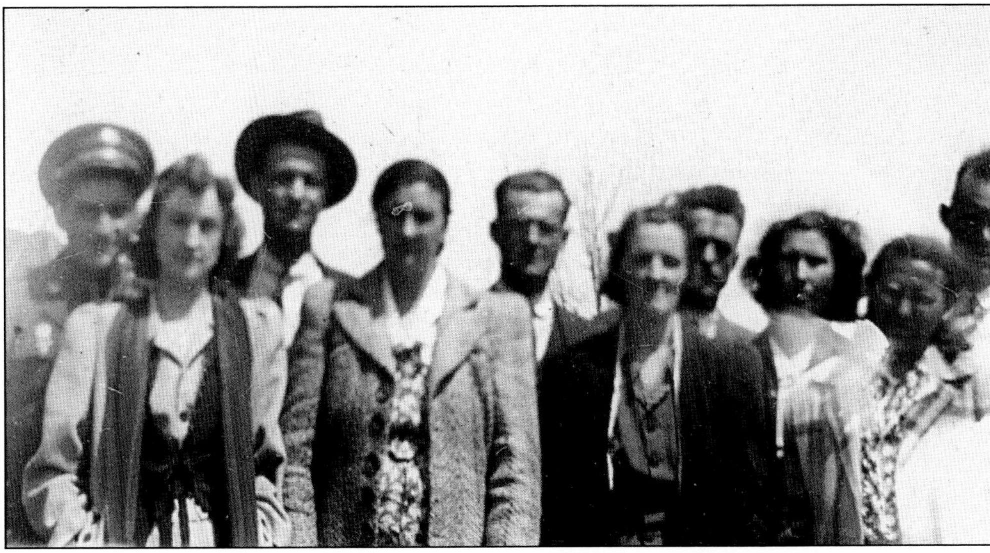

The Mullins family gathered near the banks of the Clinch near Pisgah on Easter Sunday, April 25, 1943. Pictured from left to right are Sgt. John and Edythe (Allen) Mullins, James and Pearl (Brown) Mullins, Willie and Hazel (Caudill) Mullins, Roy and Julie (Harliss) Mullins, and Maude (Mullins) and Clarence Lockhart. An Easter Sunday on April 25 is rare. In fact, that is the latest possible date for Easter Sunday. It has not happened and will not happen on that day again until 2038. (Courtesy of Mullins files.)

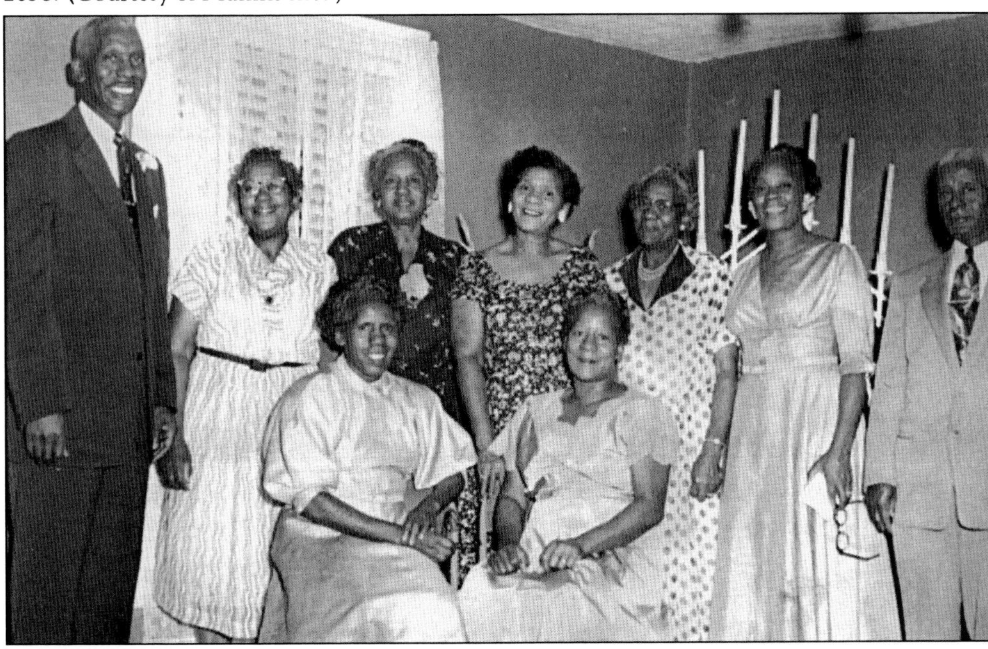

The Holley family contributed greatly to Tazewell in the early part of the 20th century, particularly in the field of education. The street in Tazewell where the family grew up was renamed Historic Holley Town Road. Also on the street sign is special recognition for Hattie Holley Heath, who was a teacher of great worth in local schools and who, along with her sister, Minnie Holley Barnes, was an integral leader in erasing racial barriers. The Holley Quartet is remembered for its inspirational singing style. (Courtesy of Nancy Peery Olson.)

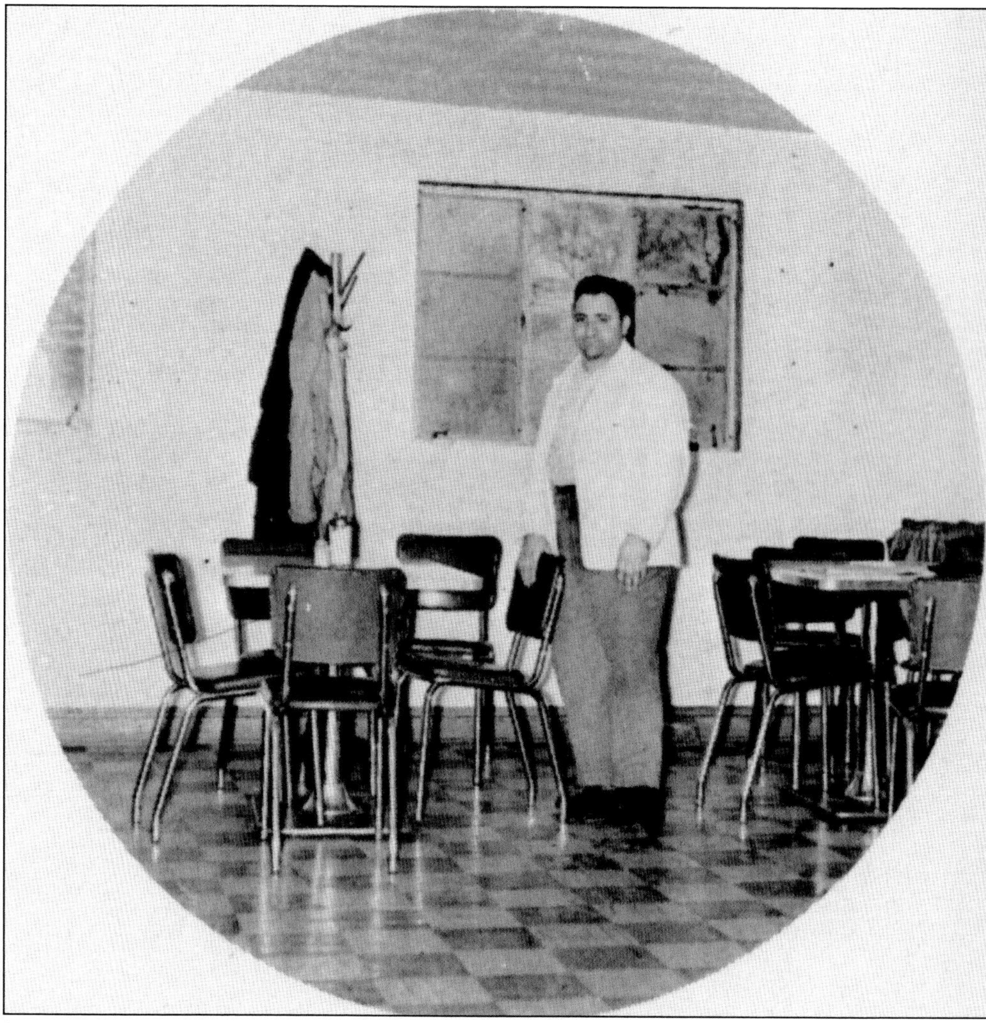

Joe Ianni, a native Italian who moved to Tazewell in the 1950s, was the owner of Joe's Drive-in, which was located near Burke's Garden Siding of Four Way. He made several trips back to his home in Italy and helped his family after becoming a successful businessman locally. On his menu, the spaghetti was a specialty. Many Tazewell young people spent hours "hanging out" at Joe's. (Courtesy of the *Peak*, Tazewell High School.)

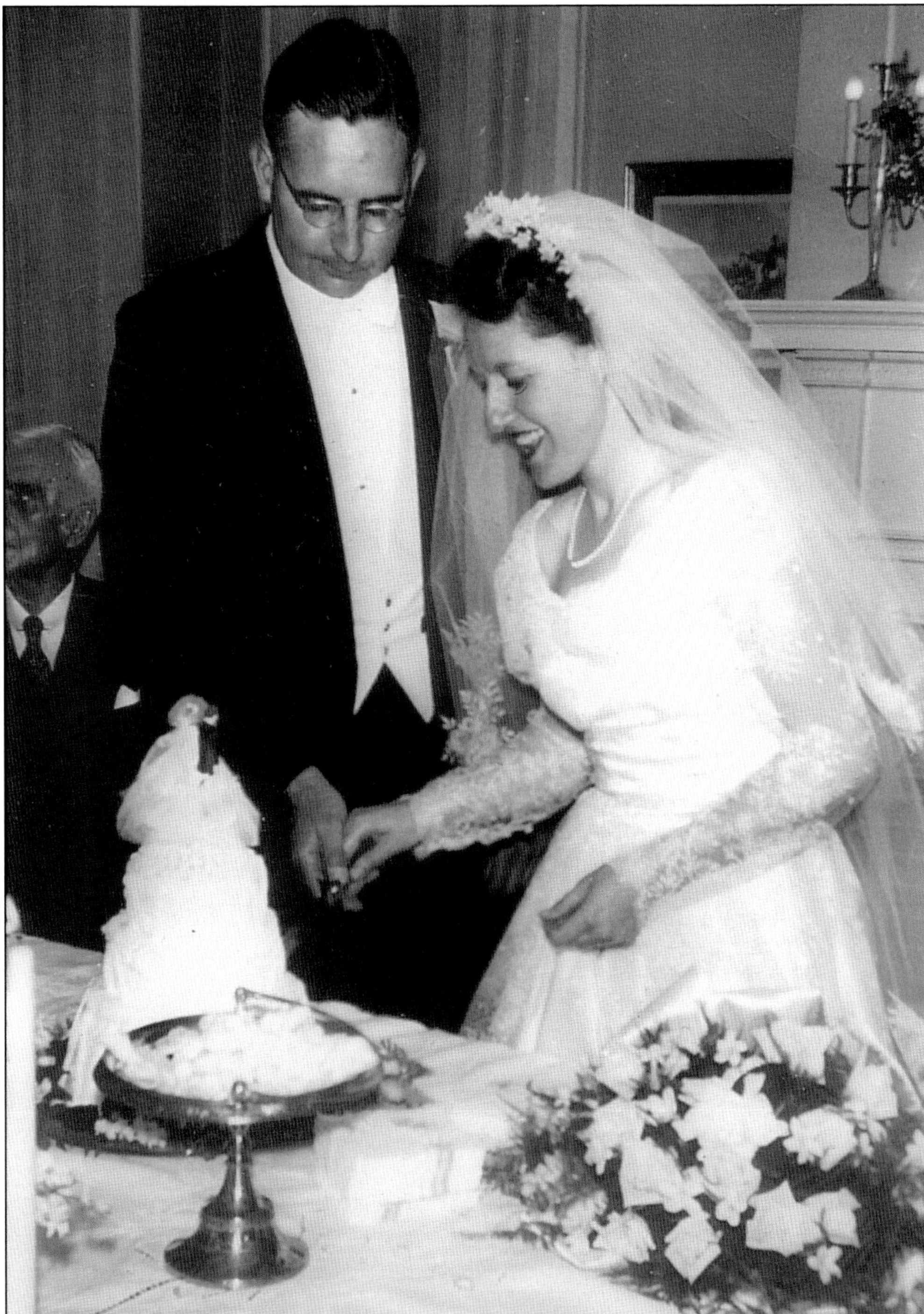

The wedding reception following the June 7, 1950, wedding of George C. Peery Jr. and Mary Bane was held at Thistleton, the home of Mr. and Mrs. W. M. Gillespie. Governor Peery can be seen in the background. Thistleton is the present home of Mr. and Mrs. Albert Gillespie. (Courtesy of Nancy Peery Olson.)

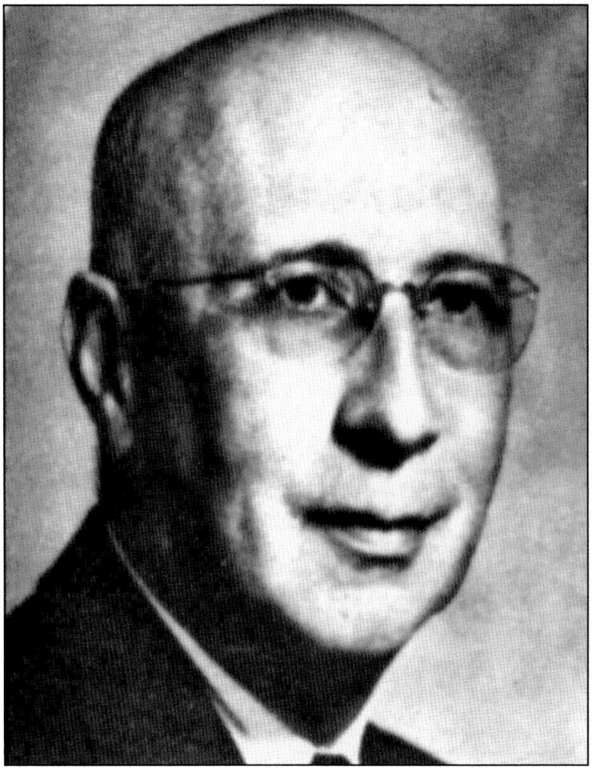

Sidney Peery, well-known Tazewell businessman, started his career in the family business at North Tazewell, the Tazewell Supply Company. He later was founder of the Acme Market and A-Mart chain of stores in Tazewell and other area towns. With his ability and quiet manner, he was a major contributor to the community's growth. (Courtesy of Leslie files.)

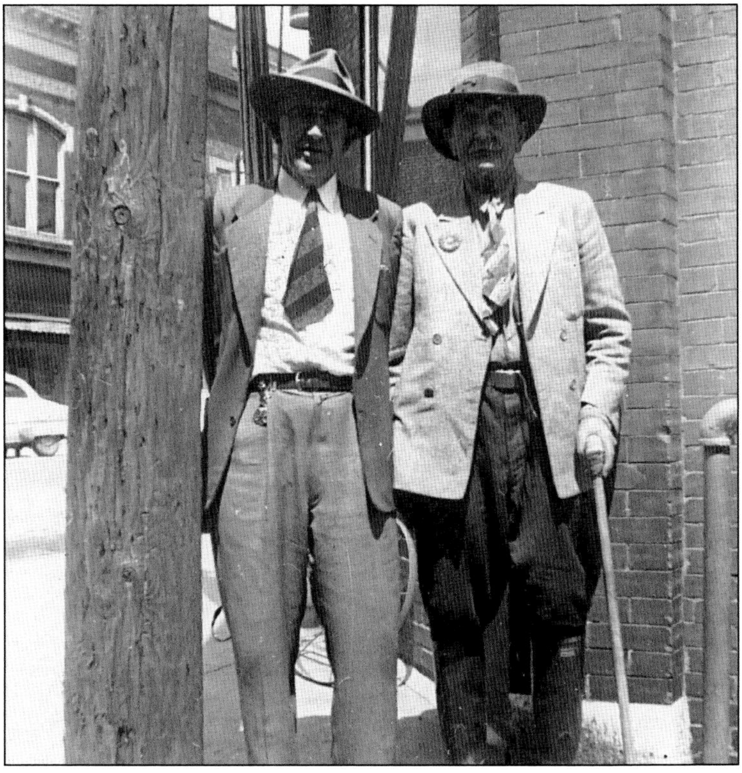

Jim Doak (left) and Charlie Helmandollar were two of the "regulars" on Tazewell's Main Street in 1955. Doak, a well-known businessman, was known for his wit and his wise observations of life around him. Helmandollar is remembered for his unique lifestyle and his amusing comments to (and about) the people he encountered. He always wore gum boots, regardless of the season. (Courtesy of June Friedl.)

Jim Higginbotham served as the chief of police in Tazewell from 1987 to 1994. He was the first African American to serve in that capacity. Higginbotham comes from a prominent African American family. The Higginbotham family has been a part of Tazewell for many generations. (Courtesy of Town of Tazewell.)

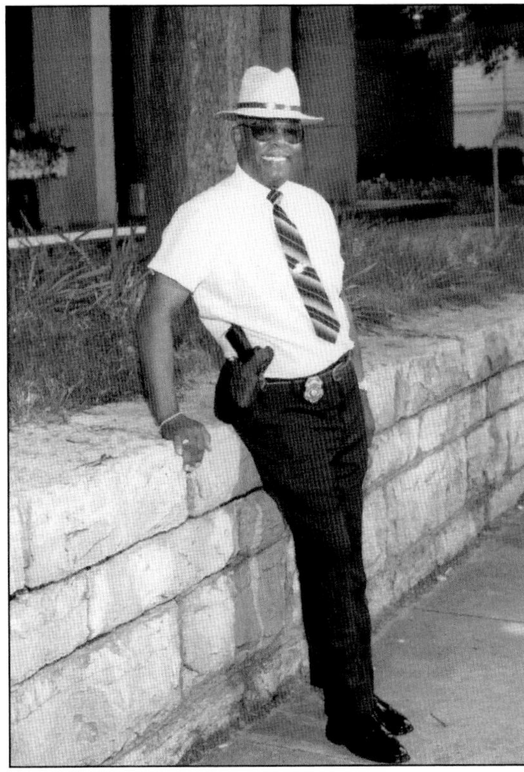

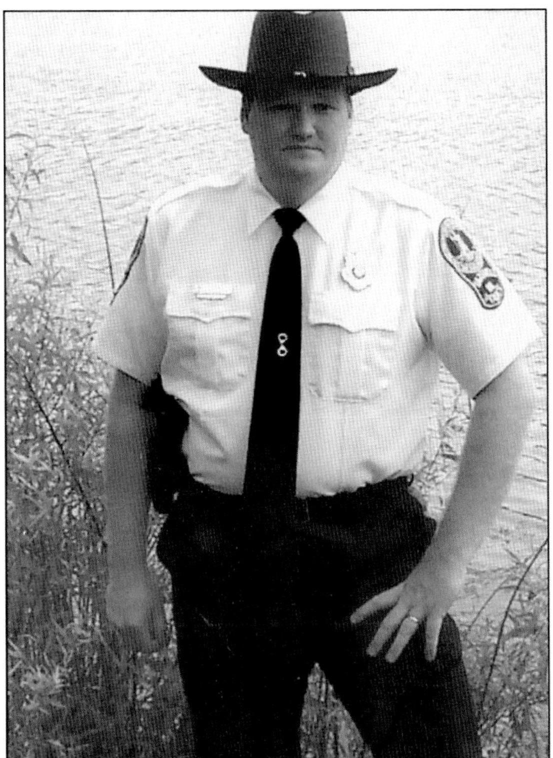

Brian Hieatt became Tazewell's chief of police in 2003. Previously Hieatt had served on the town police department, the Tazewell County Sheriff's Department, and as a DARE instructor in the Tazewell County Schools. As such, he was the first officer to be chosen as Tazewell County's Law Enforcement Officer of the Year by the Tazewell County Victim Witness Program. (Courtesy of Town of Tazewell.)

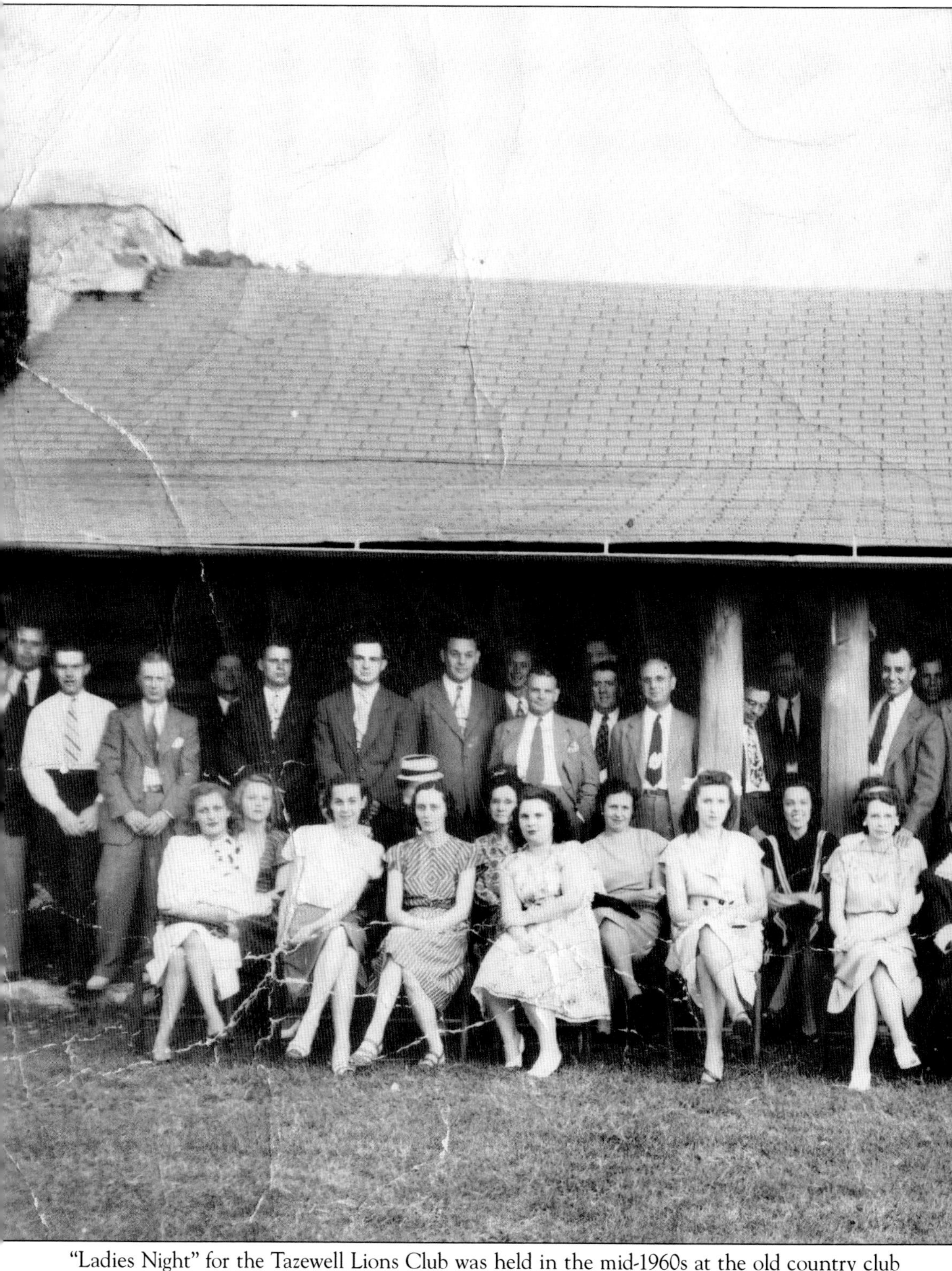

"Ladies Night" for the Tazewell Lions Club was held in the mid-1960s at the old country club building at Maxwell. This building later burned and has been replaced by a modern facility. At

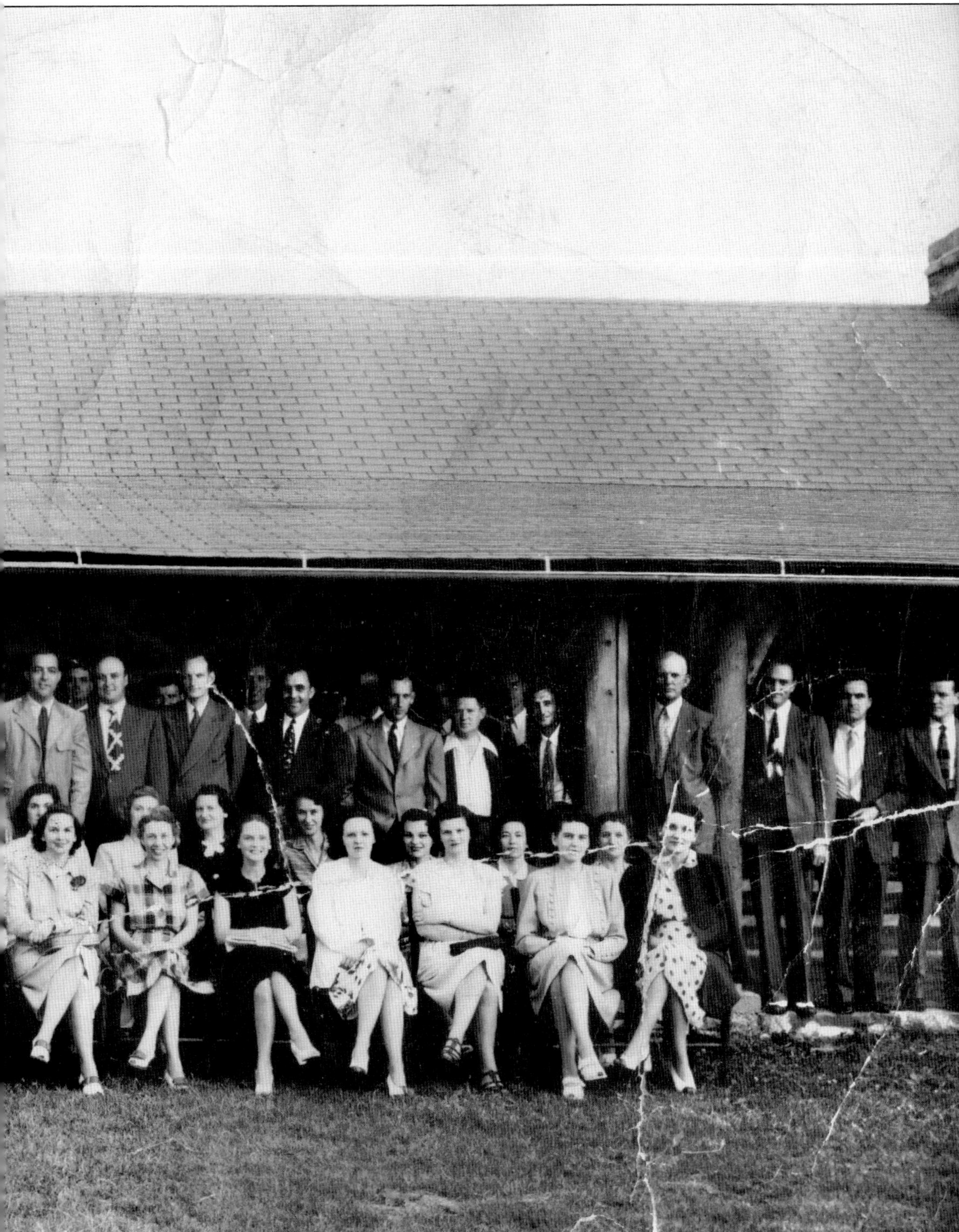

this time, the Lions Club was one of the largest civic organizations in Tazewell County. (Courtesy of June Friedl.)

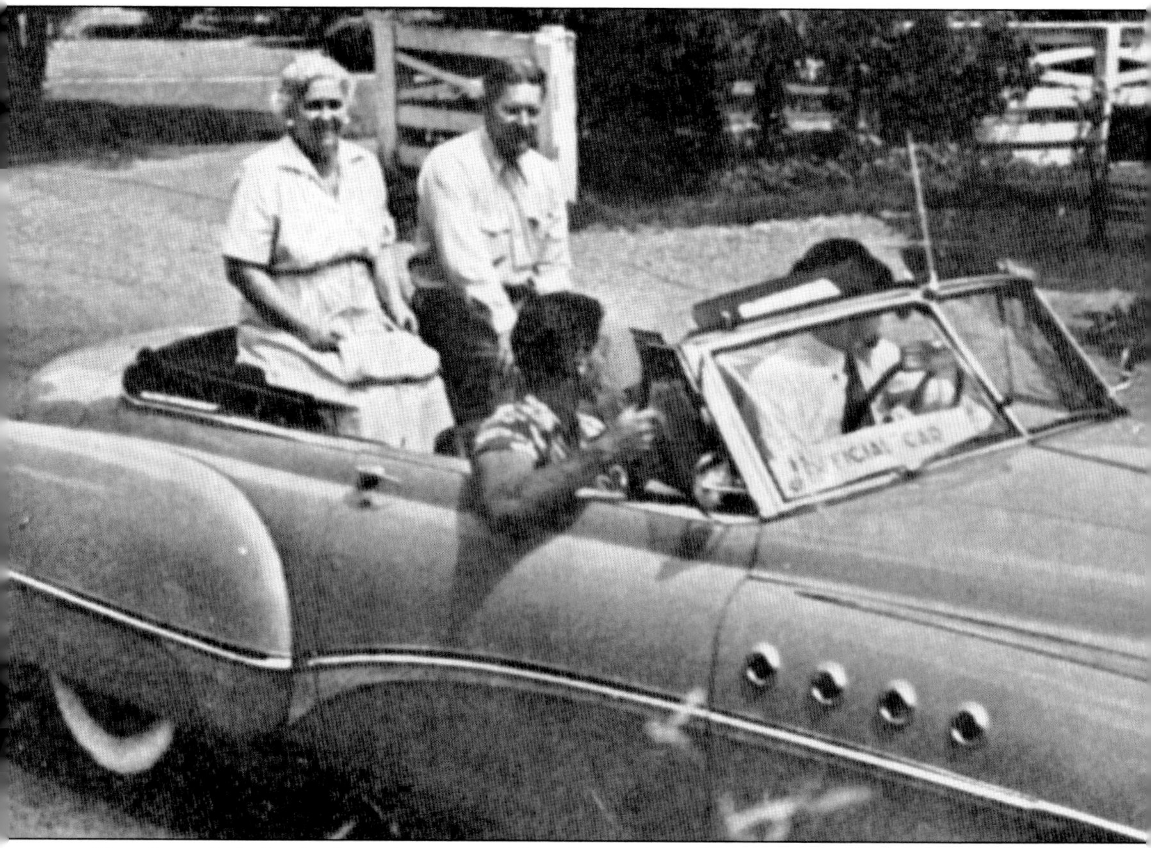

Grand marshals for the Sesquicentennial Parade were Mrs. W. B. Leslie and W. E. Hughes. Leslie was chairperson of the 1950 Sesquicentennial Celebration, and Hughes was in charge of the June 22 parade. (Courtesy of June Friedl.)

Six

The Tazewells Become One

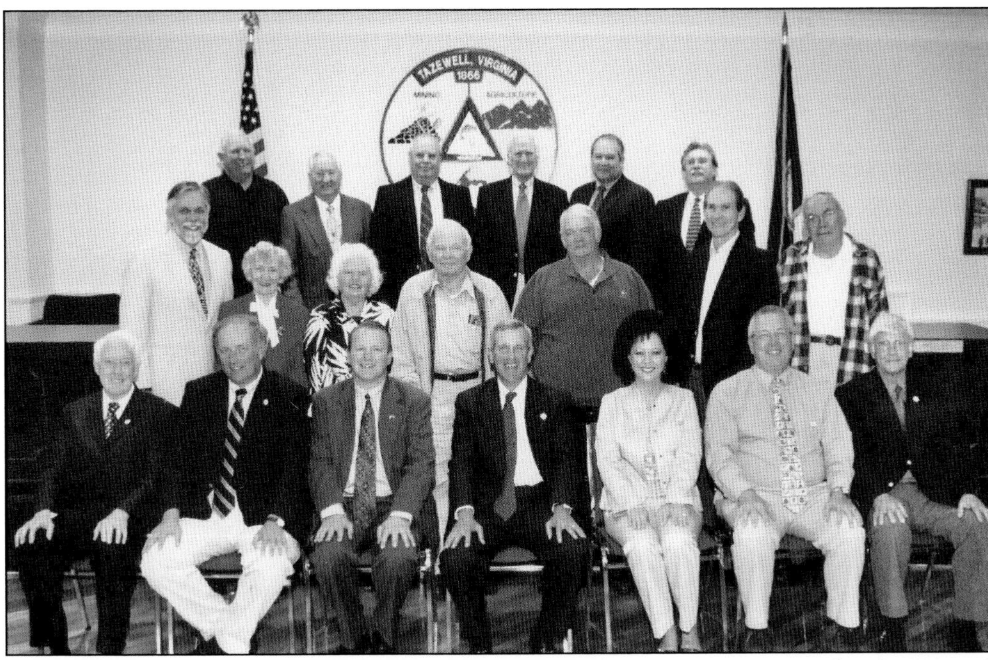

Tazewell mayors and town council members, both past and present, were pictured at the Tazewell Town Hall or Municipal Building on Thursday, May 18, 2006. Mayor Charles Green is seated in the center of the first row, while mayor-elect, at the time, Jack Harry is seated on the left hand side of the same row. Pictured here from left to right are (first row) Jack Harry, Donald Buchanan, David Larimer, Charles Green, Kim Long, Charles Grindstaff, and Jim Doak, (second row) Robert Gemmell, Bettie Byrd St. Clair, Bettye VanDyke, Bill VanDyke, Bobby Brittain, James Deskins Sr., and T. C. Bowen, (third row) Lockhart Conley, Jerry Galliher, Ed Thomas, Jack Hawks, James Deskins Jr., and Jerry Wood. (Courtesy of Bryan Warden.)

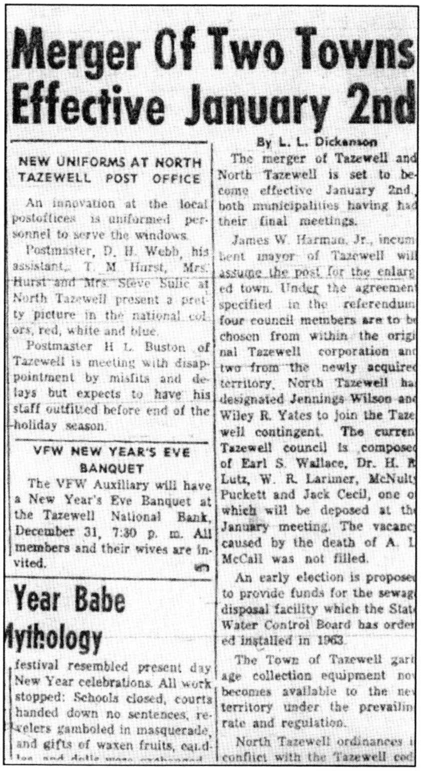

Merger Of Two Towns Effective January 2nd

By L. L. Dickenson

The merger of Tazewell and North Tazewell is set to become effective January 2nd, both municipalities having ha[d] their final meetings.

James W. Harman, Jr., incumbent mayor of Tazewell wil[l] assume the post for the enlarg-ed town. Under the agreemen[t] specified in the referendum four council members are to b[e] chosen from within the origi-nal Tazewell corporation an[d] two from the newly acquire[d] territory. North Tazewell ha[s] designated Jennings Wilson an[d] Wiley R. Yates to join the Taze-well contingent. The curren[t] Tazewell council is compose[d] of Earl S. Wallace, Dr. H. R. Lutz, W. R. Larimer, McNult[y] Puckett and Jack Cecil, one o[f] which will be deposed at th[e] January meeting. The vacanc[y] caused by the death of A. L. McCall was not filled.

An early election is propose[d] to provide funds for the sewag[e] disposal facility which the Stat[e] Water Control Board has order-ed installed in 1963.

The Town of Tazewell garb-age collection equipment no[w] becomes available to the ne[w] territory under the prevailin[g] rate and regulation.

North Tazewell ordinances i[n] conflict with the Tazewell cod[e]

NEW UNIFORMS AT NORTH TAZEWELL POST OFFICE

An innovation at the local postoffices is uniformed personnel to serve the windows.

Postmaster, D. H. Webb, his assistant, T. M. Hurst, Mrs. Hurst and Mrs. Steve Sulic at North Tazewell present a pretty picture in the national colors, red, white and blue.

Postmaster H. L. Buston of Tazewell is meeting with disappointment by misfits and delays but expects to have his staff outfitted before end of the holiday season.

VFW NEW YEAR'S EVE BANQUET

The VFW Auxiliary will have a New Year's Eve Banquet at the Tazewell National Bank, December 31, 7:30 p. m. All members and their wives are invited.

Year Babe Mythology

festival resembled present day New Year celebrations. All work stopped: Schools closed, courts handed down no sentences, revelers gamboled in masquerade, and gifts of waxen fruits, cand-

The towns of Tazewell and North Tazewell officially became one on January 2, 1963, with the consolidation of the two towns and their governments. One day prior to the consolidation, the Town of North Tazewell annexed the Riverjack section and the Town of Tazewell annexed the Four Way section. The "new" Tazewell was, therefore, nearly four times the size in area and in population than the "old" Tazewell. (Courtesy of *Clinch Valley News* files.)

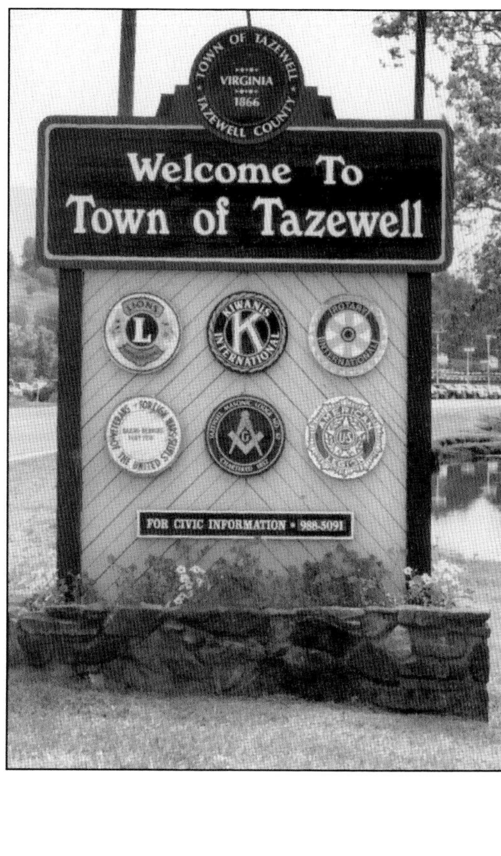

Signs around town welcome visitors and honor important Tazewellites. The bridge near the original home of George A. Martin was named for him, the county's first road engineer and surveyor. He was vitally interested in Tazewell and helped plan many of the road sites used today. His home was used for many years as the Martingale Restaurant before it burned. The outstanding career of Sen. George F. Barnes and his many contributions to Tazewell and Southwestern Virginia were also recognized by the naming of a bridge on U.S. 19/460 Tazewell By-pass in his honor. He served as a Virginia state senator for 12 years. Along with his political interests, he was a well-known farmer and coal operator in the area. (Courtesy of Mullins files.)

The Main Street pictured here gives one a glimpse of Tazewell at the time of the Tazewell–North Tazewell consolidation. The consolidation was based on a court order of July 2, 1962, and took effect on January 2, 1963. Tazewell's Main Street seems aglow in this twilight picture. This photograph was included in the 1964 edition of Tazewell High School's yearbook, the *Peak*. Through the years, the exact location of Main Street has been noted for its perfect alignment with Deskins Mountain. At sunset, it is a scene of beauty often captured by the photographer's lens. (Courtesy of the *Peak*, Tazewell High School.)

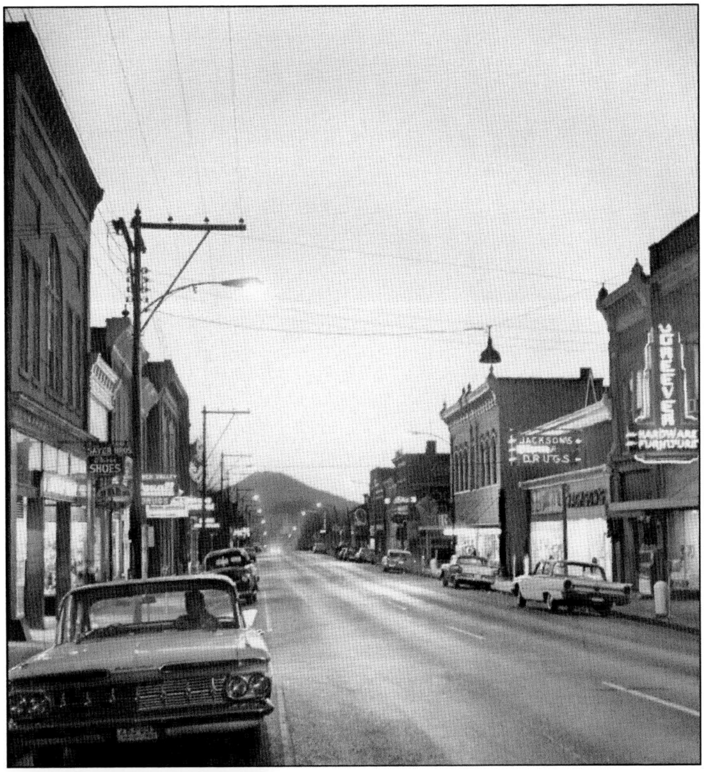

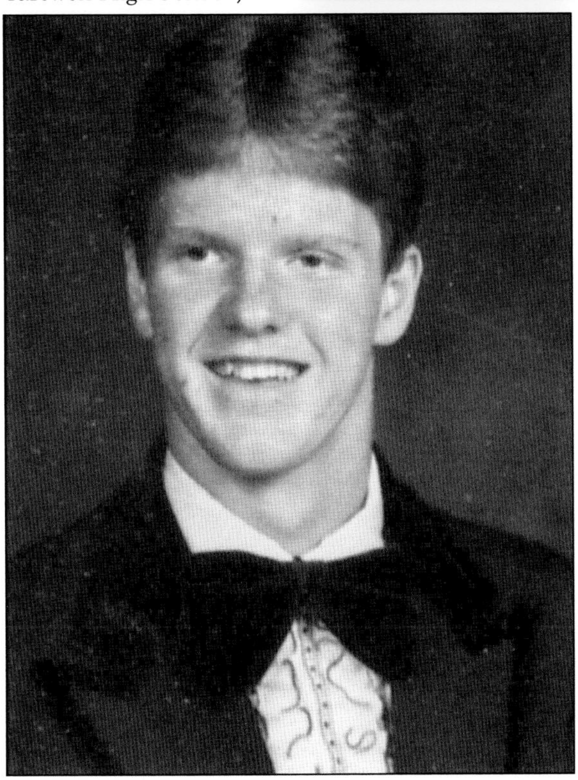

Billy Stanton graduated from Tazewell High School in 1983. Stanton created the seal for the town of Tazewell, found at the beginning of this book, as a part of a competition sponsored by the town in the early 1980s. He is the son of Dr. and Mrs. W. P. Stanton. Dr. Stanton was a well-known Tazewell dentist for many years. Billy Stanton was also an outstanding art student under the guidance of longtime Tazewell High School art instructor Richard Smith. (Courtesy of the *Peak*, Tazewell High School.)

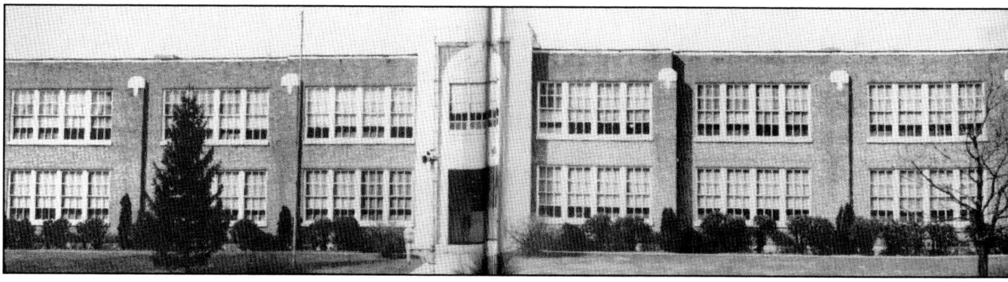

Tazewell High School students moved into this building on School Street in 1931. Before that time, the high school students shared the 1909 building on Main Street with elementary students. The 1931 building, designed to accommodate 500 students, cost $80,000. In 1954, the present Tazewell High School building was completed at a cost of $1 million. A later addition was built for $341,880 in 1978. Tazewell High School continues to be known for its high standards in academics and athletics. (Courtesy of Mullins files.)

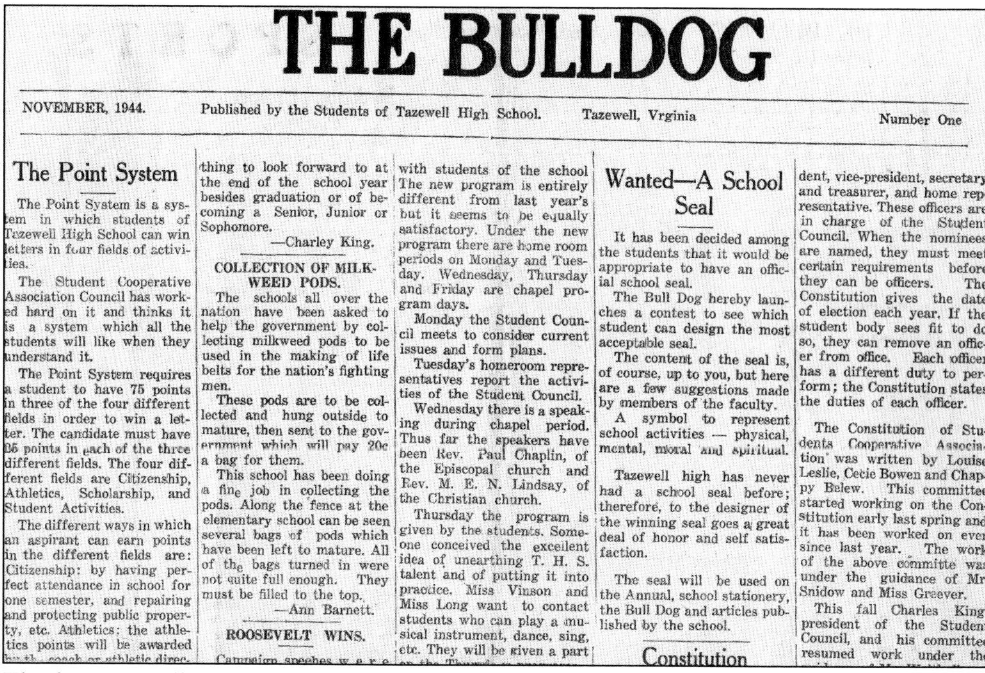

THE BULLDOG

NOVEMBER, 1944. Published by the Students of Tazewell High School. Tazewell, Vrginia Number One

The Point System

The Point System is a system in which students of Tazewell High School can win letters in four fields of activities.

The Student Cooperative Association Council has worked hard on it and thinks it is a system which all the students will like when they understand it.

The Point System requires a student to have 75 points in three of the four different fields in order to win a letter. The candidate must have 25 points in each of the three different fields. The four different fields are Citizenship, Athletics, Scholarship, and Student Activities.

The different ways in which an aspirant can earn points in the different fields are: Citizenship: by having perfect attendance in school for one semester, and repairing and protecting public property, etc. Athletics: the athletics points will be awarded

thing to look forward to at the end of the school year besides graduation or of becoming a Senior, Junior or Sophomore.

—Charley King.

COLLECTION OF MILKWEED PODS.

The schools all over the nation have been asked to help the government by collecting milkweed pods to be used in the making of life belts for the nation's fighting men.

These pods are to be collected and hung outside to mature, then sent to the government which will pay 20c a bag for them.

This school has been doing a fine job in collecting the pods. Along the fence at the elementary school can be seen several bags of pods which have been left to mature. All of the bags turned in were not quite full enough. They must be filled to the top.

—Ann Barnett.

ROOSEVELT WINS.

with students of the school The new program is entirely different from last year's but it seems to be equally satisfactory. Under the new program there are home room periods on Monday and Tuesday. Wednesday, Thursday and Friday are chapel program days.

Monday the Student Council meets to consider current issues and form plans.

Tuesday's homeroom representatives report the activities of the Student Council.

Wednesday there is a speaking during chapel period. Thus far the speakers have been Rev. Paul Chaplin, of the Episcopal church and Rev. M. E. N. Lindsay, of the Christian church.

Thursday the program is given by the students. Someone conceived the excellent idea of unearthing T. H. S. talent and of putting it into practice. Miss Vinson and Miss Long want to contact students who can play a musical instrument, dance, sing, etc. They will be given a part

Wanted—A School Seal

It has been decided among the students that it would be appropriate to have an official school seal.

The Bull Dog hereby launches a contest to see which student can design the most acceptable seal.

The content of the seal is, of course, up to you, but here are a few suggestions made by members of the faculty.

A symbol to represent school activities — physical, mental, moral and spiritual.

Tazewell high has never had a school seal before; therefore, to the designer of the winning seal goes a great deal of honor and self satisfaction.

The seal will be used on the Annual, school stationery, the Bull Dog and articles published by the school.

Constitution

dent, vice-president, secretary and treasurer, and home representative. These officers are in charge of the Student Council. When the nominees are named, they must meet certain requirements before they can be officers. The Constitution gives the date of election each year. If the student body sees fit to do so, they can remove an officer from office. Each officer has a different duty to perform; the Constitution states the duties of each officer.

The Constitution of Students Cooperative Association was written by Louise Leslie, Cecie Bowen and Chappy Belew. This committee started working on the Constitution early last spring and it has been worked on ever since last year. The work of the above committe was under the guidance of Mr. Snidow and Miss Greever.

This fall Charles King, president of the Student Council, and his committee resumed work under the

The first Tazewell High School newspaper, the *Bulldog*, was published in November 1944 under the guidance of the principal and teacher J. L. Walthall. The first editions were printed, free of charge, by the *Clinch Valley News* printing plant. Members of the editorial staff of the first edition of the *Bulldog* were editor Louise Leslie, business manager Danny Myers, assistant business manager Charlie King, advertising manager Janice Sayers, circulation manager Tommy Altizer, and assistant circulation manager Margaret Clarke. The first edition was free to all students. The second edition (December 1944) sold for 5¢ per copy. The third (January 1945) and subsequent editions were available for 25¢ each. (Courtesy of Emmy Dennison.)

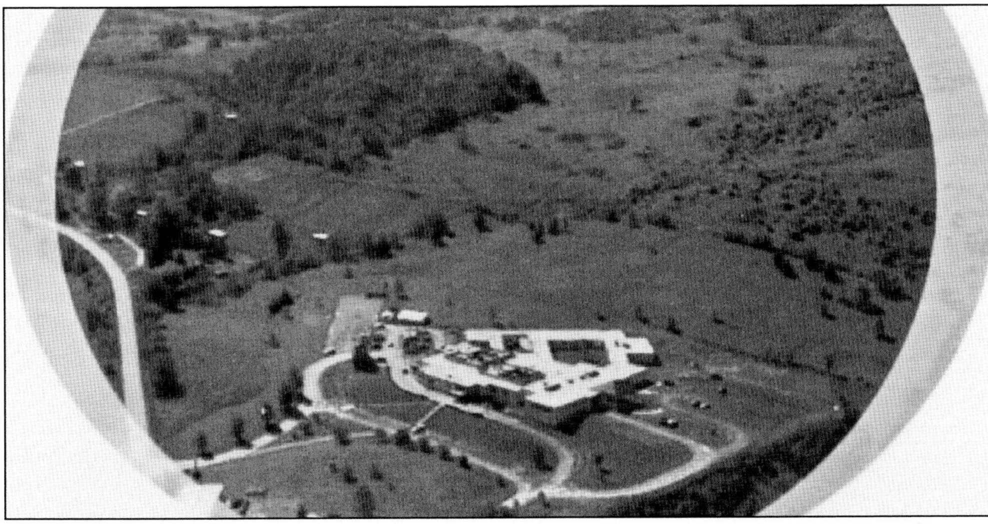

Tazewell Community Hospital opened its doors to the public in 1973. Its immediate predecessor was Jeffersonville Hospital located on Tower Street and owned and operated by Drs. Mary Elizabeth Johnston and Rufus Brittain. The hospital is located at the east end of Tazewell on an expansive campus, which will soon include the new Four Seasons Wellness Center. Stanley Omwake was the hospital's first administrator in 1973. Chris Wearmouth is the current Tazewell Community Hospital administrator. (Courtesy of Tazewell Community Hospital.)

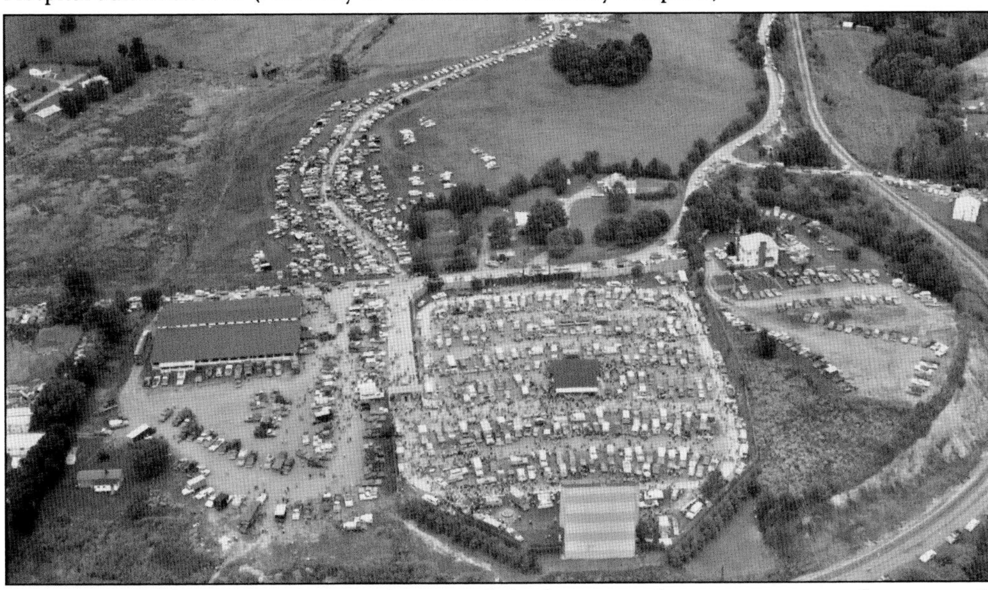

The Tazewell Flea Market grew to be one of the largest such expositions in a large area. It expanded beyond the Tazewell Livestock Market and Sunset Drive-In Theater to encompass much of the Four Way section of town on Mondays. More than 1,000 people regularly attended the flea market. On this special day, perhaps Labor Day or the Fourth of July, the crowd swelled to several thousand. This Four Way section had originally been known as Burkes Garden Siding, since this was the closest spot the Clinch Valley Line of the Norfolk and Western Railway came to the agricultural community of Burkes Garden. The Sunset Drive-In Theater was established in 1951 with a capacity of 300 cars. The drive-in theater closed in 1984 and was demolished a few years later. (Courtesy of June Friedl.)

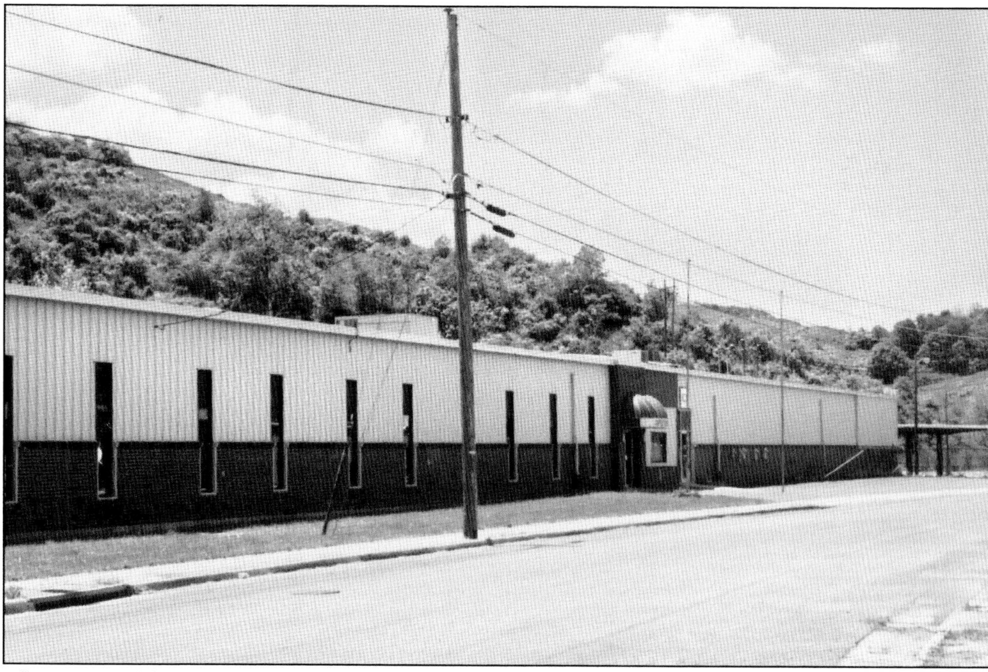

The Micamold Corporation occupied the town's industrial site at Four Way. In 1956, the General Instrument Corporation bought out Micamold. These businesses are now closed, but many workers who moved to Tazewell in the 1950s and 1960s to work at the plants stayed to make their homes here. The Clinch Valley Printing Company now occupies the former electronics plant site. (Courtesy of Mullins files.)

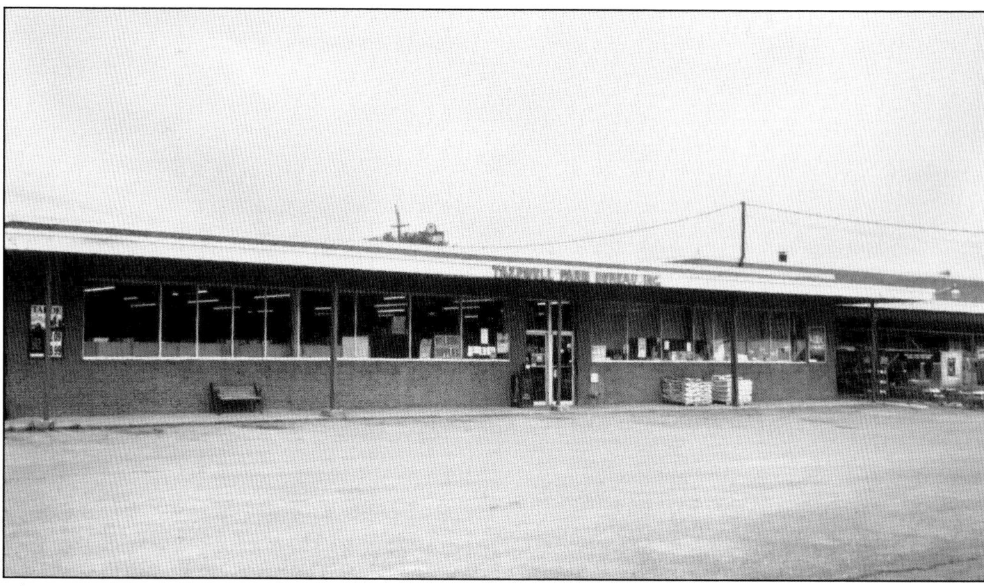

The Tazewell Farm Bureau's local store is a thriving business located at Four Way close to the railroad tracks and the area formerly called Burkes Garden Siding. The manager of the Tazewell store, now part of a five-store cooperative, is David Morrison. This location is also the site of the Tazewell Farmer's Market on Saturdays during the summer garden season. (Courtesy of Mullins files.)

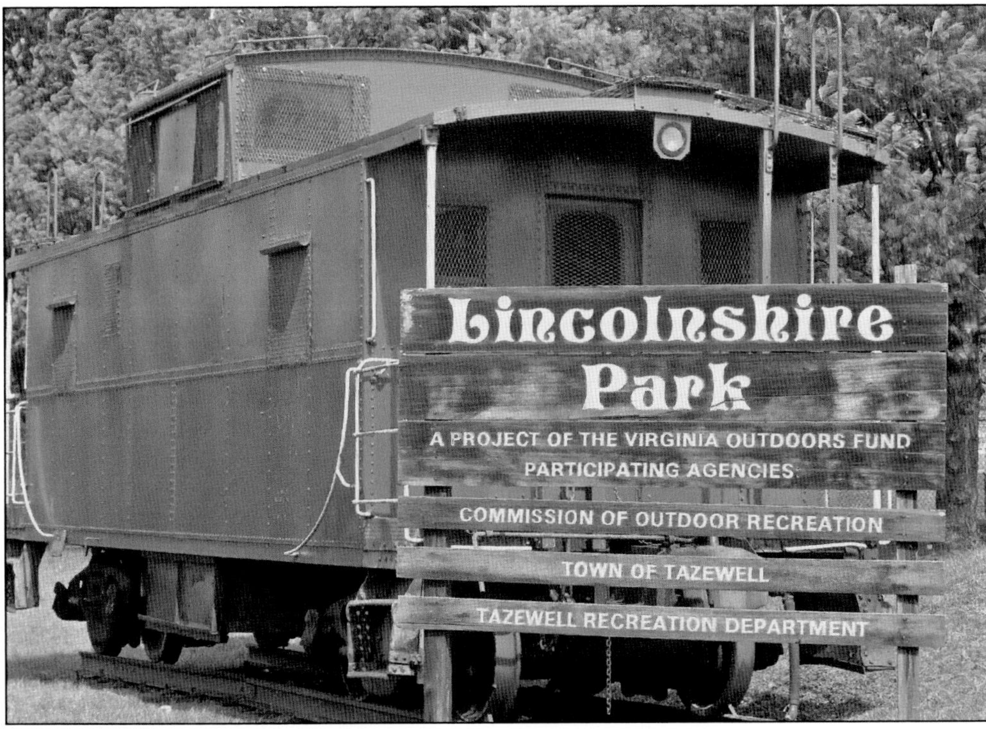

This caboose, donated by the Norfolk and Western Railway, greets visitors to Tazewell's Lincolnshire Park. The railroad car is used to hold the name of the park in full view. The caboose is also open to the public. Betty Conn now serves as recreation director for the town of Tazewell. (Courtesy of G. Michael Alford.)

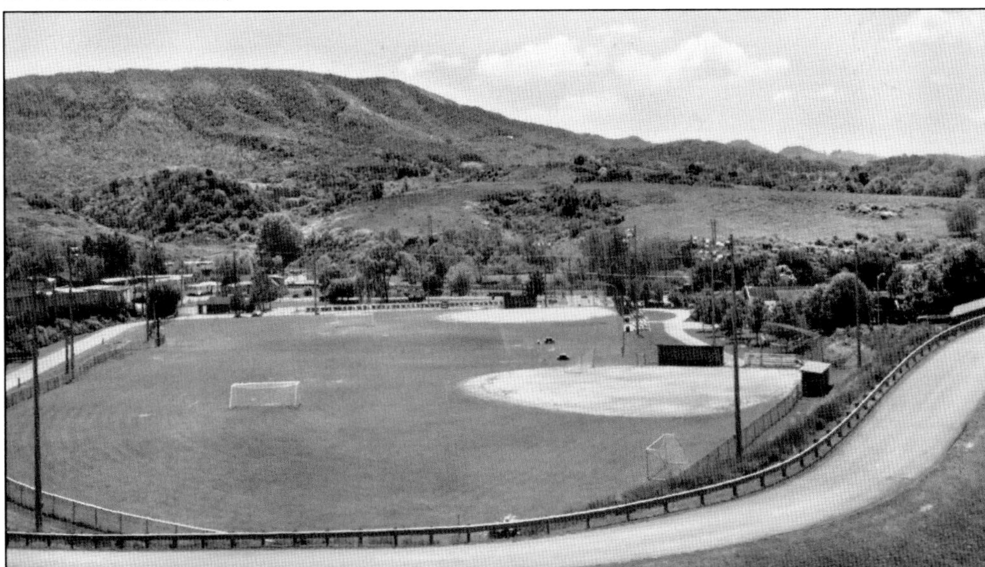

Just east of Tazewell, Lincolnshire Park is located where Georgia Camp played an important role in Tazewell's contribution to the Civil War. A group of Georgia infantry men was first stationed here, giving the camp its name. Other units used this encampment as a rest camp during the duration of the war. A baseball park now occupies the same site. (Courtesy of G. Michael Alford.)

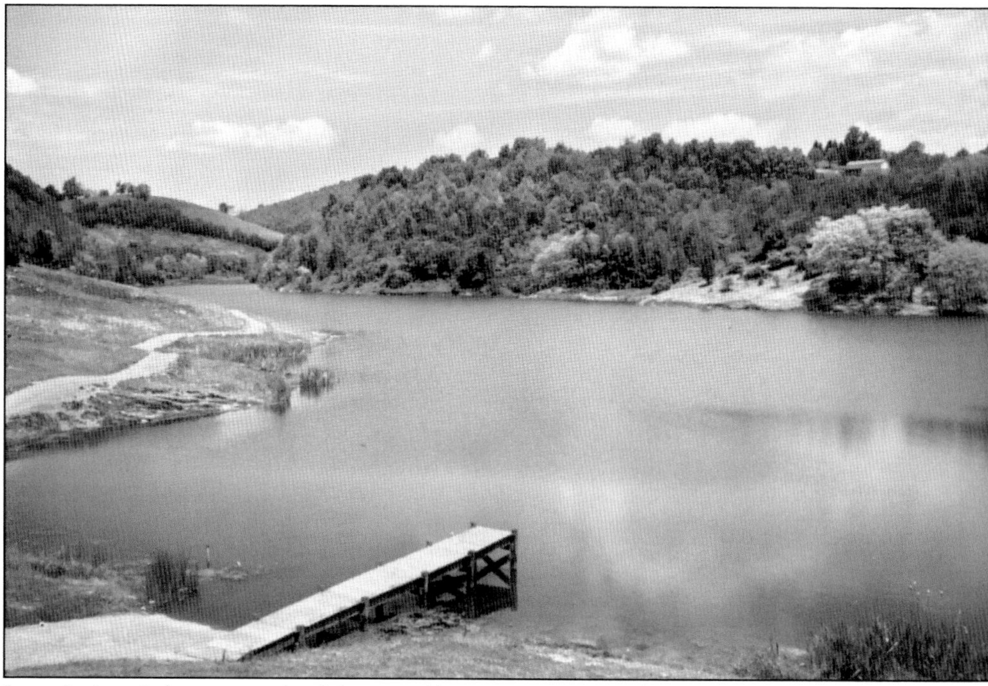

Lincolnshire Lake is a popular fishing and boating recreational area, part of the public town park at Four Way. The lake and dam, along with the Cavitts Creek project, are also part of an overall flood control plan formulated several years ago. (Courtesy of Mullins files.)

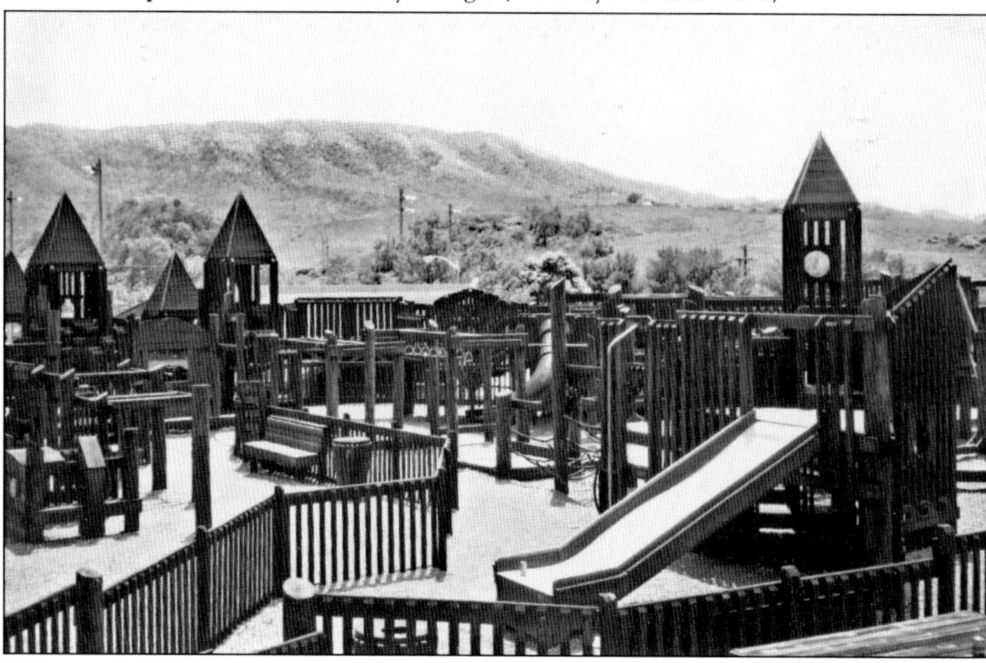

Kidzown was created by and for "kids" of Tazewell as an addition to Lincolnshire Park in the 1980s. In fact, the Kidzown playground was built almost entirely by community volunteers and, according to the county website, is a great example of neighbors helping neighbors in Tazewell County. (Courtesy of G. Michael Alford.)

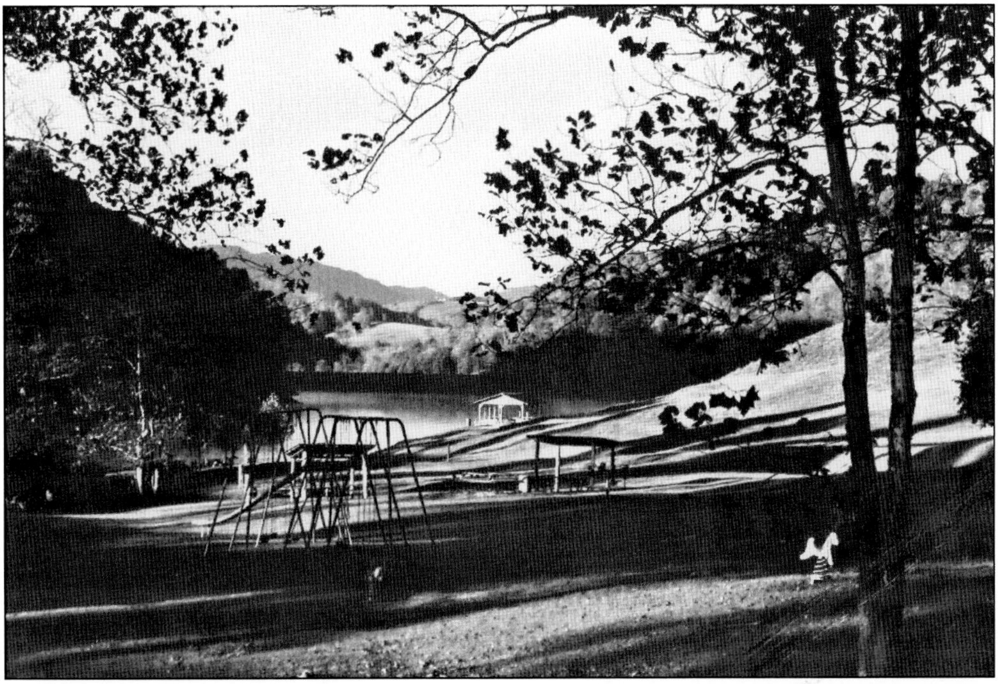

Lake Witten, a popular fishing place, has become a mecca for those who like to spend the day on the lake and (usually) catch their supper at the same time. The name of the lake honors "Doc" J. Walter Witten. (Courtesy G. Michael Alford.)

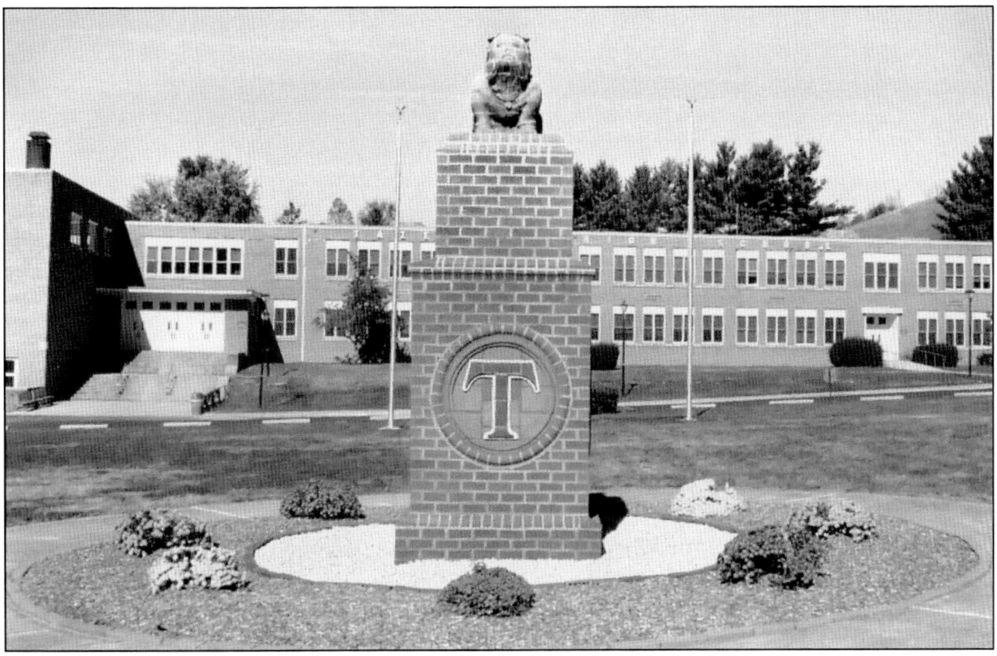

Tazewell High School's Bulldog monument is a source of pride for those students who remember their alma mater and the Bulldog teams, which have given the school a wide reputation in sports since the 1920s. Local artisan Johnny Hagerman crafted the monument from brick. (Courtesy of G. Michael Alford.)

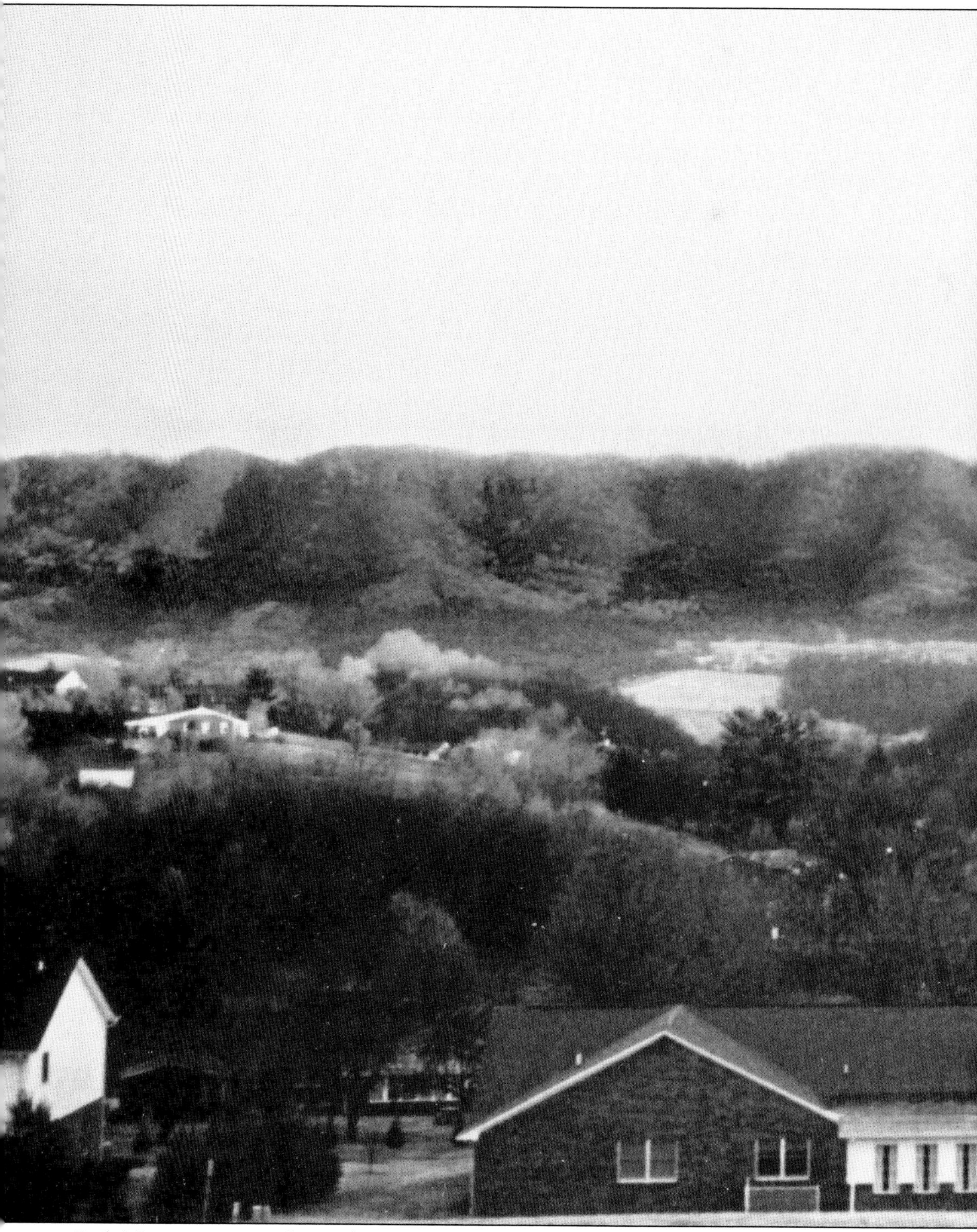

Rich Mountain is one of many beautiful mountains visible from the high elevations within the town of Tazewell. It is a branch or spur of Clinch Mountain and is named because of the richness of its soil, according to early Tazewell historian George Bickley. The principal mountains in Tazewell County include Clinch, Rich, East River, Brushy, Paint Lick, Deskins, Garden, and Flat Top. In

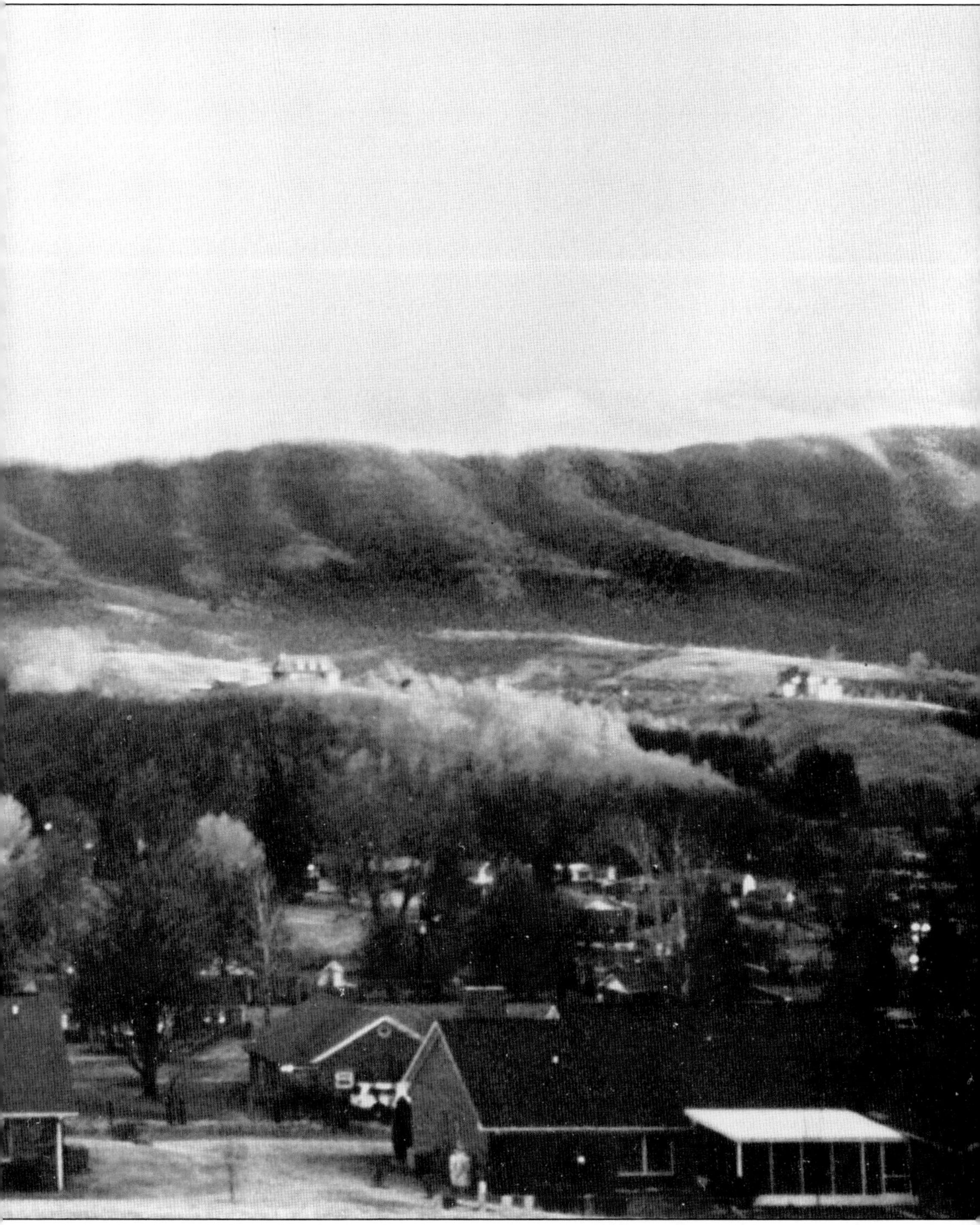

fact, the elevation of Tazewell County varies more than 3,000 feet from an altitude of 1,670 feet where Dry Fork enters West Virginia to 4,710 feet at the top of Beartown on Garden Mountain between Burkes Garden and Thompson Valley. Rich Mountain, shown here, provides a splendid backdrop for the town of Tazewell. (Courtesy of Mullins files.)